SHARING
SPACE

life

SHARING SPACE

An Astronaut's Guide
to Mission, Wonder,
and Making Change

Cady Coleman

PENGUIN LIFE

VIKING
An imprint of Penguin Random House LLC
penguinrandomhouse.com

A Penguin Life Book

LIBRARY OF CONGRESS CATALOGING-IN-PUBLICATION DATA
Names: Coleman, Cady, 1960- author.
Title: Sharing space : an astronaut's guide to mission, wonder,
and making change / Cady Coleman.
Description: New York : Penguin Life, [2024]
Identifiers: LCCN 2023037690 (print) | LCCN 2023037691 (ebook) |
ISBN 9780593494011 (hardcover) | ISBN 9780593494028 (ebook)
Subjects: LCSH: Sharing. | Self-confidence. | Self-realization. | Success.
Classification: LCC BF575.S48 C654 2024 (print) |
LCC BF575.S48 (ebook) | DDC 158.2—dc23/eng/20240207
LC record available at https://lccn.loc.gov/2023037690
LC ebook record available at https://lccn.loc.gov/2023037691

Printed in the United States of America
1st Printing

Designed by Cassandra Garruzzo Mueller

With love to my mother and father,
Anni Doty and Jim Coleman,
who were responsible for getting me
to the launchpad, each in their own way

CONTENTS

Why I Love to Share Space

"If Hollywood wants to tell better space stories," the blockbuster movie director told the NASA PR folks, "we need to share space the way Cady shares space."

It was one of the most meaningful compliments I'd ever received. I'd just given a short presentation about my experience living for six months on the International Space Station (ISS)—the most magical place I've ever been. As I spoke, I tried to convey the delight of waking up in space every day; the exhilaration of flight; the awe I felt each time I gazed at the Earth, with its infinite variations of light and color, never the same view twice. I also shared some of the everyday details—what we ate, how we brushed our teeth, and even a few bathroom details. I wanted people to hear my stories and feel like they could have been there themselves. Too often, when we hear about space exploits, we relate to astronauts as heroic, larger-than-life figures. But that's just an image. Astronauts are regular people who have worked really hard for the privilege of doing something rare and extraordinary.

My name is Cady Coleman, and I am an astronaut. Even after twenty-four years at NASA, two space shuttle missions, and six months living aboard the ISS, it thrills me to say those words, and yet there is a part of me that's still surprised by them. Like many astronauts, I tend to think of myself as "unexpected." We can't help but wonder, how did *I* get to do *THIS*?

That's the way I want to share space: relatably. I want people to realize that if I could become an astronaut, maybe they, too, could be something they never imagined they could be.

Sharing is also part of how I process life. It's one thing to have an extraordinary experience—and I've had some of the most awe-inspiring ones it's possible to have—but if I don't get to share it with anyone, it would feel like an important piece was missing.

My experience changed the way I look at the world and what it means to be a citizen of planet Earth. My missions to space took a lot of work, good fortune, and support from friends, family, the whole team at NASA, and beyond. Because of this, I feel strongly that I have a responsibility to share those experiences. They belong to other people too. So I hope this book can be an up-close-and-personal guide for you to the beauty, strangeness, and wonder of living hundreds of miles above the Earth.

It's been a wild ride. I've gotten to perform hundreds of space experiments that can't be done here on Earth; launch the Chandra X-ray Observatory (a telescope that is sending us fascinating information about black holes to this day); capture the second-ever free-flying supply ship with the ISS's Canadian robotic arm; train for spacewalking in a three-hundred-pound suit that was way too big (after NASA eliminated the suit that fit me); and play the first-ever duet between Earth and space, with Ian Anderson from Jethro Tull. And in the midst of it all, my husband and I managed to keep our family together and raise two wonderful sons, despite living in different states!

I learned valuable lessons while training for missions and living in space that—perhaps surprisingly—can be applied to many aspects of life here on Earth as well. When I look back on my experiences, certain themes keep showing up that resonate strongly with what I hear about from people in other fields, especially people who are forging new ground. Working for years in environments that weren't designed for people like me, I had to learn when to make the best of things and when to challenge the status quo and catalyze real, lasting change. I learned to build deep bonds with teams of very different people while working under extreme conditions, often in remote locations and close quarters. I learned lessons about trust and collaboration that are useful in every situation that involves working with, living with, or loving another person.

If you are passionate about your home life, your work, your personal time, or all of the above, then you might find we have a lot in common: juggling priorities when the missions are more important than we are, and yet if we don't care for ourselves, we can't bring our best to any of it.

Sharing space, to me, means including more people—both in the privilege of going to space and in so many of our endeavors here on Earth. When I applied to be an astronaut, very few women had flown in space. Today, that number has grown to 79, of 676 human beings in total. Newer NASA astronaut classes have averaged 50 percent women, and the current astronaut corps is 40 percent women. Space flight is making progress in terms of including people with a greater diversity of backgrounds, fields of expertise, and physical abilities. But we have a long way to go. And the same is true in countless fields—the barriers that we struggle with in space exploration seem to be ubiquitous in the working world.

If there's one thing I learned above all else from my time in space, it's that we're *all* sharing Earth. No one else is coming to solve our challenges and ultimately save our planet. It's so clear from up there that we're one family—or, as many astronauts think of it, we are all the crew of Spaceship Earth. If more of us could see it that way and rise above our differences, I have no doubt that together we'd find creative ways to solve the problems that affect all of us. I hope that what I share in these pages—from the magical to the mundane—can contribute in some small way to that oh-so-important mission. Perhaps by sharing space, and our stories, we can all get a little better at sharing Earth.

Chapter 1

Just Another Day in Zero-G

Reimagining What's Possible

0700 GMT, International Space Station,
250 miles above the Earth

Slowly, I open my eyes. *I'm still here.* That miraculous fact hits me the moment I wake up, every morning, floating. *I'm in space. And I'll be in space tomorrow and the next day, and the next—for six whole months. I LIVE here.* It's a kind of bubbly, never-gets-old feeling that floods my body and banishes any notion of slipping back into sleep.

My next thought: *Which way is up?*

My cabin is not much bigger than a bathroom stall, with soft white panels lining the walls, floor, and ceiling. It resembles nothing so much as a padded cell, but I love every inch of it. It's a bedroom, of sorts, though there's no actual bed. Many astronauts hook their sleeping bags securely to the wall and slither inside each night, but I like to sleep with my bag untethered. I tuck my knees to my chest, zip the sleeping bag up so it holds me in a ball, and float off to sleep, literally. So when I wake up, adrift, it takes a minute to figure out where I am.

Today, my cheek is bobbing gently against something solid, and as I shift my head backward, my eyes focus on a small barcode sticker. Aha! I'm under my desk—a tiny shelf just big enough for my laptop computer. Looking up—or what I think of as "up," at least in relation to the floor—I see my photographs, each inside a ziplock bag, Velcroed to the wall. My ten-year-old son, Jamey's, impish grin. My husband, Josh's, warm smile. My whole family, posing on the rocks on Rhode Island, the way we did every summer. Josh's family at Christmas. Jamey's stuffed tiger, Hobbes, is tethered to the wall with a bungee cord attached to his small Velcro collar. If my son couldn't come with me to space, at least he knows that Hobbes is up here keeping an eye on me. It means a lot to both of us.

I gently push off from under the desk and float upward, unzipping my sleeping bag and stretching out my legs. Checking my watch, I see that I'm cutting it close, as usual. I am a night owl, and my strategy is to use the late-night hours to prepare the things I'll need for the following day and enjoy the feeling of solitude that descends on the space station after everyone else is zipped up and sleeping. So I've mastered the art of waking up just minutes before the Daily Planning Conference (DPC)—our morning meeting where we talk through the upcoming day with the Mission Controls around the world.

Wearing my favorite long-sleeved pajamas—a Russian-issued outfit in soft dark-green cotton—I open the cabin door and with a gentle push I'm flying through the lab and into Node 1, the center of the space station. When people try to imagine zero gravity (or zero-g, as we call it), they think about us floating around, but in reality, it's more like flying. This weightless freedom is truly one of the most magical feelings I've ever had. In space, the lightest touch of a finger can propel you across a module. And the ISS has plenty of room to enjoy the freedom of flight: ten modules, each the size of a bus. There are handrails strategically positioned along the walls that you can use to give yourself a little push in the direction you want to go or correct your course midflight. When you get to where you want to be, you can tuck your toes under one of the rails to keep yourself in place if the task at hand requires it. Staying still actually takes effort—without holding on, you would float away.

I hook a right into Node 3, toward the WCS (Waste Collection System, aka, the toilet), which looks like a space outhouse. A roaring sound—only slightly quieter than a jet engine—lets me know that someone's in there. In space, the toilet uses gentle suction to ensure that all the waste goes inside and stays inside. Some astronauts joke that, years after their missions, they still feel programmed, like Pavlov's dogs, to pee on command when they hear that kind of sound. (For those who are curious about exactly how the space toilet works, don't be shy—I've included everything you need to know in appendix 1.)

I fly around to the back of the WCS, where my toothbrush and a tiny square of wet washcloth are Velcroed to the wall in their ziplock bag. Just a few feet away is my favorite place on the ISS—the many-windowed hexagonal dome known as the Cupola. It juts out like a turret from the middle of the station, pointing down toward the Earth below. To enter it, you fly through a short passage into the dome with its round central window surrounded by windows on all sides—like the petals circling the center of a daisy. Suddenly (if the window covers are open) you have a jaw-dropping 360-degree view of the Earth.

Until the Cupola was added, the only way for astronauts to observe the Earth was through a few small windows. Traveling at 17,500 miles per hour, the space station orbits the Earth sixteen times per day, or about every 90 minutes. Beloved locations would flash by the tiny windows at five miles a second, so quickly that it was hard to take them in, let alone capture a photo. But from the Cupola, you can watch Earth pass majestically below, so crisp and clear it feels almost close enough to touch.

This morning, as I fly up to the Cupola with my toothbrush in my mouth, taking great care not to allow any toothpaste to escape and land on the pristine windows, I see that we're over the Pacific. I drift up so I'm parallel to the central window, and my entire field of vision is filled with the bright blue ocean-covered beauty of the planet I call home. From this angle, I feel like I'm surfing over the Earth's surface, as the ISS hurtles through its orbit. As I brush my teeth, we're passing over the broad, sweeping West Coast of the United States—so familiar and yet so mesmerizing when seen from this unique vantage point. I think about the people down there, in busy cities like Los Angeles and San Francisco, coming to the end of their day as I'm getting ready to start mine.

I still can't get used to the idea that I am one of only six human beings who are currently not on planet Earth. The fizzy feeling surges up through my body again, like I'm a glass of beer poured too quickly and about to foam over the edges.

Speaking of foam, I swallow my toothpaste. If you spit, the toothpaste becomes a sloppy projectile that doesn't stop until it hits something, or someone, or in the worst case, someone's clean shirt. Abruptly, I remember that I don't have time to dally, even though it's hard to tear myself away from that window. Earth never gets boring once you've been properly introduced. But I have things to do. If I'm lucky, I'll just have time to visit the WCS and grab coffee, though it will mean being at the meeting in my green pajamas (again). My crewmates have gotten used to me showing up for the DPC looking like a leprechaun.

Coffee, like most of what we consume on the space station, is a disappointing stand-in for the real thing. I pierce the foil packet containing the coffee granules with a needle that delivers a jet of hot water and try to pretend it's a freshly brewed cup from my beloved coffee machine back home, rather than a boring, weak imitation. I glide into place among my crewmates just in time, like a baseball player sliding into home base—something I always dreamed of doing on the ground.

"Houston, we're ready for the DPC," Scott Kelly, our commander, says into the handheld microphone.

Once we've gotten our last-minute instructions and reminders from Mission Control, I head back to my cabin to pull my clothes on, literally. Pants: two legs at a time! My clothes are tucked behind a lattice of bungee cords attached to a kind of bulletin board on the wall. Clothes are another thing that you don't want randomly floating around up here. In zero-g, objects have a life of their own, and there's nothing more embarrassing than finding that your underwear has wandered onto someone's workstation. I grab one of the ten shirts I've been allowed to bring for this six-month stay; my favorites are the ones that are brightly colored. With the exception of Paolo, from Italy, the guys on my crew picked seriously boring colors, like navy, black, gray, or maybe forest green if they were feeling adventurous. We are constantly taking photos and filming on the station, and since part of our mission is to share the story of our work in space, I go for bright colors to bring those images to life against the mostly gray and white walls. And my big space hair doesn't hurt either!

Next up, breakfast. Again, uninspiring. No one goes to space for the food. Astronaut food is half dehydrated meals (scrambled eggs, beef stroganoff, mixed veggies) and half military grub sealed in pouches (chicken soup or BBQ beef). For the freeze-dried food, you inject water into the package and warm it inside a special heating device that looks like a briefcase. The menu, in all its glory, is generic for every space station crew and recycled every nine days.

Today, I grab an oatmeal-granola-type concoction with blueberries. And then, with just the gentle touch of a finger on a handrail, I'm flying down to the lab like Peter Pan on my thirty-second commute. The day ahead of me, like every day of my six months on the ISS, will be spent following a detailed time line. Every minute is scheduled, except for a thirty-minute lunch. And every day is different. We might be conducting science experiments, repairing equipment, exercising, unpacking or packing supply ships. Everything has written directions and procedures, so we spend our days working through checklists. Everyone's least favorite task is inventory, which involves unpacking and counting things while valiantly trying to prevent them from floating away. My personal favorite is the science experiments, evaluating new ideas about chemistry, physics, and biology that can't be tested on Earth. And on top of all that, we still do many of the same mundane tasks that people do on Earth every day. But one thing—or rather, the absence of one thing—makes it all magical. *Gravity.*

As I pass the now-familiar storage lockers and instrument panels, letting myself do a slow roll as I fly down the module—just because I can—I think the same thing I've thought every day since our Soyuz capsule launched, the day after my fiftieth birthday: How did I get so lucky that *this* is my job?

Maybe I Could Have That Job . . .

I still remember vividly the exact day when it first occurred to me that I *could* have this job.

Cady Coleman, astronaut, was not something I doodled in the margins of my grade school textbooks or confided in my girlfriends as a teenager. It never occurred to me that *I* could be *that*, until one day during my junior year at the Massachusetts Institute of Technology (MIT) I met someone who *was* that—and to my great surprise, seemed pretty much like me.

It was the spring of 1982, and I was hurrying down what is known as the Infinite Corridor, connecting many of MIT's buildings across the sprawling campus. The chemistry labs, where I spent much of my time, were all the way at one end. Since most of the student population used this corridor daily, it served as a useful bulletin board in that pre-internet and pre-email era. The walls were lined with posters for campus events, including talks by speakers that I'd enthusiastically plan to attend until I'd wake up on the day of the talk and realize that, given my backlog of classwork, it just wasn't realistic. On this day, however, something different caught my eye.

The poster, as I recall, showed a smiling woman in a flight suit, holding a helmet by her side. I recognized her immediately: Sally Ride, one of America's first group of female astronauts. It had just been announced that she would be part of the crew for one of the upcoming space shuttle flights, making her the first American woman in space. And while she was visiting the Lincoln Labs for training, she would be giving a speech and attending a reception hosted by the MIT Women's Alumni Association. A woman speaker was still a novelty at MIT in those days. But a woman *astronaut*? I knew this was one event I had to attend. I couldn't pass up a chance to meet her.

At this point in my education, I'd landed on chemistry as my major. Of all the things I'd studied, organic chemistry was the one that I was the most curious and excited about. It just seemed to fit naturally with the way my brain worked. I loved running chemical reactions in the lab to create new compounds. Even though there were procedures and "recipes," there was a certain amount of intuition or instinct about what might be happening in the reaction flask that seemed to come in handy. And I was good at figuring out what would make these different molecules literally want to dance together and form bonds. (Turns out, the secret is usually to get them to give up something that neither of them cares about as much as they care about connecting with each other. A good lesson for relationships outside the lab as well!)

The more I learned about chemistry, and in particular the chemistry of special molecules called polymers, the more I wanted to be part of creating new materials that would improve people's lives in our changing world. That kind of research has led to everything from new ways to deliver medicine to specific parts of the body to new, lightweight protective clothing to help keep people safe.

As much as I enjoyed the lab work itself, however, I didn't think that spending my whole career in a lab would work for me. I wanted to continue to pursue chemistry, but I wanted a job that involved adventure as well as the sense of being part of something larger. I just wasn't sure how all those things could go together.

On the day of Sally Ride's talk, I hurried into the lecture hall—a large, theater-style auditorium that sits under the big dome that is the emblem of MIT. Sandy Yulke, the chair of the Women's Alumni Association, was already onstage introducing Sally. *Sally.* Just a first name. As if she were *one of us.* I slid into an empty seat just a few rows back as Sandy talked about how proud she was to welcome the soon-to-be first American woman in space. And Sally was standing there, right where our professors stood every day. A woman. And an astronaut.

Growing up in the 1960s, the image I'd had of astronauts—or any kind of explorer, for that matter—could not have been further from the figure before me that day. And I'm not just talking about images I saw in the media—I had one much closer to home. My dad, James Joseph Coleman, known as JJ, was a career naval officer who ultimately led their Experimental Diving Unit. A legend among navy divers, he had also been a project officer for the navy's SEALAB program, building the first underwater habitats, allowing men—and it was all men at the time—to live and work in the deep seas for extended periods. The spirit of exploration, the desire to understand fascinating and challenging environments, seemed normal to me as a child. But because none of the explorers I saw looked like me, it didn't occur to me that I could be one. My dad worked in a male-dominated world where I'm sure few people imagined that people like me might belong too.

My older brother, Jamey, longed to be a pilot until he learned that his eyesight would disqualify him, shattering his dreams at the age of seven. When we were little, I remember him showing me the famous photo of the Mercury 7—America's first astronaut class, selected the year before I was born. Clean-shaven, athletic-looking military types with their silver spacesuits and short haircuts. Every one of them male, and every one of them white. As were the Apollo astronauts we saw making history in the 1960s and '70s. Much later, I'd learn about pioneering Russian cosmonaut Valentina Tereshkova, who was the first woman in space, back in 1963, but it would be nearly two decades before another woman launched. So I guess it's not surprising that when the moon landing occurred on July 20, 1969, I almost missed that historic "small step for a man" and the giant leap it represented.

We were staying at my grandparents' house that night, sleeping on the hide-a-bed in their TV room with its plush mint-green carpet. My mom woke my brother up to watch the events unfold but didn't think to wake me too. In so many ways, she was a fiercely independent woman who championed my dreams, but in that instance, she reverted to the cultural norm. Space was for boys. Luckily, little boys who are about to see a man walk on the moon have a hard time keeping quiet, so I woke up too, in time for that extraordinary moment.

By the time I got to MIT in 1979, only six women had been selected as NASA astronauts. But seeing Sally Ride on the stage that day turned a possibility into a reality—a reality that could include *me*. She was a young, bright-eyed woman, with wavy brown hair kind of like mine, wearing a blue flight suit and black boots. She seemed a little shy, looking down at her hands as she was introduced and applauded. I was captivated.

I don't remember much about her speech, though I do recall being struck by one story. Preparing for her flight, the NASA folks asked her about things they'd never had to consider before, like how many tampons to pack, and would they need to include a makeup kit. Sally told them, "I can't answer those questions. There are six of us now—six women astronauts—and we're all different. So we'll talk about it together and come up with an answer for you." That really struck me—that even though she, as an individual, had a voice and was being heard, she didn't assume she should speak for everyone. Her instinct was to listen and to bring others along.

Another thing that struck me about Sally was her obvious expertise. She had this amazing job where she got to fly jets and practice space-walking and be assigned to go on missions, yet it clearly counted that she was an accomplished astrophysicist too. A scientist who used her knowledge and skills to solve important challenges. A scientist who was *also* an adventurer and part of a crew with a mission. She might have seemed larger than life, but instead she was surprisingly real and relatable. She was accomplishing something that no American woman ever had and, in the process, opening the door for the rest of us. As I listened to her speak that day, an utterly unexpected idea popped into my head: *Maybe I—Cady Coleman—could have that job.*

I didn't say it out loud to anyone. I'd have felt foolish or naïve. I knew the selection process was tough. I didn't know what it would take to be qualified to apply, or if I could pass the physical. I knew the odds of being picked were ridiculously low. It felt almost taboo to consider it seriously. All the same, I couldn't seem to let it go. Couldn't this be me? I was training to be a scientist. I was planning on entering the Air Force (I'd gone to college on an ROTC scholarship, which meant I'd be serving four years after graduation). Okay, I was not the most organized of students. But I was smart, persistent, and not afraid to challenge myself. The idea began to glow like a little ember inside me. My secret, quiet, joyful thought. *I could have that job. At least, I could try. Maybe, just maybe, I, too, could be a scientist who went to space and made a difference there.*

At the reception after the talk, I got in line with my friend Megan Smith and dozens of other young women to meet Sally. Megan remembers that I asked Sally a question and she answered it. But I can't recall any of what was said. What I do remember, as tangibly as if it were yesterday, is the feel of her hand when she shook mine. Small. Strong. Female. The ember glowed a little brighter.

If You Can See It, You Can Be It

That day, without even knowing it, Sally gave me one of the most precious gifts we can receive from another human being: *permission*. It wasn't explicit—I certainly didn't tell her that I wanted to be an astronaut, nor did I ask for her blessing. But nevertheless, her example made something real that had not been real for me before. Sure, I'd known it was possible, but in a possible-for-someone-else kind of way. Sally showed me that an astronaut could look and feel like me. And in doing so, she made it possible for me to imagine that I could be one too.

I'm sure that some of you read that word—*permission*—and cringe. It doesn't sound very empowered or liberated. Why should we need anyone's permission? And probably we shouldn't. In a perfect world, we would be beyond all that by now. But this isn't a perfect world, and I needed that permission as my catalyst. Maybe you do too. And I can guarantee you that despite real progress in making opportunities more inclusive, there is someone, even in this day and age, who will need that unspoken permission from you or from me. It's extraordinary what a difference it can make to see someone like us—someone who looks like us, who loves like us, whose background is like ours—doing things we might never have even considered that we could do.

If you can see it, you can be it. Representation doesn't fix everything, but it changes, on a visceral level, the menu of options that you feel you can reach for. No matter how many people tell us we can be whatever we want to be—and my mother told me that from the moment I was old enough to understand—some of us need more than words. Representation matters. A lot. We are enormously influenced by the signals that we get from our surroundings. What do people expect of us? What models do we have? What limitations do we internalize without knowing it? In her quiet, matter-of-fact way, Sally Ride shattered assumptions I didn't know I'd taken on—those same assumptions that my mother didn't know she held, but that led her to almost leave me sleeping while my brother watched the moon landing. As Sally spoke about the mission she was about to undertake, I let myself dream.

Chapter 2

Please, Underestimate Me

Leveraging Your Insecurities to Beat Expectations

"You would have to be some kind of exception, Miss Coleman."

The tone of Mr. Peterson's voice made it perfectly clear that in his estimation, I was anything but exceptional. My heart sank.

Anyone from the Air Force who applied to become an astronaut in the 1980s and '90s knows the name *Mr. Peterson*. You didn't get to be an astronaut—or even to apply for selection—without talking to him. I'd never met him in person (we were speaking by phone), but I could picture him clearly. He probably wore a tolerant but kindly expression, as if it were his job to prepare naïve young officers like me for the inevitable. No doubt he was sitting at one of those government-style gunmetal gray desks with a heavy piece of glass on top. I imagined that he would put phone numbers under that glass that were going to be important for a long time.

No one just *becomes* an astronaut. Every astronaut is something else first. A scientist. An engineer. A pilot. A doctor. And fewer than half are members of the armed forces. I checked two of those boxes: I was a chemist, and I was serving in the U.S. Air Force. At this point, I was working at the Air Force Research Laboratory as a research chemist, which meant I was developing materials for airplanes, like new versions of Kevlar and smart materials for windshields. In my spare time, I was also completing my PhD dissertation and getting ready to apply to NASA. However, Mr. Peterson, whose job was to oversee all the "special flying programs," including the Air Force's preselection of astronaut candidates to send over to NASA, had just finished explaining to me that I wasn't qualified to apply for the 1990 astronaut selection. Military applicants needed to have served for a full four years before they were eligible for selection to apply to the NASA astronaut corps. Most, in fact, were test pilots with at least ten years of experience. Having delayed my Air Force service to go to graduate school, I only had two years under my belt. But I'd thought that my doctorate would put me in a strong enough position to apply regardless.

"If I were a civilian, I'd be well qualified," I protested.

"But you're not a civilian, ma'am," he replied.

I sat up a little straighter. I hated that he was right, but he was. I was not a civilian. I was a first lieutenant in the Air Force, and proud of it. My scientific qualifications wouldn't change the fact that there was a regulation, Mr. Peterson explained, so I would need to obtain a waiver. A waiver would at least get my application looked at by the USAF board, and hopefully it would be one of the ones they selected to forward to NASA. But to get one, I would have to be "some kind of exception," Mr. Peterson had said. Period. End of conversation. The notion was clearly beyond his imagination. *Why*, I could almost hear him thinking, *would NASA pick someone so . . . unlikely?* He wasn't being mean; he just knew something I'd only learn later: that very few scientists had ever been selected and passed on to NASA from the military. He also recognized, in a way that I didn't fully grasp at the time, how different I was from the typical test pilot or flight-test engineer applicant. I could tell that he was a caring man who no doubt thought he was helping me by being realistic.

Familiar feelings of insecurity and inadequacy began to scratch around the edges of my mind. *Perhaps I'm not astronaut material after all. And even if I can get around the bureaucracy and apply, my chances of getting picked sound like they are minuscule.*

By this point in my career, I'd learned a thing or two about dealing with people who underestimated me, and the feelings they evoked in me. This wasn't the first time that I'd been told I couldn't do something, it wasn't going to happen, it was a long shot, the chances were too small, it would require a miracle, and all the other discouraging things people say when you dare to imagine you could do something beyond their ability to envision. Indeed, I'd come to anticipate being underestimated. Happily, I'd learned to use it to my advantage.

Here's how it works. Whenever someone underestimates me, doubts me, or implies I'm not up to a task, I begin to doubt myself too. But it also triggers a slow burn deep inside me. Determination begins to simmer. That slow burn turns into a driver, a motivator—it makes me want to *do* that thing to prove to them, and to myself, that we were *both* wrong. If you tell me I can't do something—I don't have the experience; I'm the wrong type; I'm too small; I'm too female; I'm just too different—that slow burn ignites. Before I know it, I'm putting pressure on myself to do everything I know I'm capable of, plus things that surprise me.

In this way, insecurity has served as a catalyst in my life—maybe not the healthiest one, but a catalyst all the same—for accomplishment. Many people assume that I must be very determined to have done what I've done. And I am. I'm naturally persistent, tenacious, and optimistic. But what people don't realize is that I can also get discouraged easily. I doubt myself at times that might surprise you. In those moments, determination becomes a compensation strategy to keep my insecurity at bay. It reminds me of something I've heard said about courage: Courage is not the absence of fear; it's acting in the face of fear. In the same way, grit and determination, for me, are not the absence of self-doubt and insecurity. They are acting in the face of self-doubt and insecurity.

I often wonder how other people deal with their own moments of self-doubt. People you'd never guess were inwardly insecure. It's easy to look around at others and assume they're supremely confident. I can't tell you how many times I've misjudged someone. I look at the way they're acting and think they couldn't possibly feel the way I do. It is easy to make the mistake, as the writer Anne Lamott puts it, of comparing our insides to somebody else's outsides. Maybe those who look most outwardly determined and focused are in fact acting that way in proportion to the intensity of their inner insecurity. Maybe they are just doing a really good job of proving their own doubts wrong.

That's exactly what I did during that phone call with Mr. Peterson. My treasured dream of becoming an astronaut seemed to be slipping further out of reach, and everyone who'd ever doubted me (including myself) was in danger of being proven right. But as Mr. Peterson uttered that word—*exception*—I felt the slow burn start.

I was polite—when am I ever not polite?—but I didn't back down. In fact, I spoke cheerfully, as though we were on the same team—a team that was going to be successful.

"Well, Mr. Peterson, I *am* an exception," I said firmly, as much to myself as to him. I assured him that we'd be talking again. "In fact," I added, "I think you should write down my name and my phone number on an index card and put that card under the glass on your desk. Because you are going to be calling me. You and I will be talking *a lot*. And maybe someday I'll be calling you from my desk at NASA."

After that conversation, I was more determined than ever. I *would* get that waiver; I *would* apply for astronaut selection. Mr. Peterson's kind but discouraging attitude, and the very real obstacles he'd pointed out, only fueled my commitment. It helped me to picture that index card with my name and phone number staring at him from under the glass on his desk as he made his important phone calls to the kinds of exceptional people NASA was looking for. One day, I vowed, one of those calls would be to me.

Motivation Comes in Many Forms

When did that slow burn first ignite? Certainly my dad played a part in that story. It wasn't so much that he underestimated me; he simply didn't know *how* to estimate me. He was proud of how smart I was, but it didn't occur to the people in his world that girls or women could do risky, adventurous, consequential things like they did every day as deep-sea divers. But I persisted nonetheless, spurred on by my own innate sense that I was supposed to do such things, and by my mom's unflagging confidence in me. And perhaps the upside of my dad's attitude was that from an early age I felt an inner pressure to make something of myself, to exceed his expectations.

By the time I was in high school, our parents had divorced, and my siblings Jamey, Cari, Kip, and I were living with our mom in Fairfax, Virginia, just outside of Washington, D.C. The public schools there were among the best in the country, and often had accelerated classes that I gravitated toward. When I showed up for Advanced Physics class, it was me and five boys. On day one, our teacher, Mr. Van Mater, proposed that we'd begin on chapter 4 of the textbook. "I'm sure all of you have those first three chapters down, right?"

Well, no, I didn't. And I didn't want to start out the class being hopelessly behind. I'd come here to learn, not to pretend I already understood. So I raised my hand and confessed that there were certain things in chapters 2 and 3 that I hadn't grasped yet. I could feel the eye rolls from my classmates and imagined that Mr. Van Mater was mentally rolling his too. Clearly, I'd established that I didn't belong there. I sensed his disappointment, and the irritation of the boys, as he turned the pages back to answer my questions. I wonder if others in the class were secretly relieved to review the opening chapters. I'm betting they were. Now, looking back, I've realized that feeling compelled to voice questions that others were reluctant to ask has been a role I have played throughout my life, in contexts that ranged from NASA mission briefings to local town council meetings. I've found I can make surprisingly powerful contributions that way, catalyzing important conversations and connections.

It didn't take too long for Mr. Van Mater to realize I was smart, eager to learn, and teachable, and he became a supportive and encouraging figure. But my classmates were another story. Most of those boys had one overriding goal: to attend MIT. They made it sound like some earthly paradise for smart future innovators and Nobel Prize winners (all of them men, of course). It clearly never occurred to them that I would apply there. Actually, it had never occurred to me either. Why would I want to go to a nerd school where people did nothing but study? But something about their certainty that I wouldn't apply, that it wasn't a place for me, just made me mad. They seemed to think it borderline hilarious that I would dream of going to MIT. *I'm pretty sure I could get in,* I thought. *My grades are just as good as theirs.* So I applied—partly to prove them wrong; partly to see if I could prove myself right.

When the letter came, I was working at my after-school job at the local library, shelving books. My mom had opened the envelope.

"Hey, Cady, you got into MIT!" She sounded thrilled.

To my surprise, I felt thrilled too—much more than I was prepared to let on. "Mom, you know I get in trouble when you call me at work," I told her, keeping my tone casual and speaking quietly from the phone behind the checkout desk. "And I can't believe you opened my mail. I'm not going to go to that nerd school anyway." But . . . they wanted *me.* What would it be like? Despite myself, I was curious.

My mom—who seldom underestimated me—was the one who insisted that I get on a train to Boston (a six-hour trip) and visit the campus. So I did. A guy who'd gone to my high school kindly agreed to show me around (I think *his* mother insisted), and as we toured the various buildings and dorms I realized that it wasn't just a bunch of guys like my physics classmates. There were people like me, who were interested in science but also liked to have fun, hang out with friends, and play music. Maybe I could fit in here after all. And it turned out I did. But if it hadn't been for those obnoxious boys in high school underestimating me, I might never even have applied.

There's an upside to being underestimated. But that doesn't mean it hurts less in the moment. It's no fun being stereotyped or dismissed out of hand because you aren't what people were expecting. It stings not to be taken seriously or to be judged lacking before you've even tried. It's frustrating not to even be invited to a meeting because people can't imagine why you would need to be there. And unless you're an unusually self-confident person, those judgments can set off internal judgments as well.

Would I prefer to live in a world where everyone was encouraging, supportive, and free of bias? Would I rather be surrounded by people who see and affirm my potential and challenge me to live up to it? Of course. And today, my strategy is to proactively create that environment, to gather people around me who will help me succeed and to be part of that supportive circle for others as well. But looking back, I wonder, would I personally have gotten so far without the extra boost I got from my need to prove my doubters wrong? As long as we live in a flawed and biased world—and given human nature, that may always be the case— it's helpful to learn how to use the uncomfortable experience of being underestimated as a spur to success rather than a reason to quit.

I confess I've been guilty of underestimating people myself, as much as I try not to. I believe we all need to work to reveal and deconstruct our unconscious biases so that we don't unknowingly discount people who don't "fit" our narrow expectations. Case in point, not long after I got to MIT, I had to choose a lab partner for organic chemistry. Picking the right partner was critical. On the first day, I spied a new transfer student across the room. She was blond. Beautiful. Smiley. *She looks like Miss California*, I thought, followed by, *I'll bet she can't be that good at chemistry.* I ended up partnering with Steve Kim, a guy who *did* look the part of Serious Science Person. He and I turned out to be a great team. But to my surprise, I quickly became friends with Miss California, otherwise known as Laura Kiessling, who was actually from Wisconsin. She and I ended up working together in the lab almost every day for the next three years. Whenever we were together, we couldn't stop laughing. We also couldn't stop getting top grades. These two things in combination puzzled our classmates. If we were as unserious as we came across, why were we doing so well?

Today, Laura Kiessling is an internationally respected chemistry pioneer who heads up her own lab as a professor at MIT. She's a MacArthur "Genius Grant" fellow. And she's still one of my closest friends. We have fun recalling our MIT days, including how when she laid eyes on *me*, Laura's first thought was, *She's too cute to be any good at chemistry.* We're even, I guess.

As a member of ROTC, my MIT education was paid for, in exchange for serving in the Air Force after getting my undergraduate degree. But when I graduated, I was given the opportunity to postpone my commitment in order to study polymer chemistry at the University of Massachusetts, the best place in the world for that field. Five years later, I'd finished all the research for my PhD, and it was time to start my military service, which meant that I'd be writing my dissertation in my spare time.

I was thrilled to be assigned as a research chemist at the Air Force Research Laboratory in Dayton, Ohio. It was the perfect place for me, a chance to do the kind of research I had trained for. But completing my dissertation while working full time was one of the hardest things I've ever done. And I've done a lot of hard things.

Don't Forget to Breathe

"You think a *girl* can do this?" Tommy would ask, drawling out the word *girl* as he looked me up and down, as if measuring my five feet and four inches from the vantage point of his much larger frame.

"Well, let's see!" I'd reply.

Tommy ran the Air Force Research Laboratory's human centrifuge testing panel, for which I was a volunteer medical subject. We had this conversation, a ritual of sorts, before every test run. He liked to tease me about being female—never in a mean-spirited way; he just liked to give everyone a hard time. Tommy, in fact, had great respect for the women in the program, most of whom had excelled in the tests. I enjoyed the camaraderie and never took his teasing personally. But nonetheless, his jokes felt close to the bone. The voices of my inner insecurities sometimes sounded just like him. Did I think *I* could do this? Well, there was only one way to find out, and that was to do it. Start with facts and actions, not assumptions.

I think I was at the bar on the Air Force base when I first heard about the centrifuge program. Occasionally, on a Friday night, I'd take a break from writing to go out with friends, just so I could remember how it felt to be a person rather than a person who hasn't finished their dissertation. At the bar, I heard people talking about how the centrifuge program was looking for volunteer subjects. It sounded challenging. It also sounded pretty cool. I don't think anyone ever suggested it would be too hard for me, but it sounded like the kind of thing they wouldn't expect a small, female person to sign up for, let alone do well at. And even as my inner voices clamored their agreement with this imagined judgment, the slow burn began. *Maybe I could do that. I could be a centrifuge subject.* It would be a way to prove to myself—and to the people at NASA, never far

from my awareness in those days as I worked to build my application—
that I wasn't just a chemist. I could learn what it meant to be a medical
subject and to test new flight equipment, both important parts of an astronaut's job. It would make me more qualified and show that I was
tough. Tougher than I looked. Tougher than I imagined people thought I
was. Tough enough to go to space.

The minimum qualifications for becoming an astronaut these days
are having a master's degree in a technical field and passing the flight
physical. There isn't a standard checklist for the other, less tangible qualifications, but the job itself includes flying high-performance aircraft
and carrying out space missions, both of which require skills and experiences that demonstrate an operational perspective. This was a strength
for applicants with aviation backgrounds, like military pilots and navigators, who had already learned what kind of training and attention to detail are necessary to successfully complete high-stakes missions.

As a scientist, my lab experience with fire and chemical safety and
detailed procedures was valuable, but I lacked some important aspects of
that operational perspective, so I looked for opportunities to gain that
experience. I learned to fly and to scuba dive—adventurous activities
that I'd always wanted to pursue. Now I was also excited to be building
skills that would make me a stronger astronaut applicant. I also made
new friends, including Jackie Parker, one of the first woman test pilots,
and Eileen Bjorkman, one of the few women test engineers, both of whom
made that world of flight operations more real and exciting to me. Volunteering for the centrifuge program was another way to show myself,
and NASA, that I could operate effectively as a member of a test team in
stressful and physically challenging situations.

The point of the centrifuge program is to test what happens to the
human body and to various kinds of equipment in high-acceleration situations, up to 9gs (or nine times the force of gravity). If you're going to fly
a high-performance jet, you need the right protective equipment to help

you withstand g-forces and perform your mission without losing consciousness. It's also important that the equipment you are using in the cockpit functions well in a high-g environment. The last thing the military wants is pilots passing out or equipment malfunctioning during combat. The same goes for NASA, since flying T-38 jets and space shuttle launches also involve g-forces.

So I applied to be a medical subject, underwent the required physical, and was thrilled to be accepted. There were about a dozen people in the centrifuge testing group at the time, including four women. On my first day of training, I showed up at the giant, circular building feeling nervous and a little giddy with anticipation. First, there was a meeting where they explained to me what would be happening, including instructions for what to do if you felt like you were going to pass out or throw up. Until that moment, I'd been fairly confident being hurled around in this contraption wouldn't make me lose my breakfast. I guess I am a born optimist, and my default setting in the face of new experiences is delight. *Oh well*, I thought, *good thing I've always had a pretty strong stomach.*

Getting my first flight suit was a great milestone: coveralls with a dozen zippered pockets that pilots wore to fly airplanes and casually referred to as their "bag." The suit was a dark army-green, and before I put it on, I was fitted out with electrodes and sensors so the folks in the control room could monitor my vital signs during the centrifuge run. Looking at myself in the mirror, I could hardly believe it was me. But it felt right—like I was supposed to be wearing all this gear and helping with research that was critical to the Air Force mission. On top of the flight suit, they helped me put on a g-suit, which is a special pair of leggings that come up to midthigh. It is constructed with a pattern of panels and tubing so that air can be pumped into the panels, creating compression around your legs, like a blood pressure cuff. When a fighter jet accelerates through a turn at high speed, the g-forces can be intense, causing your blood to rush from your head down to your feet. The suit is designed to counteract that effect.

The hub of the centrifuge sits in the middle of a cavernous circular facility, its thirty-foot-long arm extending outward from the center. It looks a bit like something you'd see at an amusement park, only much bigger and more intimidating. At the end of the arm is a capsule the size of a ski-resort gondola car, known as the cab. Inside the cab is a replica of a cockpit, complete with an actual seat from whatever jet we are testing. The technicians helped me into the seat, which leans back at an angle, just as it would in a plane, strapping me in securely with seat belts over my shoulders, across my lap, and from the floor to my waist. In front of me was a camera that the control room would be using to watch my face closely during the test. They could also speak to me through my headset. They reminded me that this first ride would be an easy "orientation run," just to get me accustomed to the sensation of "pulling gs." The main purpose was training, but in retrospect, I realize it may also have been a test. I took them at their word, however, and didn't feel much anxiety about needing to perform. I was so excited!

The cab closed, the centrifuge started to spin, and I felt the pressure begin to build, pushing down on my head and pinning me back into my seat. I had no sense of which way the centrifuge was moving or which direction was up or down. The voice from the control room told me, "Breathe. Breathe. Relax your face. That's it. Don't forget to breathe."

As the speed increased, I felt the blood leaving my head, and my field of vision began to narrow into a tunnel that seemed to shrink with every revolution of the centrifuge. They kept this intro run at amusement park ride levels, about 2gs, so that I could experiment with techniques to stand my ground and keep those encroaching gray edges of the tunnel from reaching the center. The fight to stay conscious is a very particular athletic challenge. The closest comparison is the experience of pulling your stomach in tight and straining with your core. Somehow the combination of those motions forces the blood to stay up in your head. It's easy to forget to breathe in the midst of it. When you see the video footage, your face looks strange and distorted. I found it fascinating to watch my face getting flattened and smooshed, as if I were directly in front of the world's most powerful wind machine. (Dating tip: do not let the video of your squished face in the centrifuge be the first way you are introduced to your future mother-in-law.)

Once the machine came to a stop, it still felt like everything around me was in motion—not spinning around me as can sometimes happen when you're dizzy, but when I bent my head down, the ceiling and the walls rushed downward with me, like a wave crashing over my head. The operators came and opened the cab door to help me, holding me on either side as I stepped out. They had me sit down on the step at the base of the cab until I could get my bearings. In some ways, the aftermath was more challenging than the run itself, the first few times. Fortunately, with every ride, my head learned to compensate, and soon I barely noticed the transition.

In the centrifuge, we weren't just testing our own physiology; our mission was to test equipment. For example, there was a new pair of night-vision goggles that had been designed for pilots. They were heavy. And in a high-g situation, heavy things get heavier. How would a pilot feel wearing these goggles at 3, 4, or 5gs? Would they still be able to see their controls and fly the airplane? Would the goggles slip down their nose and obstruct their breathing? That's the kind of thing we tested.

During my time as a volunteer, the g-suit itself was being redesigned, and they wanted to test a couple of different configurations—one that didn't come up so high on the leg, and one that included sleeves as well. For these tests, they had us play a video game during the run—something like today's *Candy Crush*—so that they could measure how well we could focus. The test profile alternated between thirty seconds at 3.5gs and thirty seconds at 7gs—back and forth until you couldn't handle it anymore.

They don't tell you how long they think that will take. I'm not good at keeping track of things like that; I always lose count of the laps when I'm running on the track. Eventually, I just got to a point where I was tired and decided it was time to stop. I came out, and the guys were all looking at me kind of strangely. *Oh no*, I sighed, *not long enough*. But I tried to be matter-of-fact.

"You know, I'm still figuring this new g-suit out. I'm sure I'll do better next time."

"No, it was okay," one of the guys responded quickly.

"Okay, good," I said, my mind already occupied with how I'd do better next time and prove that I wasn't a lightweight.

It was only later that night that I found out through the grapevine that everyone else had only been lasting about six minutes. I had done eighteen. I had broken a record! It turns out I did well under the pressure of gs.

When the folks at Boeing wanted to try out a new seat geometry for their fighter jets, they brought it to our facility for testing. And I heard that they were quite concerned when they were told they would only get one subject for a series of five runs, and that it would be me.

They told Tommy, "If we only get to try this with one person, we don't really want it to be the girl."

Tommy stared at them. "Listen, if anybody can show that your idea works, it's the girl. She can do anything." Later, he also wrote me a rec-ommendation for the astronaut program.

Who Are You under Pressure?

The pressure in the centrifuge is artificially created in order to replicate particular real-world situations. But it's real pressure. I feel it, just as much as a fighter pilot does. Of course, I can push a button to stop it, unlike the pilot hurtling through the air in a small plane. But even knowing that, the forces are still intense. And there's nothing like pressure to show you how well something—or someone—really works. In the case of the centrifuge, understanding how we, and our equipment, functioned in that simulated high-g environment was critically important for avoiding costly and even deadly incidents in real life.

Throughout my career, in large and small ways, I've intentionally created or sought out pressure in order to test, challenge, or improve my performance. In the centrifuge, I learned that I'm good at staying focused and bringing all my skills to bear when things get intense. The same is true, I've discovered, in other high-pressure situations.

I'll admit, I'm a world-class procrastinator. I've often relied on the old college-student trick of leaving an assignment to the very last minute, using the pressure of the impending deadline to motivate myself to finish the job. That time pressure can also be a way to force my way through an uncomfortable or difficult task that I care about. Not only do I *have* to finish by the deadline, but the only way to do so in a short time is to give it my all.

The pressure of being evaluated is one that also works well for me, although it's not much fun. This goes back to insecurity, of course. In those situations, reminding myself that I'm prepared, that I've practiced all that I can, is the key to being free to perform at my best, proving to myself and others that I have the skills to succeed.

Of course, pressure can be positive too. When people around me have faith in me and expect me to do well, their expectations create a pressure that keeps me focused and energized. Once I start doing well at something, the positive feedback gives me the momentum I need to continue to improve. Motivation and inspiration, whether they come from outside or inside, can be positive pressures pushing you forward.

Another kind of pressure comes with accepting tasks that have serious consequences attached to success or failure. I thrive in those jobs, because I know that they are precisely the circumstances in which I feel compelled to bring everything I have. I'm all in. I do whatever needs to be done. Knowing this has given me the courage to sign up for these high-pressure missions and tasks, to put myself in situations where failure could be costly, or worse.

None of us excel under pressure all the time. But the mistakes we make under pressure, as one of my instructors once told me, are the greatest gifts. They teach us about ourselves. Sometimes a mistake is just random. But we each have certain kinds of mistakes we're more likely to make, or situations that tend to trip us up. By embracing high-pressure opportunities, we can observe our mistakes, look for patterns, and decode our particular triggers and our vulnerabilities. Those experiences help us anticipate and avoid making mistakes in situations where they might put the mission or lives at risk.

That's why training in high-pressure simulations is so critical for people in high-risk jobs. You can never fully replicate an actual crisis in a training situation, but the pressure of being evaluated and judged on your performance in a simulation is surprisingly effective in highlighting areas that might need improvement for you and your team. When you're performing an emergency simulation for a fire or a toxic leak inside a mock-up of the space station, you know that the smoke is artificial and the air you're breathing is perfectly safe. But knowing that you're being graded adds another level of stress that can bring out your most likely mistakes. You might skip a critical step in a procedure, or not hear or listen to a crewmate's suggestion. These are valuable insights, applicable across all of your training, and it is best to learn them early and while you're safely on the ground. I've come to look at pressure as an ally and a teacher.

There are many ways in which we can choose to create or embrace pressure to learn about and enhance our own capacities. But sometimes in life, both at home and at work, the pressure is there whether we want it or not. Sometimes it can seem like life is cranked up to 9gs and we're spinning out of control. We didn't choose our circumstances; it's not a test; and it's hard to turn it into a positive. These are the times when I hear Tommy's voice from the centrifuge control room. *Don't forget to breathe.* Sometimes, the only thing you can do about the pressure that you're under is to stay present, stay conscious, and keep breathing till the spinning stops.

Wrong Number, Right Guy

Not long after I joined the centrifuge program, I had one of those chance encounters that occasionally come along in life—the kind that can make even a rational-minded scientist like me believe that something can be written in the stars. I met the love of my life by dialing a wrong number.

I already knew Josh Simpson by name and reputation—he is a world-famous glass artist who is known for his otherworldly glass spheres that he calls "planets." I'd loved them for years and had always wanted to meet Josh, whose studio was in a small town nearby, although as a starving grad student, I had never bought one of his planets for myself. I had given one to my stepsister as a wedding gift; and my friend Amy Marsters, whose husband was also an artist, had started working at Josh's studio just as I was leaving to start working with the Air Force.

That fateful day in December 1990, I was celebrating having successfully defended my dissertation, after five years of grad school and two more hermit-like years of writing while working full time. Whenever I meet a major milestone in life, I like to commemorate it in some way, and this was a big one indeed. So I decided this was the day I would buy my very own Josh Simpson planet—just a small one that could sit on my desk and remind me that I could do hard things like finish my dissertation and that now it was time to work on my next big goal, becoming an astronaut. I drove to the gallery that sold them, but by the time I got there, it was late and the sheer number of cool planets to choose from overwhelmed me. Not wanting to rush the decision, I resolved to return the next day. Looking at the planets made me think about Amy, who I hadn't talked to in ages. I decided to call her.

A man answered. Amy's husband, Peter? But the voice on the other end of the phone was heavily accented—something Slavic. Bulgarian, perhaps?

"I guess you're not Peter," I said.

"Oh, no!" the man replied. "I am Olga Ezneechko Eahvorskyah Gupta Mehmet Ali Aghar Manop Boonyavatana. You look for Peter? You look for Amy? Amy work here no more. You look in phone book, Ash-Field."

At this point, I realized that I'd called Amy's work number by mistake. The artist's place. This strange guy must also work there.

"Okay, thanks," I said, about to hang up the phone.

"But wait!" he exclaimed. "You must tell them hello from Olga Ezneechko Eahvorskyah Gupta Mehmet Ali Aghar Manop Boonyavatana." Knowing that I would never be able to say this convoluted mouthful of syllables, I told him politely that I probably couldn't do that. I might be able to manage "Olgi Nichki."

"Oh no!" he declared. "Muzt be whole name. We praaactiiiice!" I held the phone away from my ear and looked at it suspiciously, wondering if this guy was for real. And he proceeded to coach me through the pronunciation, making me repeat his name over and over.

Meanwhile, I was shaking my head at the phone in my hand with the giant Slavic voice booming over the speaker and trying not to laugh. And for once, I wasn't in a hurry to be doing anything else. After months of being chained to my lab and my desk, I was coming up for air, just for a day, before diving into corrections on my dissertation tomorrow. I was feeling more playful than I had in a long time. I finally pronounced the name to the man's satisfaction, thanked him for his time, and hung up. If nothing else, at least I had a funny story to tell Amy.

As soon as she picked up, I relayed the whole encounter, building up to my carefully rehearsed message: "He wanted me to tell you hello from—" I took a deep breath and launched into the name.

Amy cracked up. "Oh, that's just Josh."

Josh? In my mind, he was this old, famous, serious-artist guy who lived up in the hills. She went on to explain that the studio phone also rang in his house, and he hated answering machines and liked to "screen" his own calls at night.

I was immediately intrigued. I'd been known to play a practical joke or two myself, and someone that funny should have someone be funny back. Grinning, I dialed the studio again. Adopting my best Russian accent, I told him I was from the KGB.

"Vee have numerous reports of glass breaking in the area," I declared. "Your number eeez up."

"Oh, but I not Russian. I am Bulgarian!" he protested.

"We do zem too, and you are heestory," I insisted.

He started laughing, and I introduced myself as Amy's friend. We chatted for a while, and he invited me to visit the studio any time I was in the area. "I will," I promised, fully intending that I would—someday. And that might have been the end of it, except that the next day, while at the library making corrections to my dissertation, I had lunch with Sally Prasch, a scientific glassblower at the university's glass shop who had designed much of the glassware I used in my research. I knew that she must know Josh, so my first words to her were, "You'll *never* guess what happened to me yesterday. . . ."

Rather than laughing at my ridiculous story, her face grew serious and a little dreamy. Sally, as well as being an incredibly skilled glassblower, is an incurable romantic. "Cady," she said, "You *have* to meet this guy."

"You know, I've always wanted to," I said. "But maybe sometime when I'm not crazy busy correcting my dissertation and haven't slept!"

"No, no," she insisted. "Here's what you're going to do. You're going to hustle back to that library and finish those corrections like your life depends on it, and then you'll have an extra hour at the end of the day, and you're going to drive up to the studio and meet this guy. We're calling him right now." And she picked up the phone and dialed his number.

Josh was friendly on the phone and said it was a great time to tour the studio, but apologized that it would have to be quick because he had dinner plans with his seven-year-old son, Josiah. Privately, I was thinking, "What does he think this is, a date?" But I thanked him, said I'd see him later, and hurried back to the library. And then I drove out to Shelburne Falls, Massachusetts, where Josh's studio sits beside a farmhouse on a beautiful hilltop. I can still picture myself, wearing an ugly, itchy sweater, standing just inside the studio door and locking eyes with the not-so-old and actually-quite-attractive artist himself. Turned out I'd done that underestimating thing again.

He showed me around his studio, a big barn filled with roaring glass furnaces and an amazing array of glass pieces—not just planets, but vases and platters, all evoking the wonder of the night sky. I remember thinking that we definitely shared a love of chemistry when he explained how he achieved the jewel-toned colors in his glass. And then he asked me about myself and my work. What was I planning to do now that I'd gotten my doctorate?

"I'm applying to be an astronaut."

The words came out of my mouth without a moment's hesitation. I had barely told anyone at this point, and I definitely hadn't told anyone with such conviction and confidence. But it just seemed evident to me that this visionary artist—an explorer in his own way, who had defied the odds and become successful—would understand. And he did. He didn't even look surprised. For the first time, I felt like I had company on my quest, someone beside me who also believed in the impossible and delighted in seeing it happen.

I went to dinner with Josh, and his son, after all. And I came back to visit a few days later. He called every night for months. And pretty soon it was clear that in dialing that wrong number, I'd found exactly the right guy.

Unexpected Astronaut

Human beings are quirky creatures. I know I am. We each have unique personality patterns and habits, some of which help us thrive and others that may become vulnerabilities. Sure, there are some bad habits we can change and some unhelpful psychological knots we can untangle. But for those that are more stubborn, rather than pretend we're someone we're not, we're better served by honestly admitting them (at least to ourselves) and finding ways to work with or around them.

In some cases, we can find ways to use those traits to our advantage, like with my insecurity. While I still work to improve it, I can also leverage its power to motivate. You may be surprised how far this strategy can take you—I know I have been. My relationship to insecurity has been reshaped by those times when it has served me well. When feelings of self-doubt get triggered, they are less daunting, and I can stay steady, knowing that they don't have the power to derail me.

After that conversation with Mr. Peterson, I applied for and received the waiver to exempt me from the military service requirement. I still missed the 1990 selection—it took time to complete my doctorate and make my case for the waiver. Mr. Peterson eventually came around (indeed, he became one of my greatest advocates). In March 1991, I submitted my NASA application to the Air Force, and in June I was thrilled to learn that it had been selected for forwarding to NASA. Technically, it was still the very beginning of the selection process, and a total of 2,054 people had applied that year, but I was on my way!

I got to know several of my fellow Air Force applicants, and we dubbed ourselves the Astronaut Hopefuls, or ASHOs. We'd share updates anytime we heard something that indicated a step forward. *They checked my references! That means I made the cut. Now there are five hundred.* The second-to-last hurdle was being selected for an interview at the Johnson Space Center. Only about ninety of the applicants would get this call—and I was one of them. When a kind-voiced woman named Teresa Gomez called from the Astronaut Office in mid-October to tell me the news, she asked, "Would you like to come down in December or later?" December?! That seemed like forever. I wanted to come right now! But I swallowed my impatience and told her that December would be great, thank you very much.

As soon as I hung up, I couldn't wait to tell my parents. I'll never forget my dad's reaction. He was so clearly pleased. But he was also so clearly surprised.

The "interview" consisted of a weeklong trip to Houston in early December as part of a group of twenty hopefuls. Once all five groups had been interviewed, NASA would select the new class. We had no idea how many would make that final cut. It was common knowledge that during the week we'd be asked to write an essay. For years, the topic had been "Why do you want to become an astronaut?," so it was worth preparing that in advance, which I did (after some procrastinating). I recruited the help of my running partners so I could show up in the best shape of my life. On the night we arrived, we underwent a three-hour psychological evaluation, and then, sure enough, we were informed that we'd need to write an essay. The topic? "Are we building the right space station?"

WHAT?! The one thing I'd actually done in advance, and they changed the question! But then it dawned on me: NASA wasn't just interviewing for a new class of astronauts. They were interviewing for *space station astronauts.* The plans for an international space station, to be built in partnership with Canada, Russia, Japan, and Europe, were already underway. If I got chosen, I wouldn't just be going to space; I'd potentially get to *live* in space. I borrowed a computer and stayed up all night writing about what kind of space station a scientist would build, envisioning myself up there.

The interview itself was just a small part of what was essentially a weeklong physical, but it was certainly the most nerve-racking sixty minutes of the trip. I'd carefully selected a black skirt suit with a red shirt. What I hadn't realized was that my interview was scheduled directly after I was wired up with electrodes all over my torso for the twenty-four-hour heart monitor test. I hurried over to the interview building with just minutes to spare and ran into the ladies' room to change. I hadn't exactly envisioned how my suit would look with wires sticking out in all directions. Oh well. I was ready on time, but the bathroom was a shambles. No time to clean up my clothes or do my makeup before the interview. I hurried out, madly tucking wires out of sight as I passed a woman headed for the bathroom. When I sat down in front of the committee a couple of minutes later, my heart dropped. That same woman was one of my interviewers. And she had seen the bathroom!

That woman turned out to be Rhea Seddon, one of the six original female astronauts. She had a kind, quiet manner, and I don't think she judged me for the state of the ladies' room. Sitting beside her on the panel was her husband, Hoot Gibson, who opened up the interview by saying, "Tell us about yourself, starting with high school."

High school? I was floored. Everyone had told us they'd ask about college. I'd rehearsed and refined the highlights of my time at MIT and UMass. I felt unprepared to wind back the clock any further, but I did my best, stumbling through my academic interests and how I had played the flute in the jazz band.

At my mention of the flute, Hoot interrupted me.

"So, could you play the intro to 'Stairway to Heaven'?"

Surprised, I nodded yes and told him I could, and he immediately made a little note on his pad. "Good!" Little did I know that he was the lead guitarist in the astronaut band. But his enthusiasm put me at ease, and the interview flowed more smoothly after that.

On the final night, there was a dinner at a restaurant called Pe-Te's Cajun Barbeque, where all the candidates got to talk with astronauts and management folks who they might not have met. After dinner, Rhea Seddon took me aside.

"Hey Cady," she said warmly, "have you had a good week?"

I was thrilled that she had taken the time to check in with me. And then she said something I've never forgotten. "You may or may not be thinking about having kids," she said, "but if you are thinking about it, I just want you to know that it is possible to have a family in this job. Many of us do, and we're a community that really supports each other." At the time, I really hadn't given it much thought. I knew I wanted to be an astronaut. I didn't really know if I wanted to be a mother. But it meant a lot to me that she took the time to talk to me about it. I felt like she was saying to me, "We see you. You could belong here."

At the end of the week, I flew home, and the phone watching began. They'd told us we'd be informed of our acceptance or rejection in February 1992, but as February and then March came and went, we still heard nothing. The Phone Call, I knew, would come from Don Puddy, the head of Flight Operations at NASA—*if* it was good news. If you didn't get selected, someone else on the committee called you. A lot of my work time was spent in the lab, in the center of the building, far from my office. I could forward my calls from the office to the lab. But inevitably, in that pre–cell phone era, there would be times when I was between phones and might miss The Phone Call. That's where my officemate Clyde Mitchell came in.

It was April 1 when Clyde came running toward the lab, making dramatic phone gestures with one hand through the glass of the door. For a moment, I assumed it was an April Fool's prank, but when I ran back to the office and picked up my phone, the voice on the other end said, "Hello, Cady, this is Don Puddy. How are you doing today?"

"Well, sir," I stammered, "that depends. But I heard it was really good if you called."

The answer I'd been waiting for all these months came in the form of a question: "Would you still like to come and work with us at NASA?"

"Yes, I'd like that. I'd really like that," I replied, feeling as if I were no longer attached to the floor.

"Okay, so here's the thing," he said. "You can't tell anyone for twenty-four hours."

"Not even my mom?" I tried to imagine how it would feel to keep this news to myself for a whole day.

"Is your mom the kind of mom who's likely to tell a lot of people?"

Reluctantly, I said yes.

"Then not even your mom."

As I put the phone down, some part of me was wondering, *Did that just happen?* But another part of me was glowing with a kind of validation I'd never experienced before and have never forgotten. In that moment, all the people who'd ever underestimated me—including myself—were proven wrong. Of course, this wouldn't be the last time I had to prove myself, or the last time I'd be underestimated. It wouldn't be the last time I had to battle my own self-doubt. Far from it. But in that moment, those thoughts and feelings all faded into the background. NASA had picked *me*. You don't get to be an astronaut unless you're qualified—unless you have the right stuff for the job. And NASA had decided that I did.

Chapter 3

Launching Is Not the Beginning

Celebrating the Legwork, Not Just the Liftoffs

"T minus thirty-one seconds. We are GO for auto sequence start."
The space shuttle's computers are now in control of the launch sequence. The countdown continues and I brace myself, knowing that in just seconds, the shuttle's main engines will start, the solid rocket boosters will ignite, and for the first time, I will be on my way to space.

Imagine you are sitting in an airplane seat, but the plane is tipped back ninety degrees so that its nose is pointing straight up and you are lying on your back. That's the position we are in during the space shuttle launch countdown. For the past two hours, I have been tightly strapped into my seat, directly behind the pilot's seat, while the Launch Control team works through the rigorous sequence of safety checks and preparations. I'm wearing a bright-orange spacesuit and helmet. A parachute is strapped to my back in case of emergencies. On my lap is my knee board, a kind of small clipboard with my checklists, a pencil, and pictures of my family. It also holds a small plastic mirror, pointed at the ceiling so I can see the switches there, and also see the view from the window above me because my helmet won't tip back to allow me to look directly up.

A few hours earlier, on the morning of October 20, 1995, I stepped out of the launchpad elevator with my crewmates, marveling at the view.

From twenty stories up, you can see for miles, out over the enormous spaces of Cape Canaveral and up and down the Florida coastline. With that vista, it seemed like we were already on our way to space. We were dressed in our launch and entry suits, and now the "suit techs" (our spacesuit technicians), along with one of the astronauts from my class who worked at the Cape, were waiting to help us get strapped into the shuttle, one by one. When my turn came, I was ushered into the "white room," which is not really a room but more of an open-air canopied hallway at the end of the orbiter access arm, outside the shuttle hatch. There, the suit techs helped me into my parachute harness and then performed a comical procedure in which they hold you up in the air and shake you vigorously while pulling at the wrinkles in your suit to avoid material bunching up between the harness straps.

Now, sitting in my seat, I'm glad they did this. I'm strapped in tightly, trussed up like a turkey, and my harness feels secure and snugged to my body, not just to my bulky suit. Plus, those innocent-looking wrinkles can be wildly painful. It's loud in here—the metal of the external fuel tank creaks and groans under the extremely cold temperatures of the liquid hydrogen and oxygen fuel. It feels strangely like the shuttle is alive—anticipating the launch along with me and my crewmates. And the moment is coming. Any . . . moment . . . now.

Ten . . . Nine . . . Eight . . . Seven . . . I've rehearsed this sequence dozens of times, but no simulator in the world can replicate the deafening roar as the countdown reaches six and the shuttle's three main engines kick in, one after another. The thrust from those engines forces the shuttle's nose to tilt forward six feet (it can't go anywhere yet because it's still attached to the launch platform) then swing back to vertical (a motion known as the "twang"). The pilot's voice is calm as he reports on the status of the engines. "Three at a hundred." That's good: all at full power. The force below us is overwhelming, and liftoff feels inevitable. It's clear in a visceral way that once we launch, there will be no stopping us. There is only one direction possible, away from Earth. The 4.4-million-pound vessel strains against the bolts that hold it to the launchpad, and then . . . *Three . . . Two . . . One.* The solid rocket boosters ignite—startlingly loud, even through my helmet—then the bolts explode, the shuttle leaps off the pad, and we are off. Spacebound.

I can't help but let out a whoop of celebration, and around me, my crewmates are hollering too. Five of our crew of seven are rookies, and this is our first launch. And after seven launch attempts over thirty days, we'd started to think we'd never get off the ground.

Our commander Ken Bowersox's very grown-up voice comes over our headsets: "Settle down!"

The launch of a space shuttle is a truly sensational event. My sister-in-law, not easily impressed, called it the eighth wonder of the world. From television and movies, most of us know what it looks like and sounds like from the outside—the countdown, the anticipation, the flaming boosters, the sudden propulsion skyward. The heart-stopping moment when the shuttle disappears into a cloud of smoke and water vapor and it seems like a lifetime before it emerges. I've watched many launches over my career, and I find myself tearing up at almost every one with the wonder of it all and, at the same time, the acute awareness that so much needs to go perfectly.

And yet, from the inside, it's nothing like that. I don't worry about any of those things—I'm just *launching,* and the sheer power of being in a rocket on its way to space engulfs everything. It feels less like a violent leap and more like a steady, irreversible surge. It's *relentless.* Like nothing could stop it—nothing could stop *me*—from being propelled into space. Everything shakes intensely, but I'm strapped in so tightly that my body is motionless in the seat. It's as if I'm part of the rocket. Looking in the mirror on my lap, I see the clouds shrinking into the distance as we fly past and the blue sky turns to black, but that's my only visual indication of our speed. After two minutes, which feels like forever, there's a loud bang as the solid rocket boosters (SRBs) detach, about 150,000 feet aboveground. The shuttle, freed from that extra weight, is powered upward by the main engines for another six and a half minutes. The ride is so much smoother now. It feels like we'll just keep going and going, but then . . . the engines cut off and everything seems to stop. We're in orbit around the Earth.

It's an otherworldly moment. For the past eight and a half minutes, I've felt nothing but power and momentum, so their sudden absence is shocking. All that pressure has turned to lightness. All the noise gives way to silence. I'm still strapped tightly to the seat, so my body feels the same, but inside my helmet, my head feels curiously weightless. Looking around the cabin, I see checklists bobbing at the end of the braided tethers that hold them. I glance at my crewmate Mike, sitting beside me, and he's grinning uncontrollably. I realize that I am too. For a moment, catching one another's eyes through our visors, we wordlessly celebrate. We are HERE.

There's not much time for celebration, though. In fact, we need to get right to work, doing all the things we've been practicing and training for. You see, for a crew of astronauts, a launch isn't really a beginning. It's an exciting interlude in a multiyear journey of training and preparation. People often think of the launch as the start of the mission, but the mission starts much earlier than that—both for the astronauts and for the numerous people in the space program who support that mission.

An astronaut's job begins years before the countdown starts and continues long after they land safely back on Earth. I think the same is true in many fields of life and work. Think of an entrepreneur who has an idea for an innovative product or company. They work for years developing the idea, testing it, refining the design, raising money, and finally they launch it. So the launch is not the beginning—it's just a moment when the public eye is turned on the hard work they've been doing and will continue to do. The same goes for a social activist or politician who works behind the scenes for years before launching a public campaign. Or an artist who spends years perfecting their craft before "opening night." Those dramatic moments that everyone sees are just a step on the journey. And those who succeed in their endeavors are those whose commitment to the legwork is every bit as strong as their love of the lift-off. Those who make it are the ones who are willing to create their own momentum when there are no flaming boosters propelling them forward. They're in it for the long haul—even when nobody is watching, cheering, or counting down.

My career at NASA lasted more than 24 years—that's 8,888 days to be exact. Of those days, 180 were spent in space, over the course of my three amazing missions. And only 25 minutes and 34 seconds were spent launching.

Training Begins

My journey to space began in earnest on August 3, 1992, a little over three years before my first launch. When my class of twenty-four reported to NASA for our first day of work as new astronauts, we were presented to the public at a press conference. I can still picture us standing there, unaccustomed to either our business attire or the limelight, but eager to meet one another and literally grinning from ear to ear.

After the ceremony, I climbed three flights of stairs in Building 4 South with my classmates to the floor where all the astronauts had their offices. My desk was a nondescript, institutional gray metal that made me think fondly of Mr. Peterson. Sitting on it was a stack of paper manuals at least two feet high. *Workbooks*, I was told. *I guess I have a lot to learn*, I thought. I met two of my officemates: Dave Wolf, a fascinating and sometimes gruff medical doctor, and Shannon Lucid, one of the six original woman astronauts, a biochemist. A warm, down-to-earth woman from Oklahoma, Shannon was immediately welcoming, and I was thrilled to be sharing an office with her.

Just a day or two after I arrived, Dave asked me, in what I would soon learn was his charmingly abrupt manner, what was on my schedule for 5:00 p.m. that day. When I told him I was free, he asked, "Could you come back here and hold a camera?"

"Sure," I replied.

"Good," he said, offering no more information.

I showed up at five to find Dave wielding a syringe over Shannon's arm. He handed me a camcorder and said, "Film this, but don't say anything," and then he proceeded to draw blood. It turned out that the two of them had been assigned to a Spacelab mission that focused on the effects of the space environment on human physiology—the kind of mission that highlights the role of astronauts as medical test subjects. There was a move afoot to have Shannon taken off the mission due to a perception that because she was a bit older than the other crew members, her veins might not stand up to all the blood draws needed. Clearly, Shannon and Dave thought the higher-ups were underestimating the performance of Shannon's veins. The purpose of the film was to keep the discussion focused on facts, instead of assumptions.

It clarified something for me: as space shuttle operators, we astronauts had a different perspective than our trainers and managers. That meant we had a responsibility to speak up when our experience could provide important insights.

My class was the fourteenth group of astronauts selected by NASA: nineteen Americans and five foreign astronauts. I was one of three women, along with Wendy Lawrence, a navy helicopter pilot, and Mary Ellen Weber, a materials engineer. Our class nickname was the Hogs, after *The Muppet Show* skit "Pigs in Space," and because we sponsored some Vietnamese pot-bellied pigs at the Houston Zoo. (We also sponsored some snow leopard cubs, and I campaigned hard that we be named after them, but to no avail.)

The first few months of our training felt like being freshmen in college again, except we weren't kids—most of us were in our thirties or early forties. At thirty-one, I was one of the youngest. About half of the class were from the military; the other half were scientists and engineers. I was proud to be both. One thing we all had in common from the get-go was our exhilaration at finally being here. We'd been dreaming of this for so long. When I looked at the faces of my classmates, I saw the same beaming smile on them that I glimpsed in the mirror each morning.

Within just a few days of our arrival, all the new astronauts (known as ASCANs, as in astronaut candidates) would be flying up to Fairchild Air Force Base in Washington State for land survival training. Astronauts need survival skills in case we have to bail out somewhere unexpected when returning to Earth, among other reasons. Importantly, as part of our training we'd be flying T-38 jets on a regular basis, so we needed to be prepared for emergency-landing or ejection scenarios. Little did I know that over the coming years I'd learn how to stay alive in the desert, the ocean, the forest, and even the frozen plains of Siberia.

Clearly, for the military pilots and navigators who'd already gone through a series of much more intensive survival training courses, our first session was child's play. But for those of us who were newer to aviation, this four-day trip was quite a challenge at times. We practiced navigation skills and shelter building. Knots were tied. Food was scavenged. Worms were eaten. Tired, grubby people made hard decisions together. Rules were broken, fun was had. And we got to know one another. I think that's likely why they scheduled the trip so early—there's nothing quite like facing adversity together to bond a team. Our class emerged with more trust and cohesion, ready to navigate the rest of our ASCAN year together.

Our survival training didn't stop on dry land. We also had to learn water survival skills, like disconnecting from your parachute, climbing into a raft, and making the most of the supplies we had in case we had to eject from the T-38 or bail out of the shuttle over water. This started in a swimming pool. We were wearing flight suits, boots, and parachute harnesses, all of which would quickly become waterlogged and heavy, as if we really had jumped out of the plane. Of course, we also had life vests, which are supposed to inflate automatically but can also be inflated manually if needed. That day, they told us in advance that we would need to inflate our vests manually, just like the flight attendants demonstrate on commercial airline flights. At the instructor's signal, we jumped into the pool with our heavy gear, and all around me I saw everyone's vests inflate automatically. It was clearly a mistake, and everyone started laughing, myself included, until I looked down and realized that my vest hadn't inflated and I was having trouble staying afloat.

Flustered and feeling behind, I rushed to try to inflate my vest, but I was having trouble. To my embarrassment, the divers came over and gave me a float to hold on to so I could catch my breath and then try again. "Don't worry," one of them said to me. "You can do this. You don't have to be in a hurry." Still, it was humiliating to have to get up on the side of the pool in front of twenty-three people I didn't know very well yet and try again. That time, I did fine.

Later, Mike Lopez-Alegria, one of the pilots in my class, came up to me and said, "Listen, I know it sucks to be the person that couldn't do this on their first try. And then you had to do it again in front of everybody, which you did nicely. But I'm telling you, you're the lucky one. Because in the real emergency, it's going to be worse. It's going to be scarier, and you're going to feel like you need to rush. You learned that you have more time than you think, and you learned it while you were scared. And that makes you the lucky one." I never forgot those words. In the years since, I've realized that forcing yourself to slow down is almost always good advice when faced with the unexpected.

Those early months of training were an avalanche of new information to process: for perspective, the condensed manual for the space shuttle is five inches thick. (I still keep a copy of it in our bathroom for light reading.) We learned about each of the shuttle systems, and then worked together in teams of two or three in simulators (sims) to practice the normal procedures and, importantly, learn how to react when the systems malfunctioned. We practiced mission scenarios that showed how the various systems affected one another. We memorized the function of every switch and circuit breaker. The rule of thumb was that if something was important, then we probably had three, so we'd still be okay if two of them broke. It became normal to speak in sentences like, "AC1 is down. Now critical to AC2 on the center, AC3 on the right"—kind of like playing a card game where you have to figure out which cards have already been played and which ones might still be available to save you. We learned a whole new astronaut language, including words like *nominal*, which sounds boring but is really the word you want to hear, because it means that everything is performing as expected.

Some simulators resembled wild amusement park rides, like the motion-based one that we strapped into for launch and landing sims. We'd start off lying on our backs for launch, and the sim would shake, pitch, and roll just like we could expect from the real shuttle. Other simulators weren't physically exciting, but they taught us to work with Mission Control and showed us what a day in space on a real mission could be like. Those often included lessons from "flown" astronauts, meaning those who had flown in space, as we all hoped to do. They shared stories about what it was like being part of a space crew that wouldn't be found in any workbook or manual.

There were always new skills and technologies to master, all while adjusting to the culture of NASA. We learned the basics of robotics, rendezvous (how to dock with other spacecraft without colliding), and spacewalking, and we spent time at the gym. That usually happened outside of work hours, but being in shape to work in heavy spacesuits was important, as were the conversations that you'd have there with other astronauts who you might not meet in the office. We took classes at the NASA Food Lab to sample the space food; classes on the bathroom to understand how to use it and how to fix it; and last but not least, classes on video and still photography in hopes that we wouldn't return home with America's Funniest Far-from-Home Videos. And in the midst of all that, as ASCANs, we were also constantly being evaluated, just as we would be on an actual mission. It was daunting, but having our work observed also allowed us to practice solving problems without allowing the inevitable public attention to be a distraction.

We learned the power of our position as well. At NASA, when astronauts speak, people pay attention, sometimes too much attention. So we had to be mindful when we spoke, to use our influence with care. Part of our job—and one of my favorite parts—was to listen to people at every level of the space program, encouraging them to confide their ideas and concerns and making sure those perspectives were heard.

Among so many memorable firsts, I'll never forget the day I tried on a spacesuit for the very first time. Astronauts wear three different suits— our blue flight suits, which are the coveralls we wear to fly the T-38; our orange spacesuits, which we called our "pumpkin suits," that we wore for launching and landing on the shuttle; and then the big white spacewalking suits. The schedule called this appointment my "Orange Suit Fit," and the suit techs started a file with detailed notes on how the different sizes (meant to fit guys) could be made to work for me. You'll be shocked, I'm sure, to hear that those one-piece spacesuits weren't designed for people with boobs or hips. But the technicians tried hard to find the best options to fit me up top and on the bottom without having too much material bunched up. They also took measurements for how short the arms and legs of the suit needed to be. The result? Compromises were made. The phrase "good fit" was dramatically redefined. Did I care? Not a bit. It was *my* spacesuit! Okay, technically it wasn't really my pumpkin suit (no one has their own), but it meant that they knew exactly how to configure one for me, and NASA would have a Cady-size suit ready whenever I was scheduled for a suited training exercise.

When I looked in the mirror that day, all suited up, I saw an astronaut, with a huge grin, looking back at me. My face said it all: *This is REAL!*

Learning the Operational Mindset

There were so many exciting milestones during that first year of training, each of them reinforcing the still-surprising fact that getting selected hadn't been a dream. A much-anticipated day for me was the first time I got to put on my blue flight suit (just like the one Sally Ride had been wearing when she stepped onto the stage at MIT) and fly in the T-38—a supersonic high-performance acrobatic jet that is used to train Air Force pilots and also used by NASA for astronaut training. I already loved piloting small planes, and now I got to train as a copilot (meaning I did everything but take off and land) in one of the coolest planes imaginable. I felt like one of the pilots in *Top Gun*. We don't often fly faster than the speed of sound (it's illegal over populated areas and uses a lot of fuel), but we each got to do it the first time we flew. After that first orientation flight, we spent many hours learning about the T-38 systems and practicing airport approaches and procedures in the plane. I was thrilled to be learning how to control the jet, but even more important, I was learning how to *think*.

What does flying jets have to do with thinking? Training in a high-performance aircraft is a terrific platform for developing an operational mindset—learning to make decisions and solve problems in high-speed, high-pressure, real-risk situations that can't be simulated, like the ones we might encounter when we are in space. For a scientist-astronaut like me, without an operational military background, this was invaluable. The moment you're strapped into that airplane, you are on a mission. I had to be 100 percent present. It didn't matter if I'd had a bad training session earlier that day, or if I was worried about something Josh had said on the phone earlier. All of that had to be left on the runway so that my attention was available for the moment-to-moment demands of conducting the flight safely. Among other lessons, flying the T-38 taught me the art of compartmentalization—something that would be critical when I went to space.

Fortunately for me, my friend and housemate Mark Polansky was an accomplished instructor-pilot who was always generous with his time. He helped me learn to always look ahead to the next thing that needs to be done, and the next; but not think so far ahead that you skip critical steps. I realized that I had a tendency to do just that—to consider too many possible scenarios and get ahead of myself, losing sight of the task at hand. When I got caught up in theoretical thinking, Mark would bring me back to our next step by saying, "Ah, so, how are we doing?" It became a joke between us.

"Coleman," he said to me one day after we'd flown in a formation flight just a few feet away from another T-38, matching its every move. "You were doing a fine job up there. But I'm betting that your shoulders were up around your ears. You need to relax so that you can make fluid movements with the throttles and controls, avoiding any sudden changes to your speed or position, and so you don't get tired." He was right. In fact, my shoulders were still up around my ears, even though we were on the ground. Taking a deep breath, I relaxed them. Mark continued, "Here's my suggestion: as often as you can remember to do it, wiggle your toes, because you just can't stay tense if you're wiggling your toes!"

It was a great tip and became a habit I've used many times in tense situations. Many years later, when I was launching telescopes and capturing supply ships in space, if you'd looked at my feet, you'd definitely have seen my toes moving (especially because we seldom wear shoes in space!).

Flying in the T-38, the stakes are always real, but sometimes an actual emergency happens and without any notice, you may get to test the skills you've been developing. I was flying from Houston to Cape Canaveral one day with Rick Hull, an experienced Marine instructor pilot. I liked flying with Rick; he was easy to learn from, and when we weren't too busy, it was fun to exchange stories and joke together in the cockpit. As we checked the weather in Florida, I noted that it was good at the Cape, but not looking so good in Orlando, where thunderclouds were amassing. "Good thing we don't need to stop in Orlando!" I told Rick.

As if on cue, an orange warning light appeared on the caution and warning panel at my right knee. I knew exactly what that light meant, and so did my stomach, which dropped through the floor of the aircraft. We'd lost one of our two electrical generators, and if we had lost the other one, we'd be flying solely on battery power. And the battery only lasts eighteen minutes.

I knew we'd be fine as long as we kept our heads and followed our checklists. Despite my stomach's initial response, my by now well-trained mind remained clear. As quickly as the plane could switch from the generator to the battery, Rick and I switched from light banter to focused operational mode. We pulled out our checklists, confirmed the right page, and began to work through the procedure for making a safe, expedited landing, in poor weather conditions, in Orlando.

It was only after we were safely on the ground that I felt a little shaky from the adrenaline rush. But I also felt a new kind of confidence—the kind that only comes when a real emergency puts you to the test, and you rise to the challenge, because you have *trained* to do so.

A Different Kind of Rocket Science

After the busiest twelve months of my life, all twenty-four of us in the 1992 class had completed our initial astronaut training and were considered eligible for flight. Each of us proudly received a silver astronaut pin signifying that we were no longer ASCANs but full-fledged NASA astronauts. None of us had been assigned to a space flight yet, and as eager as we were to get those assignments, we understood that it would be quite a while before anyone in the class would fly. So you can imagine how I felt just a few months later when I received a phone call out of the blue from a man who introduced himself as a mission manager from NASA's Marshall Space Flight Center:

"I'm calling to congratulate you on being selected for the crew of STS-73, a Microgravity Laboratory research flight."

I was astonished. And so excited! I was going! I was really going. In those first few seconds I was already thinking about what it would be like to tell my mom and dad the news. But I was also worried. Every astronaut knows that there is a very specific way you're supposed to hear about official mission assignments. And this was definitely not it.

"Thank you, sir," I replied, taking a deep breath to calm myself and trying to be very polite, "but I don't quite know what to say. I've never been assigned to a flight before, but I've been told that when I am, I'll hear it from the chief of the Astronaut Office. And when he tells me that I'm assigned to STS-73, I'll be *very* excited."

There was a brief pause, and then he said, "Well, I've got the whole mission management team here on speakerphone to congratulate you."

Now I really didn't know what to say. "That is so great! And I can't wait to meet everyone. And of course, I am thrilled to be assigned to a science flight," I added, not wanting any of the people listening to think I was unenthusiastic. "However," I concluded firmly, "I think that I will have to wait to hear it officially from my chief."

But I couldn't just wait. I knew the process wasn't supposed to work this way, and I figured that Hoot would want to know. I walked down the hall and poked my head into his office. Hoot Gibson, like most of the chief astronauts before him, had an open-door policy, and I'd felt comfortable with him ever since he brought up "Stairway to Heaven" in my interview. After I told him about the call, he shook his head, exasperated. Clearly, the different parts of NASA were not always good at communicating with one another.

"Well, Cady, you're right about the way you're supposed to find these things out. And I'm going to get this cleared up. In the meantime, you should just know that eventually you'll be assigned to a flight." And that was the end of that conversation.

I felt a little deflated—I'd have loved to get confirmation that this was indeed my mission assignment—but I knew better than to complain. Every astronaut accepts that the who, what, and when of crew selection at NASA is a black box, because it is a complex process that has to balance factors ranging from international relations to mission requirements to preparing newer astronauts for future flights. It's never transparent, it's not predictable, and it doesn't always seem fair. But that's just the way it is.

At this point, I was working as the assistant to Dr. Carolyn Huntoon, the director of the Johnson Space Center—every astronaut is assigned a job within NASA—while continuing to train. I tried to put STS-73 out of my mind, but couldn't help but look for everything I could find about the mission. Two weeks in space doing science experiments! It sounded amazing. A couple of months passed, and our class was training on the landing simulator at the Ames Space Center in San Francisco when Hoot called me. The faces of my classmates made it clear: either I was assigned to a mission or I was in big trouble.

When I picked up the phone, Hoot said, with a wry note in his voice, "Well, I am looking at a draft press release announcing the first flight assignment for the class of 1992, and that's you, Cady! So, I'm officially letting you know that you will be flying on STS-73. You'll be part of the science crew and also one of the EVA crew members if a spacewalk is needed. You'll be spending sixteen days in space, the longest shuttle mission ever planned." And just like that, it was official.

The mission wasn't actually scheduled to launch for two and a half years, but they were assigning the "lab crew"—that is, the scientists—early, because we had a lot of experiment training to do for the long flight. The shuttle would spend sixteen days orbiting the Earth, while the crew performed thirty different experiments back in the Spacelab module that filled the shuttle's entire payload bay. In addition to launch and entry, we'd have to learn all about the Spacelab systems, but much of my mission-specific training would involve learning how to conduct the numerous experiments, which ranged from growing potatoes inside a locker, to using sound to manipulate large liquid droplets, to growing protein crystals.

Why do we perform science experiments in space? Essentially, it's because the space environment is different from the one here on Earth. There is almost no gravity! Officially, it is called microgravity, but you'll also hear it referred to as zero-g. We say that we are weightless up there, but the truth is, we are *almost* weightless. We are still affected by the Earth's gravity, but it is only a tiny fraction of what we are used to on Earth.

The microgravity environment gives us an opportunity to study how natural processes work under conditions we can't simulate on Earth. Think about it this way: Gravity is a large and dominant force here on Earth, so we can't easily see the effect of weaker forces. A good example is looking at how liquids behave. When we spill liquids on Earth, gravity forces them to spread out into a puddle. In microgravity, the weaker forces dominate and liquids can form spheres, floating around our cabin. On our planet, those forces, though small, still have an effect and are important for us to understand. The lack of gravity in space makes those effects easier to measure and interpret.

Microgravity also effectively slows down certain processes, allowing us to observe them and take more measurements than we'd be able to take on Earth. When it comes to processes like combustion, this is important. By studying the way flames burn in space, we can better understand how pollution forms on Earth, helping us develop new fuels that burn more sustainably.

Additional experiments are related to growing food and other plants. This matters for space exploration, so we can eat fresh food when we're on our way to Mars, but also, and more important, our space experiments help us learn how to grow plants in places on Earth where the conditions are challenging, which is critical for food sustainability.

Sometimes, the subjects of our experiments are ourselves. The human body performs differently in microgravity, and I am not talking about our ability to do endless somersaults in the world of weightlessness. We lose bone density much faster than we would on Earth—about ten times faster than a woman with osteoporosis. Because the process is accelerated, it is easier to measure the changes. We can learn a lot of critical medical information this way and use that information to keep people healthier on Earth. That's why Shannon's veins had to be up to numerous blood draws for her flight, which was focused on medical experiments.

On STS-73, there was another important reason for doing all these experiments, quite separate from gathering data from the experiments themselves. We were a pathfinder mission—a "practice run" of sorts— for the way that science would be conducted on the International Space Station. The lab where I hoped to work one day. At the time I received my STS-73 assignment, in 1993, construction of the various modules of the station was well underway in all the partner nations, although it would be five years before the first segment launched into space. It meant a lot to me that our mission was playing a part in that process. Our mission patch, the logo we designed to wear on our spacesuits, featured a geometric design to represent the future ISS's Cupola window.

Not only did we have to learn the experiments; we had to put them to the test, thinking ahead about how the equipment itself would behave in the weightless environment, far away from the scientists who had designed it. We had to make sure the procedures were clear and easy to follow, and that the experiment hardware was robust enough to withstand our attempts to perform the experiments in space. Jokingly, this is referred to as "astronaut-proofing." If a piece of equipment were to break or malfunction in a lab on solid ground, it was very likely to break or malfunction on orbit when it was being operated by an astronaut while circling the Earth at 17,500 miles per hour. None of it was rocket science, but it was science done onboard a rocket ship, far from Earth, where spare parts would likely be hard to come by. Conducting an experiment in a weightless context is always tricky, since we can't re-create that environment for long periods of time on the ground in order to practice.

Years, even decades, of work by scientists and engineers had gone into creating these experiments. Some brilliant, hardworking scientist might have spent her entire career developing one particular experiment and be waiting for the chance to test it in zero gravity, and now she was counting on me to see it to its conclusion. Each of us on the crew felt an intense responsibility to all of those men and women as we prepared for the mission, and we took extra care to let them know that we understood what mattered to them and were honored to be their eyes, ears, and hands in space. Those scientists are among the countless hidden figures behind every mission, along with the engineers and the ground crew who make it all possible. Just as the public only sees the launch, not the work that goes into it, they also only see the astronauts, not the folks behind the scenes.

Some astronauts were not so eager to be assigned to laboratory flights, which lacked the excitement of spacewalks or robotics. As a scientist, however, the assignment felt like a gift. I was also happy to learn that our payload commander would be Kathy Thornton, an experienced astronaut, mother, and fellow scientist whom I admired but did not know well at the time. She had done two spacewalking missions, one of them to repair the Hubble Space Telescope, and I felt fortunate to be able to learn from her during our training. We were joined on the lab crew by Fred Leslie, a fluid physicist from the Marshall Space Flight Center, and Al Sacco, a university professor known for his zeolite crystal growth experiments, and their backups, Glynn Holt and Dave Matthiesen. They were all "payload specialists"—full-time scientists who were becoming part-time astronauts for the mission. The lab crew would be rounded out with the flight crew, two pilots and a flight engineer. They had not yet been assigned, which grew increasingly inconvenient as decisions about launch and landing became pressing. As a joke to emphasize the urgency of filling these assignments, Kathy signed herself and me up for training to land the shuttle. (This involves landing a plane that has been modified to look and feel like the shuttle, and that dives toward the runway at an angle seven times steeper than a typical commercial airliner.) It was a ludicrous idea—Kathy and I were trained to fly, but we were scientists, not shuttle pilots—which was exactly her point. The message was received, and soon after, Commander Ken Bowersox (Sox) was assigned to our flight along with my fellow rookies, pilot Kent Rominger (Rommel) and flight engineer Mike Lopez-Alegria (LA)—who'd given me that great advice during water survival training.

The lab crew—me, Kathy, Fred, and Al, plus Dave and Glynn—became especially close because we spent several weeks of each month together in Huntsville, Alabama, during the twenty-two months before we launched. It was my first real taste of the close bond that can be created among a crew who come together with a shared mission of great importance. We don't get to pick our crewmates, and sometimes those relationships aren't easy, but my first crew was a wonderful group of people who worked hard and had a lot of fun together too. We were like a family, and during Spacelab sims we lived together for days at a time in a replica of the shuttle—eating, practicing our experiments, and entertaining ourselves. The first time we did one of those sims, we didn't realize until afterward that our entire three-day sim was broadcasting live on the NASA channel all day long. We were mortified, and an inventory of goofy facial expressions I may have made flashed through my head. But on the bright side, it was yet another good reminder that on a mission I'd be performing my job in public.

Our crew quickly discovered that we shared a love of elaborate practical jokes. Because one of our experiments involved growing potatoes, and our final simulation required that we send a video of the potatoes growing in space back to the team that had created the experiment, we decided to surprise them with something a little different. We created a video called "10 Reasons Why Spuds Would Rather Go to Space." It featured scenes like mild-mannered Kathy Thornton wielding a chef's knife, chopping the heck out of some potatoes, and Al Sacco driving over the unfortunate tubers in the parking lot. We even rigged up a "spud gun" with a piece of PVC pipe, thanks to my glassblower sweetheart. It was surprisingly satisfying to launch those poor spuds across the field! The scientists seemed honored that we had selected their experiment for our joke, and morale was high that day in the sim control room. Joking aside, the spuds did seem to enjoy their trip to space, and we managed to grow five, a crop that we were all very proud of. Fast-forward to today, and technology from NASA's plant experiments has led to innovations like vertical farming in cities and expanded our options for growing plants without soil. And astronauts now grow lettuce and other vegetables on the space station that they actually get to eat.

Risk Is Just a Part of the Job

Our launch from Cape Canaveral, Florida, was scheduled for September 25, 1995. Before launch, shuttle astronauts undergo two weeks of quarantine. The first week starts in Houston, and then we fly to the Cape in T-38s, where we're greeted with great fanfare and questions from the press and then secluded in rather spartan motel-like rooms and fed meals that are, well, nutritious (per NASA's strict guidelines). Luckily, the motherly ladies who took care of us were also adept at baking cookies. I loved thinking about how some of these same women had tended to the crews of the Gemini, Mercury, and Apollo flights. Did Neil Armstrong and Buzz Aldrin eat these same chocolate chip cookies?

During quarantine, we weren't allowed any visitors other than our spouses or "significant others," as in my case, but we got to see family and friends from a distance at a series of traditional events before the launch.

The most inspirational was Night Viewing, when our families arrived at the launchpad to see the space shuttle *Columbia* lit up with the brightest of lights—an amazing and majestic sight, visible for miles. Something all of us loved was the traditional Wave Across the Ditch, a last chance to talk with families and friends (we each got to invite a busload!) from across the water-filled ditch around the launchpad, which, because it was Florida, probably contained alligators. We could easily talk to our guests across the five-foot divide, but of course my zany brothers insisted on some amount of charades to imitate the local wildlife and express their feelings. The Wave Across the Ditch ritual was both funny and poignant, a good chance to say goodbye to Josiah, then twelve, who was too young to come to the Beach House BBQ with our immediate families the next day. I remember looking at my mom's proud face and thinking that if she could, she would climb into my spacesuit and strap herself into my seat on the shuttle in a heartbeat. In her own way, she'd been as courageous as any astronaut—getting divorced and going out on her own at a time when very few women did such a thing.

The next evening was more of a real farewell. We gathered with our immediate families for a fun meal together at a beach house traditionally reserved for the crew during launch time. I would still get to see Josh the next day, but I cried in the parking lot saying goodbye to my parents and siblings for what I thought would be the last time before we launched. We gave each other the kind of hugs you don't ever want to end, our tightly squeezed bodies having wordless conversations about fears we hadn't wanted to voice.

Our launch did not happen on the twenty-fifth. We slipped—the NASA term for a delayed launch. And slipped. And slipped. Seven times over the next thirty days. The first time (a mechanical problem that took nine days to fix), my disappointment was mitigated by the fact that I got to go to my own launch party at Space Camp, which I had reserved for the afternoon after the launch. It's traditional for astronauts to plan these parties, which can range from picnics to wedding-scale events, but unless the launch slips, we're either in quarantine or we've left the planet when they happen. I got to hang out with several hundred of my friends and family, and as I explained the launch slip and our next steps, I experienced a surprising sense of closure. I'd been so busy getting ready, I hadn't really allowed myself time to be present in the moment and realize how special it was. Now, as people from every era of my life celebrated that I really was an astronaut on my way to space, I finally got to let it in myself.

The extra time also meant I got to take my parents and siblings and Josh and Josiah on a really cool tour of *Columbia* on the launchpad. We weren't allowed to go inside the shuttle itself, but we were able to peek inside the cabin and even stood just a few feet from the shuttle's main engines and those enormous solid rocket boosters. I think that standing on that launchpad together made the enormity of launching more real to all of us. I remember the poignant mix of joy and wistfulness on my mom's face. She'd always believed she would do great, adventurous things, and perhaps in that moment it hit her that she had not done them, but whatever regret she felt seemed inextricably mixed with her pride and excitement that her own daughter was about to embark on a space mission. On *this* vehicle. Attached to *these* rockets. Any day now.

I'll also never forget driving around the space center with my dad one night, using my badge to bring him to our launchpad and other places that were off-limits to the general public. With his navy background, that kind of access meant something, as did the tremendous historic significance of the places we were standing. I could almost see his mind recalibrating as it became real to him that his very own daughter was going to be part of that history.

These simple moments meant all the more to me because I knew they reflected a genuine shift in his attitude and beliefs—a shift that affected not just me but other women in his world and the men as well. A few years after my selection, a woman from the navy diving program, Heidemarie Stefanyshyn-Piper, became an astronaut. I like to think my dad's change of heart might have influenced others in his world and ultimately helped people like her not to be overlooked.

After so many delays, most of my guests and even my family had to leave. As a crew, being patient was easier for us, knowing that eventually, when the shuttle was ready and the weather good, we'd launch. It was hard on our friends and family as they juggled vacation time and the expense of hotels and rental cars. My mom kept asking, "When are you going to go?" And when I told her I didn't know, she said, in a conspiratorial whisper, "Come on, you can tell me, I'm your mother!"

Two of the seven attempts, we got as far as donning our pumpkin suits and getting strapped in before they called off the launch. But it's all part of the job. Thank goodness for all those cookies. I actually calculated that between the seven of us and all our guests, we ate our way through twenty-one hundred during the course of the month! It's amazing we got off the launchpad.

The night before we finally did launch, Josh and I got to spend a few hours together. We opted to go for a drive, as we had done most nights during that strange month. I never tired of exploring the Cape, with its beautiful ocean vistas and clear starry nights. The warm Florida air was soft against my skin as we stepped outside and walked to the car. I was surprisingly calm, perhaps because, after so many failed attempts, I'd had time to realize that I really was ready to launch, no matter when that finally happened. We drove through the deserted roads of Cape Canaveral, and eventually came to the historic launchpads from which previous missions had blasted off into space. When we reached Launch Complex 34, we pulled over and walked up to the imposing concrete structure. The words ABANDON IN PLACE, stenciled on the side, indicated that this site had been decommissioned but preserved as a memorial to the three astronauts who died here in the Apollo 1 launchpad fire in 1967. I traced my fingers over their names, engraved on a bronze plaque: Virgil Grissom, Edward White, Roger Chaffee. They weren't even launching on that January morning—just taking part in a routine test when a short circuit caused a fire inside the capsule and we lost them.

Josh and I stood there, hands clasped, in silence, thinking about those three men. And about the crew of the *Challenger*, who died in the nearby ocean just seventy-three seconds after launch on another January day, in 1986. I wasn't dwelling on potential disaster or stoking fear. I knew the risks, and standing in this spot made them as real and unavoidable as the vast pillars of concrete before me. But I wasn't weighing those risks or having second thoughts.

You make your decision about the risks you want to take long before you find yourself sitting on top of a rocket. That's why I say a launch isn't a beginning—by the time I put on that spacesuit and stepped onto the launchpad, I was already well along on my journey. To get to this point, I had to have faith that the entire NASA team, including me and the rest of the crew, had done our best to make the flight as safe as it could be. And I did. Being part of that trusted team was simply what I'd signed up for and what I'd been working toward for many years.

As I stood on the Apollo 1 launchpad in the Florida dusk, the moment held more hope than fear—a rich sense of the enormity and potential of what I was about to do, and the honor of following in the footsteps of the brave and pioneering men and women who had come before me. I read the words on the plaque again: "In memory of those who made the ultimate sacrifice so others could reach the stars." And in my mind, I told them, "Thank you for what you did. I promise to continue the journey."

The truth is, there's always an element of risk in launching any meaningful endeavor—perhaps not a life-threatening risk, but a risk nonetheless. And no matter how prepared we are for that moment of liftoff, we can't always control how it will unfold. Remembering what you signed up for and all the preparation that's brought you to this moment can help you navigate the unexpected. It's natural to feel nervous on the eve of a milestone event, even if it's not as dramatic as attaching oneself to a rocket. To counter that, I remind myself of three things: First, the hard work I've put in—the practice, the repetition, the anticipation of potential problems. Second, the reason I'm doing it—the mission I'm part of and the potential it has to make a difference. And third, the connection between those two—the fact that my training and skills are exactly what that mission needs. When you know you've done everything you can to be ready, and you know it's in service of something bigger than yourself, it can help you to let go when the big day comes, and trust life to unfold as it will.

Eventually, Josh and I got back into the car, and I drove him to the gate. We said our goodbyes—for real, this time—and I drove back. Cruising alone down the long, deserted roads of the Cape, under a blanket of stars, I already felt a little closer to space.

The next day, before dawn, we suited up, again, and walked out through the very same doorway from the Operations and Checkout Building through which all the historic crews—Mercury, Gemini, Apollo—had walked. It's a powerful reminder that as astronauts, we're all on one mission. It was a beautiful morning and the forecast was good. Our training team and staff were waiting to see us off as we boarded the silver bus—known as the Astrovan—that would take us to the launchpad. We entered the elevator at the pad and ascended to the "195-foot level." There, on commander's orders, we all took a scheduled pee break in the all-metal bathroom. Given our pumpkin suits, this was a complex procedure, but we did it in record time. With all these launch attempts, we'd had a lot of practice! Would today be the day we finally got off the ground? For luck, our crew decided to wear our NASA caps backward. Kathy wore her lucky socks. And I guess it worked! The countdown to launch began, and this time, it went all the way down to zero.

Getting the Job Done

On STS-73, I had a job to do the moment we reached orbit, just eight and a half minutes after launch. Mike and I were assigned to take photographs of our giant orange external fuel tank as it detached from the shuttle, an important task that allows NASA to inspect the tank for any damage that might have occurred during launch. I couldn't afford to just sit there grinning like an idiot because I was finally in space. On my knee board, I'd written out the steps I needed to take. As surgeons, pilots, and anyone else in a safety-critical role knows, it's good practice to make this kind of checklist, even when you are confident you've memorized every detail. I was very glad I'd done so, since everything seemed to have left my mind except the words *I'm here! I'm in SPACE!*

First, I reached down into the pocket beside my seat and pulled out my mesh helmet bag. Next, I opened the latches on my helmet. Immediately, it felt light—like it was dancing on top of its latches. I opened up the bag and put it over my head, while still wearing my helmet. Then, I removed the helmet, and voilà—it was in the bag. I offered a silent thank-you to Marsha Ivins, a fellow astronaut who taught me this trick, avoiding all the time-wasting madness of trying to stuff a floating helmet into a floating bag while I, too, was floating around the cabin. Once I'd stowed the helmet, I detached my oxygen and cooling hoses and my comm connection, and unhooked the harness attached to my parachute. And only then, I unbuckled my seat belt.

That's when I first felt it—the blissful sensation of weightlessness. Even in my fifty-pound spacesuit, I was floating out of the seat like a balloon at the Thanksgiving Day Parade. I'd had brief tastes of this before, in our zero-gravity plane, but for no longer than thirty seconds at a time. You'd just begin to enjoy it when you'd suddenly find yourself pinned to the floor as the force of gravity reasserted itself. Now, I kept expecting the weightlessness to end, but it didn't. Not only was I here; I was here to stay, at least for a while.

This was not the time to enjoy the freedom of flight, however. I had a time-sensitive job to do. I gently pushed off, retrieved the camera from its locker, and attached the long lens, before floating up to get myself situated at the window. In zero-g, I quickly discovered, "getting situated" is not as easy as it sounds! I wasn't tall enough to wedge myself between floor and ceiling, as some of the taller guys could, so I had to wrap my bulky spacesuit legs tightly around a seat to make sure I didn't drift away.

Taking the pictures was not a simple matter either, since the fuel tank was falling away quickly, blindingly bright, and I was using manual focus to document the surface of the tank. In the background I caught tantalizing glimpses of the Earth, but my attention was consumed by the task at hand. For those few minutes, I was just focusing and clicking, focusing and clicking, as the tank fell away.

Once the tank was out of sight, I glanced at my checklist, which was still tethered to my suit. Then I noticed something peeking out from behind the list. I pulled out a postcard with a picture of a shuttle launching. It was addressed to Cady Coleman, Low Earth Orbit. "Welcome to Space, Cady!" was scrawled on the back, and it was signed by my classmates Joe Tanner, Steve Smith, and Kevin Kregel, who worked launch at the Cape and must have slipped this onto my knee board. Smiling, I tucked it back under the checklist.

Mike and I still had one more critical job to do: opening the payload bay doors. This would expose the series of refrigeration tubes to the cold temperatures of space and allow them to release the heat load that they absorb from the computers and electronics inside the shuttle. If we failed to get them open within hours, we would have to abort the mission and return to Earth. Carefully, we opened one series of latches at a time and then drove the doors to the OPEN position. My sigh of relief as they opened smoothly turned into a gasp of awe. I could finally see out into space. With my most pressing tasks complete, I took in my first real view of our planet.

There it was: the vast curve of the Earth. Blue-green, familiar, yet utterly surprising in its beauty and crystal clarity. Above its surface, the thin layer of the atmosphere, so precious yet so fragile. And around it, space was the deepest black you can imagine. From photos and descriptions, I knew this was what our planet would look like from space. But I didn't know how it would *feel* to see it. I couldn't look away. As I gazed out of the window, I remembered that all the astronauts who had told me about this moment had a certain look in their eyes—as if they knew a secret. And now I knew it too.

Chapter 4

It's Not about You,
but It Depends on You

Embracing the Paradox of Having a Mission

What do you feel when you look up at the night sky? Does it inspire awe, wonder, curiosity? I never tire of that view. Almost every time I come home after dark to our hilltop in Massachusetts, Josh and I go straight outside to look at the stars. I love to think about how human beings for millennia have gazed upward in the same way. Today we know more about what we're looking at than ever before, yet there's still so much we don't know. I always marvel at the things we have learned—like the fact that those pinpricks of light each represent not just stars, but whole galaxies. I love to read about the mysteries of black holes and learn about the birth and death of distant stars. It boggles my mind to think about the enormous number of light years between our planet and the far reaches of space. And sometimes, even just looking up and seeing the Milky Way, like so many observers of the cosmos, I've felt that profound insignificance—the sense of being just a tiny speck in our vast and still-mysterious universe.

That newfound sense of perspective is one of the great gifts of astronomy and space exploration. As I write this, we're continuing to receive astonishing images from NASA's James Webb Space Telescope. Launched in 2022, its powerful infrared instruments allow us to see all the way to the edge of the universe, farther than we've ever seen before. Maybe you've seen some of those pictures—swirling galaxies, towering cliffs and dunes of cosmic dust, inky-black chasms of infinite darkness. Magnificent colors and shapes splattered across the heavens as if by some cosmic Jackson Pollock. These vibrant images and the stories they tell about our universe have captured the imagination of so many people around the world that it gives me hope. So many of the challenges we face stem from a lack of big-picture thinking. We all need a reminder now and then that we're infinitesimally small—that our planet is just one among a hundred billion—and that's just in our galaxy! We could all use some cosmic perspective. But when I look at those images and feel my own self-importance melting away, I'm also struck by a paradox. Those very same images that bring home such a vivid sense of our cosmic insignificance were made possible because of our marvelous ingenuity, which is one of the things that make human life so significant. They were made possible because dedicated engineers and astronomers figured out how to build telescopes powerful enough to reveal the mysteries of the universe and use rockets to launch them into orbit. And they were made possible because ordinary women and men like me trained for years to travel into space with those telescopes and release them in just the right place. In that moment, those few individuals carried an enormous responsibility upon their shoulders. I know, because I was one of them.

For my second NASA mission, I was assigned to a space shuttle flight that launched one of the telescopes that send back never-before-seen images of deep space, the Chandra X-ray Observatory. It's another member of NASA's family of telescopes, including the Hubble Space Telescope and more recently the Webb. Each one looks at different wavelengths of light out in the universe. If you've looked at data and space images showing the areas around black holes over the past two decades, it's quite likely that they came from the telescope that my crewmates and I carried with us on the space shuttle *Columbia* in 1999.

What Mission Means to Me

Insignificant, yet so significant. This sums up for me what it feels like to be part of a mission. We hear that term so much these days. Every company, great or small, has a mission statement and is proud to be "mission driven." Self-improvement books push us to clarify our personal missions. The term is overused, but the idea behind it is a powerful one when it's the authentic expression of an important goal. Being part of a mission means you are part of something that's much bigger than yourself, but at the same time, the role you play is vital. It's that strange paradox that it's not about you, but it depends on you. Without you it couldn't succeed.

Each time a crew of astronauts goes to space, we call it a mission. It's an honor to be selected for a mission, and an acknowledgment that you bring the skills that can make it successful. It might be a science mission, like my first, where we were performing experiments in microgravity in order to advance our understanding of science, medicine, and engineering. It might be an exploratory mission, like the moon landings. It might be an astronomical mission, launching a telescope or satellite to help us see and understand more of the universe. It might be a construction mission, like the flights that built the space station. It might be a mission to test equipment and processes for future flights to Mars. There are always reasons we go to space, and they are always about something bigger than us.

The power of mission is that it stretches you beyond yourself, and at the same time, it brings out the best of what makes you unique. The mix of qualities that make you "uniquely you" can be just what the larger purpose needs. In my experience, that sense of purpose has the power to bring people together, bridging our personal differences and even our disagreements and allowing us to achieve things we might never have thought possible. A crew typically spends a few years training together before the actual launch, and the shared mission is what connects us throughout—a bond that often continues even after the specific task we set out to accomplish has been completed.

Meeting Chandra

I was in Russia when I heard about my assignment to the Chandra mission, officially known as STS-93. My job at that time, in the spring of 1998, involved developing English-language labels for the equipment in the Russian segment of the International Space Station. The first segment was due to be launched, a milestone that everyone in the global space community was excitedly anticipating.

The first step of the labeling project was the hardest, meeting with our Russian colleagues and agreeing about what classes of equipment needed English labels. After spending days arguing in a conference room, I insisted that we move to the simulators used to train astronauts and cosmonauts so that we could see concrete examples of the devices we had been discussing. The modules of the ISS looked like long metal cylinders the size of buses without the seats in them. Inside the main module, it was like an industrial kitchen, with appliances lining every wall and the ceiling too. As we considered them one by one, some of the labeling choices became obvious. Suddenly the world seemed simpler and we began to resolve our conflicts more easily, agreeing on the right words and abbreviations. Particularly important was knowing where *not* to place the label. Picture your stove: it would be best not to label your burners on the burner itself. It was painstaking work, but I loved it. I got to know the space station intimately—at least the Russian segment—and in some small way, it felt like part of me would be up there, even if I wasn't selected to go right away. Despite having to haggle over almost every label, our Russian-American team became very close, and when I got that phone call telling me about my assignment, it was the next best thing to getting the news with my family.

The call came from a woman I greatly admired, Colonel Eileen Collins. She was one of the first female test pilots and became the first woman to pilot the space shuttle in 1995 for the STS-63 mission, followed in 1997 by STS-84. She and I first met back when I was at the Air Force Research Laboratory, and I was excited and proud when she was selected as a pilot astronaut in 1990. She invited some of her heroes to attend her first launch, the seven surviving members of the original Mercury 13, and she asked me to help host them. They were a group of women in the early sixties who, after receiving personal letters from the head of Life Sciences at NASA asking them to be part of a privately funded program to include women as astronauts, underwent the grueling physical tests taken by NASA's male astronauts. Despite the women performing as well as or better than the Mercury 7 astronauts on the selection testing, and the sacrifices many of them made to even pursue the tests, the program was abruptly shut down just days before they were scheduled to start the next phase of testing. It would be almost two decades before NASA selected its first women astronauts. Never had I felt more acutely aware of being part of that lineage of brave and boundary-breaking women than I did that day, standing among those pioneers, watching Eileen make history and thinking about my own first mission, scheduled for later that year. I can't know what the Mercury 13 women were thinking as they watched Eileen's launch, but I sensed that they knew how much it meant to Eileen to be carrying their legacy with her in the pilot seat of that space shuttle.

Now, I had added my name to the still-too-short list of women who had flown in space, and Eileen was calling to tell me that I would be joining her on her next mission, STS-93, scheduled to launch in July 1999. Our Mercury 13 heroes would attend that launch, too, and Eileen would be making history once again, this time as NASA's first female space shuttle commander. I would be the lead mission specialist for delivering the shuttle's precious payload, the Chandra X-ray Observatory, to orbit. I'd also be one of the spacewalkers, although no official spacewalks were scheduled.

When I shared the news, everyone I was working with was thrilled for me, except for the most senior Russian guy. I knew he was a bit of a curmudgeon, but I had come to truly like and respect him in the many months that we had worked together. It had been clear to me that he felt the same, so his response to my selection surprised me. "Katya," he said, looking me up and down, "you are so beautiful. Why you want to space-walk? Why you want to be astronaut?"

I wasn't sure whether to laugh or be offended.

I decided to laugh. "Can't I be beautiful *and* be an astronaut?"

But he just shook his head, looking earnest and regretful, and said, "No!" as if it was beyond belief to think it was possible.

Besides Eileen and myself, our five-person crew consisted of pilot Jeff Ashby, on his first flight; veteran astronaut and astronomer Steve Hawley, on his fifth; and French astronaut Michel Tognini, who had already flown once on the Russian MIR space station. He would be my partner for the telescope launch and for spacewalking. I quickly learned that Eileen had a different management style from Sox or other commanders I'd known, even though all of them came from a military background. Hers was a quieter but ultimately still firm approach. She would say, "We've got a choice to make here, and I'd like to get your input. Here are the options." And we'd talk it through as a crew and usually reach the conclusion I suspected she meant for us to reach. She'd never just say, "Here's the plan for Monday, see you then." I appreciated her consensus-building approach and the way she made everyone feel heard. Even more,

I appreciated learning that there is more than one way to be a successful leader, which helped me recognize my distinct approach as its own style of leadership.

In the meantime, I was developing my own style of understanding the electrical engineering I'd need to complete this mission. I studied the drawings and wiring diagrams created by the telescope engineers to illustrate what connected to what. It would be my job to know what would happen to the telescope or its rocket every time I flipped a switch onboard the shuttle. An experienced electrical engineer might have glanced at those drawings and grasped them immediately. But to me, a PhD chemist, it was more like spaghetti. So I came up with a solution that worked for me: I highlighted the various connections using colored pencils. Blue for cooling, pink for data, and so on. I was told that some of the instructors thought that what I was doing was a waste of time. But they were wrong. I was just taking a different route to get to the same destination—a route that made sense for the way my mind worked. Eileen took me aside and emphasized that she supported my initiative in finding the way to learn that worked for me. "If you keep your focus on the mission, you can be confident that you are doing the right thing," she said.

Mission success started with making sure that I understood the status of the telescope at every stage and could communicate issues clearly to Mission Control. In the end, I translated my colored-pencil sketches of the data communication system into a diagram that was so intuitive that it was ultimately adopted by all of the Mission Control teams.

One of our first official mission activities was meeting Chandra, as the telescope was affectionately known. Chandra was also referred to as "she," despite being named after a man, an Indian American astrophysicist named Subrahmanyan Chandrasekhar, who was beloved by his students and famous for work on stellar structure, including white dwarf stars. We flew to Pasadena, California, to meet the team that had designed and built Chandra and learn about the mission we'd be undertaking. Or perhaps it would be more accurate to say "completing," since Chandra's mission had begun decades before, in 1976, when the project was first proposed. We'd be accompanying her on the next-to-last leg of her journey before sending her off on the last.

To do that, we needed to understand everything the team could teach us about the telescope, the rocket system that would boost her into her ultimate orbit, and the deploy mechanism that would allow her to separate from the shuttle. In the shuttle's payload bay, we'd be carrying more than forty thousand pounds of state-of-the-art engineering—the telescope and its Inertial Upper Stage (IUS) rocket system. The largest, heaviest object ever to be carried into space, it filled the entire payload bay in the back of the shuttle, with only a few inches to spare. Just as heavy, in my mind, was the weight of everything that had gone into her creation: more than two decades of planning, design, and construction fueled by the expertise, skill, and ingenuity of hundreds of dedicated telescope scientists, instrument designers, and engineers. Our mission was to put Chandra into space in exactly the right place, just two hundred fifty miles above the Earth, such that the rocket attached to her could boost her into her final orbit of eighty-six thousand miles, a third of the way to the moon. Chandra would be so far away that a single orbit around the Earth would take fifty-five hours, compared to the speedy ninety-minute revolutions of the space shuttle.

Chandra was designed to detect X-rays, which are produced by very hot matter—and by hot, I mean millions of degrees. X-rays are emitted during high-energy events throughout the universe, like exploding stars and black holes, including the supermassive black hole at the center of our own Milky Way. Because cosmic X-rays are absorbed by our atmosphere, we're unable to study them directly from Earth. You have to send a telescope into orbit to study cosmic X-rays. So X-ray telescopes like Chandra must operate from well above our atmosphere to collect their data. As with Chandra, many are launched into low earth orbit on the shuttle or other rockets, and then they need additional propulsion to achieve their optimal orbit.

I was thrilled by the idea that my team and I would be launching something that would actually take on a life of her own after we sent her into space, and that her work would continue long after we were back on Earth. I studied hard for my role as Chandra's shepherd. I needed to be able to perform the deploy sequence blindfolded in my sleep. I needed to have a close relationship with the folks at the Chandra Mission Control, which was separate from NASA Mission Control, and make sure the two groups were working together. But it was equally important to me to understand *why* the telescope mattered. I threw myself into reading about the history and science of X-ray astronomy, and I also turned to one of my crewmates, Steve Hawley, an experienced astronomer. I used to joke that Steve's job was to fill the black hole in my head where astrophysics was supposed to live. And he did a great job. But I soon realized that what Steve said and what the textbook said didn't always match. For example, what I'd read in the textbook about white dwarfs was different from the way he'd described them. "Why is that?" I asked him.

"Well, when was the book written?" he asked. I opened the cover and looked at the publication date.

"Late eighties."

"Well, there you go," Steve said. "We've learned a lot since then. Just because it's in a book doesn't mean it's still true."

That might seem like an obvious statement, but it was an eye-opening reminder to me about the extent to which our knowledge of the universe was still in flux. In just ten years, our understanding of astronomy had changed so much that the textbooks *were wrong.* And after we launched this telescope, even the new textbooks might become obsolete. They'd have to be rewritten again and again to keep up with what Chandra would show us. *We were going to change what everyone knew.* And in turn, that would change what future scientists might be inspired to discover. As I sat there holding that book and thinking about white dwarfs and X-rays, our mission felt more tangible than ever before.

In a very real sense, Chandra represented the future of astrophysics—a window into a deeper understanding of the universe. When the moment came for the telescope to be deployed, all of this would be, quite literally, in my hands.

But first, it was in the hands of the launch team at the Kennedy Space Center, whose job it was to get us off the ground and into orbit. And we almost didn't make it.

Failure to Launch

Our first launch attempt was aborted eight seconds before liftoff.

That's right: Eight seconds. Not hours, or minutes. Seconds. If you remember how the countdown goes, that's less than two seconds before the three main engines on the butt of the space shuttle kick in, and only eight seconds before the solid rocket boosters ignite and the bolts holding us to the launchpad explode.

Picture this: My crewmates and I are braced for liftoff, adrenaline already surging. *This is it*, I tell myself. *We're going. I can't wait!* And then, over my headset, I hear the word that is never spoken in Launch Control unless the person saying it fully intends to bring the process to an immediate stop: *Cutoff. Give cutoff for a hydrogen leak.*

I'm seated in the middeck, closest to the hatch. Immediately, my training kicks in. Before I have time to think, I'm unbuckling my seat belts and checking that none of the straps are tangled or snagged. Later, I will be proud of how fast I accomplished this—I'd always wondered how it would go in a real emergency. If there really is a hydrogen leak, we might be in danger and need to get out fast, and it will be my job to open the hatch if instructed to do so. I'm already scanning the emergency exit procedure known as a Mode I Egress—we'll exit the shuttle through the white room, make our way across the access arm to the platform, climb into rectangular metal "slide wire baskets," and use them to zip-line twenty stories down to a safe bunker. The sliding down part is something astronauts don't get to practice, since it's considered too dangerous. Next, we'll pile into the waiting armored tank (yes, a real tank, and yes, all of us loved practicing this part) and drive away.

The launch director's voice cuts through my mental visions: "A leak of 640 parts per million." Immediately, I realize that for such a small leak, we don't have to be in any kind of a hurry, and we should wait for the closeout crew to come and open the hatch for us. I won't be driving a tank today. But neither will I be going to space.

Later, when we were debriefing the failed launch attempt, I learned that Ozzie Fish, the young man who manually triggered the cutoff, had done so because he saw a spike in hydrogen above the level considered safe for launch, which could indicate a dangerous leak. Technically, he was supposed to see two such indicators before aborting. But with eight seconds left in the launch sequence, there wasn't time to wait for confirmation. Aborting the launch would have been much more dangerous once the engines kicked in. He wasn't thinking about himself, about whether he'd be chastised for not following procedure. He was thinking about the mission, about what was at stake—the human lives, the precious cargo, the shuttle itself. It turned out that in fact the issue was a sensor failure, not an actual leak. But Ozzie couldn't have known that in the moment. He made the call to save the mission from potential disaster. He was commended for his actions, and following our incident the procedure was changed to make what he had done the correct course of action.

As late as "eight seconds before launch" sounds (and feels!), it wasn't the latest that a launch can be aborted. If one of the main engines fails—as ours could have, if there had been an actual leak rather than a sensor glitch—between six and three seconds before launch, the computers will automatically shut down the launch sequence. This has only happened a handful of times in NASA history. The engines kick in—and then they stop. The solid rocket boosters don't ignite.

NASA's engineers are always thinking ahead, building in alternate procedures to help us make the best of failure scenarios. Sometimes, none of our options are great. Let's say we launch successfully, but we lose one of the main engines just minutes after liftoff. The solid rocket boosters have already lit, so there's no stopping the shuttle. But we won't make it to space or even to one of the landing sites along our path. Our only option for a safe landing is to try to return to the Kennedy Space Center, a maneuver known as a Return to Launch Site, or RTLS. To do this, we ride those rockets until they burn out and separate. Then we turn the shuttle around, flying backward until the main engines have done their job, putting the shuttle on a path to safely glide back to Florida for landing. At least, that's the theory.

Thankfully, no crew has ever had to perform an actual RTLS, but we're grateful to our engineers that we have the option. We all trained for it hundreds of times in the simulator, and although Eileen had practiced simulated shuttle landings under these conditions, coming back to KSC would have been even more dangerous for our mission because Chandra and her IUS rocket are so heavy.

If you weren't already wondering what would possess any sane person to strap themselves on top of a rocket, you probably are now, after I've run through these various failure scenarios. And yet, two days after our aborted launch attempt, we strapped in again. It comes back to mission. I don't consider myself to be braver than most people, though I may be more optimistic than many: I take the risks that I take in my job because I believe in what we're doing together, and I trust my crew and our team.

This time, we were confidently told that at least we were "one hundred percent GO for weather." In other words, there was not even a hint of bad weather to delay us. And then . . . there were lightning strikes at the launchpad. Really. The Air Force weather officer later wrote to Eileen and apologized for their misplaced certainty. Back to crew quarters we went, tired and of course a little frustrated.

Crew quarters was like home for us at this point, one big NASA family made up of our crew plus the astronauts and management who were supporting the mission. Comic relief was abundant in between launch attempts. A friend, Rick Linnehan, was our lead astronaut support for strap-in, and he and I had a long-standing joke involving the male model Fabio, who graces the covers of hundreds of romance novels. Kandy Thomas, NASA's supreme scheduler of aircrafts and crews, used to show up at parties with a life-size cardboard cutout of a shirtless, flowing-locked Fabio as her "date." At some point during the early years of my astronaut career, that cutout began popping up in numerous places, courtesy of Rick. And then he took it to a whole new level, inviting the actual Fabio to attend the STS-93 launch as my "special guest." His invitation read, "She would have written you herself, but she is too shy!" Fabio accepted, although he didn't like the plus-one rule. "Only one guest? But I have people!" Much hilarity ensued. I enjoyed the joke, too, although I was slightly mortified to see news reports mentioning that the launch events were attended by First Lady Hillary Clinton; her daughter, Chelsea; the Apollo 11 crew; the Mercury 13; singer Judy Collins; and Fabio, special guest of astronaut Cady Coleman, a longtime fan of the King of Romance. On the bright side, though, Rick's joke brought some much-needed relief in the midst of multiple failed launches, and the ladies in our quarantine kitchen were thrilled when Fabio was allowed to call me on the phone!

For our third launch attempt, under a bright moon on a cool clear night, we strapped in and the countdown began. It was just three days after the thirtieth anniversary of the Apollo 11 moon landing. This time,

I was determined I wouldn't take anything for granted—even in those final thirty seconds after control switched over to the shuttle's internal computers. Even when the engines kicked in and I felt the "twang" of the nose tipping forward and then back. Only when the solid rockets ignited did I let myself believe that we were actually heading back to space. This time, as a seasoned second-time flyer, I kept my excitement more contained, but inside I was whooping and hollering. And then, just seconds after liftoff, my joyful inner celebration was drowned out by an angry alert tone and Eileen's voice on the radio:

Houston, Columbia *is in the roll and we have a fuel cell pH number one.*

Columbia, *Houston we'll take AC bus sensors to OFF. We see a transient short on AC1.*

Houston's reply was somehow comforting in its familiarity from sims, and yet it was incomprehensible to be hearing these words less than thirty seconds into our actual flight. An electrical short had taken out two of our six main engine controllers.

My first thought: *We know how to deal with this. We did it last week in the simulator.* It's true: we'd actually practiced this exact scenario. The difference, however, was that we weren't in the simulator anymore. This was a real, no-shit emergency, and it was only after the launch that we'd realize how close we'd come to several actual life-or-death situations. No matter how much you train for just such a moment, you can't really anticipate what it will mean to find yourself in one. I was relieved that it wasn't long before I heard the steady voice of Jeff, our pilot, confirming that he had successfully flipped the bus sensor switches to OFF, reducing our exposure to additional engine shutdowns, a potential catastrophe.

We were still headed to space, but with the loss of some of our backup capabilities, we were vulnerable. Now there were various milestones along the way that would tell us which options we still had. I tried not to hold my breath as the shuttle continued to climb.

Columbia, *Houston, Two Engine Ben.* Translation: We could lose an engine and still make it to our transatlantic landing site in Ben Guerir, Morocco.

Columbia, *Houston, negative return.* Translation: We'd gotten far enough along that it was too late to perform an RTLS and return to Florida.

Then finally, the call we'd been wishing and waiting for: Columbia, *PRESS TO MECO.* Translation: We would make it to a safe orbit and Main Engine Cut Off even if one of our engines failed in the next few minutes.

An electrical short is a serious problem, and after our launch, the shuttle fleet would be grounded for months after inspections revealed multiple cases of wire chafing on the other shuttles. Some would call us lucky, but listening to the audio from our cockpit and from Mission Control, I put the credit firmly on the shoulders of teams that were well trained to work their way patiently through multiple failures as we made our way safely to space, despite the short and the multiple failures it catalyzed, plus another unrelated but quite serious issue, a slow leak in one of our three engines used during launch. Now, we could turn our attention to our mission: sending Chandra off to her new home.

Point of No Return

Our STS-93 launch was intense, to say the least. But even in the midst of it, my sense of mission helped anchor me. My focus after making it to orbit was on understanding whether anything needed to change as a result of our wild ascent in order to launch Chandra—a process that we had to set in motion just minutes after we established that we were safely orbiting the Earth. The deploy was scheduled for seven hours, seventeen minutes, and seventeen seconds after liftoff. I also had to ensure that I was physically, mentally, and emotionally ready to play my part in that mission.

Mission eclipses so many minor inconveniences and even major challenges. At the same time, putting mission first doesn't just mean you ignore your own needs or challenges. Quite the opposite. The mission needs you to be at your best. There's that paradox again—it's not about you, but you're critically important. Part of your mission is, in fact, taking care of yourself. It means keeping yourself safe, being aware of your limits, and pulling your weight. At NASA, we even got graded on our "Self-Care" skills—our ability to make sure we were ready to accomplish the tasks ahead, both physically and emotionally. The first few hours after reaching orbit are the most critical, when all of us are adapting to being weightless. That's when we most need to take care of ourselves and one another. It's normal for more than half of us to be affected by Space Adaptation Syndrome, or SAS (translation: nausea), after arriving on orbit. The last thing an astronaut wants is to burden their crewmates or the mission with a problem he or she could have gotten help with. On STS-93, from the minute I got unstrapped, I was busy getting ready to deploy Chandra, and all that activity led to feeling nauseous a few hours into the flight. Though I recovered quickly, it was important to be honest and candid with the rest of the crew about my readiness to deploy Chandra.

Because of the fuel leak on the shuttle, we hadn't quite made it to the orbit we'd intended. Had the folks on the ground calculated whether the lower orbit was sufficient for deploying Chandra and still have her reach her destination? Or would we need to change our orbit first? Would our electrical troubles during ascent affect getting power to Chandra or the IUS? I shared my list of concerns with Eileen and asked, "Are we deploying Chandra today?"

"Cady, you are GO to start Chandra prep for an on-time deploy," she confirmed. Her words energized and focused all of us, and we settled into our tasks to get ready.

Michel Tognini and I opened the payload bay doors, where our precious cargo was mounted on her thirty-thousand-pound rocket. In my mind, I could picture how she'd looked the day she was loaded into the shuttle, on the launchpad, using a giant crane. Together with some of the scientists who had designed and built Chandra, I'd gone over to say goodbye before the payload doors were closed. There were unsentimental reasons for me being there—I needed to familiarize myself with how the telescope looked in the payload bay in case we needed to perform a spacewalk to troubleshoot an issue. But it seemed fitting that the telescope scientists would be the last people to see Chandra on Earth. It was a surprisingly emotional moment. "I can't promise to bring Chandra home," I told them, "but I promise to take good care of her and make sure she gets to space—where she belongs." Now, it was time to do just that.

My first job was to power up the telescope and the Inertial Upper Stage. Along with the Mission Control teams on the ground, I checked out her systems remotely—a kind of last-minute physical before launch—and ensured that everything was working. I could hear the voice of Bob Curbeam (Beamer), our Capsule Communicator (CAPCOM) for the deploy, relaying what David Brady, the lead payload officer at Mission Control in Houston, was saying, which included status notes from the Chandra folks in Massachusetts and the Air Force folks in California for the IUS.

The telescope was mounted on a "tilt table" that allowed it to be angled just right for deployment, ensuring that it would sail above the space shuttle with room to spare. I'd gone through the checkout process months earlier in a giant warehouse in Florida, three or four stories tall, where Chandra had been assembled, with the actual control panel I was now using to check out the telescope. I knew how these switches and levers felt in my hands, but I'd never actually seen the tilt table in action. I'd had to do my best to imagine it, as I stood on a platform high on a scaffold and looked up at the skinny end of the telescope—the part with all the instruments in it that would help us unravel the mysteries around black holes. I envisioned how it would look for this enormous instrument to rise up in front of the shuttle's windows as we tilted the table up. And I was excited to realize that right at that moment, the faces of our crew would be reflected on the mirrored top surface of the telescope. I made a mental note not to miss that cool photo.

Now, the moment had come. I looked down at my familiar checklist—the same one I'd been training with for almost two years, carefully highlighted and annotated. I could recite it in my sleep, but no matter what, I would be executing the physical checklist in tandem with Mission Control. Systematically, I began to work through the major steps we needed to accomplish in order to deploy Chandra.

Initial Systems Check. Complete.

Rotate the tilt table to 29 degrees. Complete.

Check systems with Mission Control. Complete.

Next came the point of no return. I had to rotate the tilt table up to fifty-eight degrees, the best angle for ensuring good clearance from the shuttle for deploy when Chandra and the IUS were pushed out of the payload bay. In the process, the "umbilicals"—the cables that connected the telescope to the shuttle's power—would stretch out and then break at a predesignated point where two connectors met, like pulling apart two extension cords that are joined together. There could be no reconnecting. Chandra would be without power and without data, and if we could not deploy her, we'd have to bring her home—a journey she was unlikely to survive intact. All $1.6 billion of her would be lost.

I initiated the tilt, and the cables snapped. I reported a good, clean disconnect, and Mission Control confirmed that from the ground. I was fully expecting Beamer's next call to say, "*Columbia,* you are GO for Deploy." But we had lost communication and all I heard was, "*Columbia,* you are G—" In another, less consequential circumstance, it might be perfectly acceptable to fill in the blank. But there's a very good reason that NASA confirms and reconfirms every single step for something as precise and critical as a telescope deploy or a launch.

I looked at Eileen, "That's not good enough for me, Eileen. And we still have time in our deploy window to wait for one comm pass."

Eileen concurred, and we waited an endless four minutes before Beamer came back with a chuckle and the magic words. *GO for Deploy.*

At 7:47 a.m. EDT, as my friends and family down below on Earth were getting up, eating breakfast, or beginning their daily commutes, I unlocked the "Deploy" lever and then moved it up into the Deploy position (this two-step mechanism ensures it cannot be done accidentally). Moving that switch ignites the ring of explosive powder that encircles the entire IUS. We call it an "explosive zipper," and it literally disintegrates the interface between the back end of the IUS and the shuttle. Once that happens, the five giant metal springs compressed behind the telescope push it smoothly forward and out over the nose of the shuttle.

At first, Chandra moved slowly—sailing over our heads and out into space like a graceful metallic dragonfly. She was so beautiful, I almost wished we could hold on to her for a little while longer.

I wasn't the only one performing delicate maneuvers. As commander, Eileen had the critical task of backing the shuttle away immediately—we needed to be well clear when Mission Control remotely activated the IUS rocket still attached to Chandra. She executed it beautifully, although I couldn't fully appreciate that until later, because I still had work to do.

Just seconds after the deploy, I had to switch gears and capture high-definition video of Chandra on her way to her new orbit, using one of the first HD cameras ever made. It's a human thing to want to do—but it also provides valuable engineering data as well. I felt so lucky to be one of the last people ever to see Chandra, to be wishing her luck on behalf of all the people back home who had built her, designed her, tested her, and entrusted our crew with her final deployment. The video was a marvelous source of high-definition photos of the telescope. Those images were used to show that nothing had shifted out of place or damaged during the deploy. Thank goodness I'd taken that camera home so often to practice: clearly, all those hours taking video of my cats Fitz and Markovka turned out to be integral to the mission.

I kept the camera trained on Chandra until I couldn't tell the difference between her and the stars. And even then, it was hard to look away. And then she was gone. I called the ground and said, "It was really special for all of us to watch Chandra go on her way to work."

The most important part of our mission was complete. Well, almost—there was a critical step sixteen minutes after deploy that we always used to joke I'd forget. And I did! Steve had to nudge me to command the telescope's antenna to high power. Once that was done, I could finally take a deep breath and relax—at least until the next morning.

Our Chandra duties were complete, but we still had four more days on orbit, and they were heavily scheduled, as all space shuttle flights are. I ran a plant experiment designed to help us understand how to grow food in space and eventually on Mars. We tested experimental solar array hinges for future satellites, took images with a small ultraviolet telescope from inside the shuttle, evaluated the new HD video camera as a substitute for a still camera to gather data about the Earth below, and tested the new treadmill that had just been designed for the space station. And of course, did a few interviews with the press on the ground. When Eileen and I were scheduled to do an interview together, she asked me to shake my hair free from its ponytail.

I was surprised. "But it's always been an unwritten rule that we shouldn't have our hair loose in the cabin."

She raised both eyebrows and gave me her this-is-an-order-from-your-commander look, and said, "Cady, I have short hair. We need your long hair to help all the girls out there know that they belong here too." I never forgot her saying this and would continue the "big hair" tradition on my future missions.

When the four days were up and it was time to go home once again, I was sad to leave space. But I loved knowing that Chandra was still up there and the mission was continuing, though I had no idea just how long she would go on sending her amazing discoveries back to Earth.

The plan in 1999 had been that she would last five years. But to this day, she remains up there. As of this writing, Chandra is almost twenty-five and still sending valuable data back from space. Each year, on her "birthday," the crew from STS-93 and the teams who worked on the ground connect via email, or in person for the big ones. We'll always share a bond from that mission, our experience during that time, and its continuing legacy. And what a legacy it is. Young astronomers who were still toddlers when I pulled that Deploy switch are now making discoveries based on her data. Chandra is responsible for most of what we now know about black holes, and she's still helping us advance our understanding of the universe, rewrite the textbooks, and feel both very small and very significant at the same time.

Chapter 5

You Can't Take the Baby to Space . . . or Can You?

Challenging the Playbook of Family Life

"**C**APCOM, you are GO for launch!"

The words blared into my headset. In 2001, I was working as a CAPCOM, which means acting as a liaison between NASA's Mission Control and the astronauts in space. We sit in Mission Control, which looks just like you've seen in the movies—rows of workstations, each surrounded by a cluster of monitors, and big screens on the front wall showing maps and critical data. During a mission, there can be as many as fifty people in there, including the flight director, flight controllers for the different systems, flight surgeons, and so on. Now imagine if all those people were just randomly communicating with the crew of astronauts orbiting Earth. It would be chaos—a disjointed and confusing flood of information, instructions, and questions that would be very difficult for the crew to process. That's why you have a CAPCOM and a flight director. The flight director is directing all that traffic and acting as a single decision-making authority, and then the CAPCOM acts as a single point of contact for the crew, channeling messages from Mission Control and making sure they come at an appropriate time.

The CAPCOM plays a critical role in space missions. It's up to us to translate messages into terms that will make sense to the astronauts in space, as well as to stand up for their needs or perspectives with the folks on the ground, if necessary. It requires empathy, diplomacy, great listening and communication skills, and confidence. I worked as a CAPCOM on and off for a dozen years at NASA, and I like to think I excelled at bridging the two worlds. It's a demanding role, even when you're working on simulations rather than actual missions. Sims are essential training for crew members and for Mission Control, so the idea is to make them as real as possible. That means, once you enter Mission Control and put on your headset, you're *on*, for the duration of your nine-hour shift. Lunch is eaten at your console. Personal calls are reserved for emergencies. And you can't just take a break when you feel like it to get a cup of coffee, use the bathroom—or, as in my case, pump milk for your kid.

That year I was bridging worlds in more ways than one. I was a new mother, with a breastfeeding baby boy named Jamey. And I was also a full-time astronaut. So when I heard those words over my headset—"CAPCOM, you are GO for launch!"—I knew it had nothing to do with rockets; it was directed at me. With a quick nod to the flight director, I'd sprint for the door.

There are usually hourly periods of five to ten minutes when the signal from the communication satellites is lost. During these "loss of signal" or LOS breaks—whether in sims or in actual missions—there's a small stampede for the bathrooms and the break room. I quickly realized that this was my opportunity to pump. At the beginning of each day, I would arrange with the sim supervisor and the flight director to have a few minutes tacked on to a couple of those LOS periods—times when they would not be staging any dramatic events that would require communication with the crew.

Time was of the essence, so I couldn't waste precious minutes running to the women's bathroom (which was, you guessed it, a long way away). The closest place to pump was the janitors' closet, right outside the door of Mission Control. Luckily, at the time all the janitors in Mission Control were women, and I knew them from my many years working there. They seemed to love hosting a breastfeeding astronaut. One woman brought in flowers, and another a stack of magazines.

The supervisors were generally accommodating too. It's not easy having conversations about pumping with male colleagues you don't know that well (even when carefully avoiding the words *breast* and *milk* to minimize the squirm factor), but it was quickly apparent that they liked being part of my family solution. But let's be clear: this was only one of countless such arrangements that I had to come up with, negotiate, and execute seamlessly in order to be a mother while also fulfilling a role that, quite frankly, was never designed for people like me. Thankfully, I wasn't the first to attempt this feat of world bridging, and I had role models and supporters to turn to. I knew, as Rhea Seddon had so thoughtfully shared with me, that it was possible to have a family in this job. But just because something is possible doesn't make it easy, especially when it is not to your advantage to advertise that you don't fit the mold. And when it came to my family life, that had been true for me even before Jamey came along.

Long-Distance Love

Josh and I have never had a conventional relationship. From the moment our eyes met across his studio and it was clear to us both that this was *something*, it was also clear that this *something* would not be following the typical path that many serious relationships take. Certainly, we realized early on that we wouldn't be living together anytime soon. Josh has an established glass studio in western Massachusetts, where he employs a dedicated group of folks from our local community. And importantly, he shared custody of his son, Josiah, whose mother lived nearby. And me? Being an astronaut meant that Houston would be my home for the foreseeable future. Neither of us could imagine asking the other to move!

We made regular weekend trips, at our own expense, to visit each other. I quickly got used to the conversations I'd have with strangers on planes when I'd explain our situation.

"But . . . what will happen when you get married?"

"But . . . what will happen if you have kids?"

"But . . . where will your kids go to school?"

I didn't have answers to most of those questions, but I knew the questions were just a mask for the subtext: "Well, *that* isn't going to last." I wasn't too worried, though. Josh and I would have time to figure out those things. One thing I did figure out pretty fast was that the term *boyfriend* didn't help the people I worked with (or the people on planes) understand that our relationship was a serious one. So we used the term *sweetheart* instead. We liked that it was different and charming, and its novelty interrupted the assumptions that people often made about our long-distance relationship.

Often, however, folks at NASA still struggled to know how Josh, as a significant other, fit into the more traditional classification scheme. Sometimes marital status was important for legal reasons, but Josh was also very different from the military spouses they were accustomed to. One day, I was trying to arrange for him to get a special tour of the Kennedy Space Center, reserved for "close" relatives. The tour required a significant amount of paperwork, and wasn't something you could request casually for your friends. I didn't know the astronaut who was in charge there very well, and he kept asking me, "So, you're not married, but is he a friend? A *good* friend? A *very* good friend?" Finally, exasperated, I burst out, "He's the guy I've been sleeping with for three years!" Turning beet red, he said, "Well, I guess he gets the good tour!"

Despite our long-distance setup, Josh and I were committed, but getting married had never really been on my radar. So when Josh proposed, in 1997, by a waterfall on the island of Kauai, after hiking for hours, he took me by surprise. I had to be honest—I told him I couldn't give him an answer right away. I needed to think about it and talk it through with the people closest to me. That's just how I process things. Josh, who knew my decision-making style by this point, suggested that I try on the ring just to see how it felt to be engaged. Ironically, my hands were swollen from the hours of hiking, and I had to wait until the next day for the ring to fit! But for the rest of that day and evening, I would peek frequently at the platinum ring a good friend of his had carved by hand, fitted with a sapphire Josh's grandmother had given him, and surrounded by oak leaves to remind me of our home in Massachusetts. I hadn't thought much about marriage—but it was clear Josh had, weaving his family history and our shared love of the place we met into this symbol of our fate-filled relationship.

Once I got home and had a chance to spend some time alone and think, I made up my mind pretty quickly. I had no doubt that I wanted to spend my life with this man, so why wouldn't we get married? I didn't want to tell Josh over the phone, so I waited until his next visit, a couple of weeks later. Wishing to make up for my initial indecisiveness, I made a giant sign saying YES! and put on a dress and heels to meet him at the airport. I even had a bottle of champagne in a cooler. Those were the days when you could go right up to the gate and wait for the plane. So there I was, holding my sign at the ready, expecting Josh to be among the first passengers to emerge, as he usually was.

One by one, the passengers came out of the jet bridge, but there was no Josh. I wasn't exactly lonely—it turns out that you can meet a lot of people when you are holding a sign like that—but I was definitely puzzled. Folks around me were laughing with me, though with a hint of nervousness. Finally, it was clear he hadn't been on the plane. I talked with the gate agent and she confirmed that Josh was on the next flight. So I folded up my sign, picked up my champagne, and went back to the parking garage for a few hours, putting the bottle back on ice and trying (unsuccessfully) to focus on studying space shuttle systems. The rational part of me knew that Josh had just missed his connection, but I couldn't help feeling a little rejected. Soon enough, however, I returned to the gate with my sign and my champagne to do it all over again. When Josh stepped out of the jet bridge, saw me, and realized what must have happened earlier, we both burst out laughing. Not many people get sentimental about airport gates, but to this day, seeing that first one on the right at Houston's Hobby Airport makes me smile.

Grounded—in a Good Way

Josh and I got married on a beautiful fall day on our farm in Shelburne Falls with friends and family from everywhere, including some of my NASA classmates. My younger sister, Cari, stood up for me, and Josiah for Josh, and we toasted with handblown wineglasses that looked like the night sky. Since the Coleman family was involved, there was good-natured roasting after the reception. Then it was back to our unconventional, dual-location lifestyle.

Much as I hadn't given marriage a lot of thought before Josh proposed, I really hadn't started thinking about children yet. But a few years after we got married, Josh and I both decided that we wanted to have a baby, and Josh was just sure that we could figure out how to make it work. I knew other women astronauts who had kids. Kathy Thornton had four, and when we flew together on STS-73 they were all still young. And she was a geographically single parent, as I would be. She and Steve had commuted between Virginia and Houston for years. So I knew it could be done. I tend to have a fairly naïve optimism when it comes to how things will work out, and I can multitask in my sleep, so I didn't worry too much about the geographical challenges of adding a baby to our already complicated long-distance marriage.

After STS-93, in the summer of 1999, we decided it was a good time to start trying. And before I knew it, just shy of turning thirty-nine, I was pregnant. Minutes after I read the test, and just hours before both of our families descended on us for Thanksgiving, I told Josh, "Sweetie, remember when I told you that getting pregnant at my age might take a long time? Well, it didn't!" It was both daunting and wonderful that it had happened so soon. It was too early to share the news, but Josh and I kept exchanging elated glances over the turkey and stuffing.

The timing was good, because I knew I wouldn't be assigned to another flight right away, so it wouldn't set me back too much to be grounded—temporarily unable to participate in certain aspects of training, like flying the T-38 and practicing spacewalking. The first crew was due to launch to the new space station just after Jamey was born, and I wanted to be available when they started selecting the next wave of crews. I'd been eagerly watching the assembly of the giant modular structure since it began in January 1998. The idea of actually *living* in space—not just spending a week or two aboard the shuttle—was enthralling to me, and doing that as part of an international crew seemed like the future we had always been working toward.

I'd always had the strong sense that humans were *meant* to live up there. Space felt like home to me. When I'd been up on the shuttle, I regretted having to go home. *Why are we leaving? The research we can do in space is so important—we should be working there for months at a stretch!* As a scientist-astronaut, that was what I wanted. I dreamed of performing experiments like the ones we had tested on STS-73. Of course, I knew I wouldn't be able to take a baby with me, but—well, I figured we'd work it out when the time came.

I flew to Massachusetts in July 2000, just a few weeks before Jamey was born, and stayed there with Josh through the summer. Those few months were the longest amount of consecutive time we'd ever spent to-gether! I couldn't help but smile when I found myself out on our porch—barefoot, pregnant, and shelling peas. Could this really be the same person who flew jets, launched telescopes into space, and could knock out a set of pull-ups with the guys? I still felt like myself, but I'd never imagined I could be grounded and yet feel so content.

Josiah, about to turn seventeen and start his junior year of high school, wasn't quite sure what to think about the impending arrival of a new baby brother. But he and I got along well, and I was sure that we'd figure things out. I think he knew how proud I was of the young man he'd become. That summer, he worked with his dad in the glassblowing studio while I studied space station systems and worked on a required course for the Air Force.

Jamey arrived in August, named for Josh (whose middle name is James), both of our fathers (also James), and my big brother, Jamey. I'd agreed to return to work in mid-September that year and was especially excited about my assignment to work as the lead CAPCOM for my col-lege friend Pam Melroy's second mission as a shuttle pilot to install one of the first large segments of the space station. However, Jamey had some medical issues that made me hesitate to go back to work so soon. I'll al-ways be grateful that Ellen Ochoa, who led the astronaut CAPCOM team, encouraged me to take my time.

"Jamey's only going to be six weeks old once," she reminded me, "but there will be a lot of missions to the space station." The conversation made it very clear that deciding to focus on my family would not be judged as a lack of dedication to my job. So I stayed home with Jamey, studying Russian to prepare for future missions. To this day, I attribute his gift for languages to those early months.

In November 2000, the ISS got its first long-duration crew: Bill Shep-herd, Sergei Krikalev, and Yuri Gidzenko. I'd become good friends with them during my Russian labeling assignment. Knowing they were up there was the next best thing to being there myself.

When I sat out on the porch with Jamey on the nights that were still warm enough to allow it, I'd look up and imagine them flying through the modules of the space station (still in its early stages of assembly, but already much bigger than the shuttle!), doing experiments, looking out of the windows at the Earth. And then I'd look down at my sleeping boy, overwhelmed by love and wonder. When you're pregnant, you think you're going to have a baby. But then, after they are born, the shocking thing is that you have a little person! I just couldn't get over how tiny and how uniquely himself this new arrival was. I'd whisper to him that maybe one day soon his mommy would be living up there on a space station among the stars. And I'd wonder what it would mean for him to have a mom who not only lived in a different state than his father, but sometimes didn't live on planet Earth.

Planes, Trains, Babies & Automobiles

Anyone who's balanced parenthood with a demanding job can probably guess what came next. Later that fall, when I returned to Houston with Jamey, I discovered just how challenging it would be to juggle my astronaut duties with being a geographically single mom, even with the support of a nanny for the first few months and, later, day care. I suddenly understood that feeling that moms describe, when you arrive at work already feeling like you've worked a full day. I got pretty good at the run-and-pump routine during simulations. When an actual shuttle mission was "up," the hours were long and consuming, so usually I'd send Jamey to Massachusetts with Josh, and send my milk up there on dry ice. Sprinting to the FedEx office was frequently involved.

We settled into a rhythm of sorts during Jamey's first few years, with Josh visiting in Houston, me going up to Massachusetts whenever I had a break, and Jamey traveling back and forth with one or the other of us.

Throughout Jamey's childhood, we racked up frequent-flier miles, but Jamey soon had more than either of us and was often the first to get upgraded, which led to some pretty comical situations.

Was it a perfect arrangement? No, but it worked. Josh and I were a team, trading off our parenting responsibilities so we could both pursue the work we were passionate about. Of course, I worried that even when I managed all the practicalities perfectly, I was missing something that really mattered. One time Josh sent me a photo of a two-year-old Jamey hugging the television, because he'd heard his mom's voice on the NASA Channel. I laughed and cried when I saw that picture.

Goodbyes were hard. Josh and Jamey often dropped me at the airport in Hartford, an hour from our house. I tried not to cry at the curb—I didn't think that would help anybody. Once they were out of sight, though, all bets were off. It never gets easier to leave your baby, or your husband, or your home. With some affection, I think, the nice ladies at the United counter used to refer to me as "the astronaut who cries at the airport." They would be ready with a sympathetic smile and a bag tag in hand when I came running up, damp-eyed and on the edge of late.

For the most part, we succeeded in keeping all the balls of our family life in the air, but there were times when it just seemed too complicated. One particular juggling act stands out in my memory because it followed an event that involved throwing actual balls. I'd been invited to do one of the more nerve-racking duties of my professional life. I'm not talking about a space launch or jumping out of a plane. I'm talking about throwing out the first pitch in front of tens of thousands of baseball fans at Boston's Fenway Park.

It was a Friday night and the Houston Astros were playing the Boston Red Sox. Of course, the date snuck up on me, and I felt unsuited and woefully underprepared for the task (having never learned to throw properly) despite stellar last-minute coaching from Mark Polansky. Beside me was my friend Stephanie Wilson, a fellow astronaut whose pitching skill far exceeded mine. On every side, crowds in the stands rose up—families all wearing their team colors, excited kids dreaming of the day when they'd hit a home run. As the strains of the National Anthem faded, I nervously pulled my Houston Astros cap down to shield my eyes from the glare of the stadium lights.

Moments earlier, I'd been informed that we were not allowed to stand on the pitcher's mound and would have to stand in front it, a change in plan for which I was immensely grateful. But it still seemed like the ball needed to travel halfway to the moon to get anywhere near home plate. I glanced at Stephanie, since we'd planned to throw at the same time, but she'd gotten carried away and already thrown her pitch. Calling on my very best compartmentalization skills, I focused all my energy into my left arm and threw the ball. And to my astonishment, it went into the catcher's glove. And the glove was above the plate. Feeling victorious, I made my way up into the stands and took my seat. Later, some guy came up to me and said, "You girls don't do a lot of that, do you?" But even his disparaging remark couldn't dent my happiness and pride at having thrown that ball all the way to where it needed to go.

I was relaxing and enjoying the energy in the stands during the game when my cell phone rang. Over the noise of the crowd, I could barely make out that it was Andy Thomas, the deputy chief of the Astronaut Office, calling.

"Cady, the NASA administrator is going to Norway on his European trip, where he'll present a Norwegian flag that was flown up on the space shuttle to the king. We just realized that you're the one who flew that flag on STS-93. He asked if you'd like to go with him."

Would I like to? I *had* to. First, this was a request straight from the head of NASA. And second, Norway was like a second home to me. I had spent a year there as an exchange student, and I still spoke fluent Norwegian. Since there weren't any Norwegian astronauts at the time, I felt like the closest thing.

Shouting to be heard, I told him I was honored by the invitation, but I needed to figure out some family logistics first.

"Okay, get back to us ASAP," he said. "It's wheels up on Sunday, and you'd need to get to Washington."

My mind kicked into overdrive. Sunday. That was just two days away. I'd be back in Houston, but I'd have Jamey, then almost four, with me. Josh was on a trip that week. He'd be flying home Sunday, coincidentally changing planes at Houston's Intercontinental Airport. But I would already be on my way to Washington. Someone—someone impeccably trustworthy and capable—would need to complete a handoff of Jamey to Josh in the middle of that airport, while Josh was changing planes. It was a maneuver that would need to be executed as perfectly as that ball landing in the glove. But what if . . . a half dozen ways it could go wrong played out in my head. I needed someone who was *really* travel savvy. While trying to figure out who that could be, I called the airport to arrange access passes for Jamey and a chaperone. I'd done this once before, at Newark, so I thought I knew the drill. Except it turned out that Houston had a higher profile for child trafficking and such passes were not available for nonrelatives. Now I needed not only to find the right person but figure out how they could complete the handoff without being able to meet Josh at the gate. And what if Josh's flight was late? Or canceled? And I was in the air and couldn't be reached? I was at a loss. I called Josh.

"Honey, I don't think I can figure this one out," I said. Usually I'm the logistical mastermind, expertly keeping track of babies, breast milk, nannies, planes, and training schedules. But this one stumped me. Josh, however, had faith. And he knew how much this trip mattered to me.

"You can figure anything out," he told me. "Why don't you just say yes, and we'll find a way."

And we did. In the end, Mary Lockhart, the wife of one of my fellow astronauts, heard about my situation. She was a seasoned traveler herself and knew Jamey well, so she volunteered to take him to the airport, armed with plans B and C and D and E and F in case something went wrong. Josh came out through security and found her at the curb, expertly fending off security guards who wanted her to move her car. And I got to go to Norway and put my hard-earned Norwegian language skills to use talking with King Harald. I learned that he was an avid sailor, and our conversation centered around the similarities between his experiences sailing across the vast ocean and mine sailing around our planet in a spaceship.

That handoff was a particularly complex puzzle. But it's the kind of scenario that played out dozens, maybe hundreds of times during the twenty-six years that Josh and I commuted between Massachusetts and Texas. Sometimes the logistics of our family life could seem more daunting than the process of launching a telescope into orbit. After all, I was given detailed instruction manuals for all the complex procedures I performed as part of my job. But no one gives you an instruction manual for being a parent, and a geographically single one at that. You have to figure it out for yourself—whether the challenge is handing off a small human at a busy international airport when flights don't quite align or navigating the daily irritation that the NASA day care opened at 7:00 a.m. and Mission Control shifts started at—you guessed it—7:00 a.m. Between these two locations was a three-minute car ride and a five-minute run. Had no one ever done the math? Having prearranged with my CAPCOM partner, I would read the mission logs at 5:00 a.m. from home so that I wouldn't be behind when I arrived breathless at 7:10, late through no fault of my own but knowing I was being judged for it anyway.

There is a point at which, as a parent with a career, you realize that your budget of creative problem-solving and decision-making energy is simply finite, and now has to be split between work and family. And so you need to learn to evaluate *all* your resources, mental and otherwise, and simplify and streamline what you can to stretch that budget further. You have to accept that you won't always please everyone, and that tomorrow you'll wake up and do it all over again. In those early years of motherhood, I learned that no plan is set in stone, that flight-change fees have to be accepted as part of life, and that the ladies who worked in the astronaut scheduling office were goddesses. Real, live goddesses.

The Sh*ttiest Mom Ever

"I'm so excited to meet you!" the woman exclaimed. She and her friend had stopped me in the hallway at a mommy bloggers convention in California, where I'd been invited to speak. Since I was wearing my blue flight suit, as I often do for speaking engagements, it wasn't unusual to be the object of some attention from space fans, especially women. But this woman wasn't looking for an autograph or a photo. Her next words took me aback.

"You! You're the sh*ttiest mom ever! You actually left your baby on the planet and went to space!"

Before you start imagining an angry defense on my behalf, let me clarify that this was said with the utmost warmth and a great deal of admiration. The two women, it turns out, had created a popular blog about being a "Sh*tty Mom," where they humorously subverted the ideals of motherhood and offered refreshingly honest stories of what it's really like raising a family. She definitely meant it as a compliment, and after I got over my surprise, I took it that way. But her lighthearted comment pointed to a deeper truth—how many of us secretly fear that we're terrible parents, that our choices and mistakes are scarring our kids for life. To this day, Josh and I look at each other and say, "Well, so far Jamey hasn't grown up to be an axe murderer, so I guess we did something right?"

Seriously, though, most of us need reassurance about our parenting prowess at times. One person I often turn to is Cari, because she is always there for me. My sister is a force of nature in her town, building community by catalyzing neighborhood events, volunteering at the schools long after her kids had left them, and bringing people together to solve problems. On top of all that, she and her husband, Mark, have raised their two girls, Cayleigh and Macaire, to be wonderful young women. Cari has a knack for keeping perspective and reminding me about what's truly important. So when *she* tells me I'm doing okay, I believe her.

During the early years, there were so many times when I needed Cari's reassurance because I *did* feel like the sh*ttiest mom ever. Like the day I dropped Jamey off for his kindergarten trip to the zoo, imagining that I was the only mom not going along. I called Cari in tears in the parking lot, and she reassured me: "He's okay. He's at the zoo. There are lions and tigers there. He's not even thinking about you!" Or the many times I told her how guilty I felt about not volunteering at the school. "Cate," she'd say, "you don't have a lot of time, but you are always generous about contributing money. Just be sure to thank the other moms so they know you appreciate them picking up the slack." Equally important was the less conventional example of my younger brother, Kip, who is a wonderful stay-at-home dad for his son, Calvin, and his daughter, Niah. He had great advice and would tell me stories about how dads always get left out of the mom-dominated conversations and have to figure things out for themselves—another valuable example of the ways in which our society's narrow ideas about roles affect everyone.

The reassurance of my siblings helped. But I still worried sometimes that I was doing things a "good" mom would never do. Even if we put aside leaving the planet for a moment (which I didn't actually do until my baby was ten), what kind of mom leaves her two-year-old behind for two and a half months to go hunting for meteorites in the Antarctic? Yep, me.

Adventure Calls

The purpose of the annual Antarctic Search for Meteorites is to collect meteorites and increase the number available for research. The teams are made up of about a dozen meteorite scientists and mountaineers, plus the occasional astronaut. When I first heard about this trip, I immediately wanted to go. It was a great chance to build more operational experience, and working with a small team in the middle of nowhere would be perfect training for being part of a crew on the space station. Not to mention that it sounded like the most amazing adventure imaginable! So I put my name down as a volunteer.

When the selection was made, I heard that my friend Suni Williams had gotten the spot that year. I was happy for her, though disappointed, but I told myself it was probably for the best, with Jamey so young.

Then, one day in early October, just a few weeks before the expedition was scheduled to depart, I got a phone call. Suni had been assigned to the space station earlier than planned. Did I still want to go on the Antarctica trip?

"Yes!" The word tumbled out faster than I could think, but I took a breath and quickly followed up with the kind of answer a responsible mom would give: "That's something I would love to do, but of course, we will need to talk about it together as a family. I will call you back in . . . about five minutes. In the meantime, you should be thinking the answer is YES."

When I told Josh about the call, he was almost as excited as I was. So much so that I finally said: "Sweetie, you do realize I'm not taking the baby with me, right?"

For a moment, he feigned surprise, as though he really hadn't thought it through, but then he hugged me and assured me that he and Jamey would be just fine. For the millionth time, I thanked the universe for finding me a partner who in his own creative life was also an explorer at heart and was willing not just to accommodate but to enthusiastically support the very unusual demands of my job. Even when Josh broke his leg just weeks before my departure, he still insisted I should go.

Antarctica was an unforgettable experience. We spent the first two weeks at McMurdo Station, Antarctica's largest base, a tight-knit community of about a thousand explorers and adventurous kindred spirits. We learned how to camp out on the ice, wearing three layers of clothing at all times when we were outside the tent, except for quick excursions to the "poop tent." We practiced rescuing one another from crevasses and lighting our camp stoves in sub-zero temperatures. It was a big deal for me, because growing up, I was *not* a camping girl. The mountaineering part was especially new for me, and I was a bit daunted until I realized that the operational mindset that I had been developing at NASA had really laid the groundwork for me to acquire new safety skills, even when hanging in a crevasse.

After demonstrating our skills, our four-person reconnaissance team flew in a C-130 cargo plane to the South Pole. We spent a few hours there, and then flew a few more hours in a tiny six-person Twin Otter to our first meteorite search area. We were four people in two tents, two hundred miles from the South Pole, spending hours each day driving snowmobiles slowly across the vast icy landscape in search of meteorites that were formed more than four billion years ago and fell to Earth. The folks at the South Pole Station, who came out to help us move our camp to a new location once a week, referred to us as "the Four." I thought it made us sound like comic-book heroes, and I felt like one, living on a sheet of ice and collecting rocks that had come from space. My favorite photo from the trip shows our camp from the air. It looks like a tiny speck of dirt in the middle of a vast and empty sheet of white paper.

It struck me that the people who had chosen to work and live in such an extreme outpost were not that different from astronauts who choose to live and work in space. Every supply from toilet paper to food had to be brought in, and recycling was a way of life. Everyone who lived in Antarctica lived with risk every day. It felt vast, like space, and few people had been to either one. I felt privileged to spend time in both of these amazing places. It was fascinating to learn about where the meteorites came from and what they told us about how our universe formed. Together with our mountain-based team, we found more than a thousand meteorites, including one that came from the moon. Looking at that greenish-colored piece of rock, it was hard to fathom that it had been blasted away from the surface of the moon by a large asteroid, fallen to Earth, and had been sitting for billions of years unnoticed, until our team found it.

Despite missing my family, I cherished my time at the end of the Earth. I took lots of photos and videos to show Jamey, including ones with Petey, his tiny but treasured stuffed penguin. Predictably, he was excited to see what Petey was up to, but most of all, he loved the pictures of wildly cool snow vehicles from McMurdo, some with six-foot-high tires, others with triangular tracks. Because we could only relay emails once a week, and the satellite phone cost six dollars a minute, I'd also recorded videos of me reading Jamey's favorite books to keep him company while I was gone.

Becoming a mother had changed me, but it hadn't changed my eagerness and ability to undertake important missions, on or off the planet. Indeed, if I tried hard not to let my job compromise my ability to be a mother, I worked equally hard to ensure that being a mother didn't compromise my ability to do my job as an astronaut. Sometimes, I felt as if I had to make it look like I was not just managing it all, but doing so with ease, for fear that if I showed even a hint of overwhelm, it would confirm the low expectations that women and people of color often face in a job like mine. To combat those attitudes, many of us feel the need to be not just good but exceptional. The fact that change is so slow, that this is still a reality in today's world, angers and disappoints me.

Fortunately, I found that most people in the Astronaut Office were supportive and understanding. Some of my colleagues, both men and women, became my indispensable allies. I felt incredibly useful, fulfilled, and engaged by my jobs between flights, but I did start thinking about when I might be assigned to fly in space again—when I'd get a chance to fulfill my dream of actually living on the ISS.

Eventually, one of my STS-93 friends became the lead astronaut for the space station, and he shared some information about why I hadn't yet been assigned to a long-duration ISS mission. He told me that some of the higher-ups were hesitant about assigning me to the space station because they were concerned that my "alternative" living situation would make it harder for me to be separated from my family during the years of training around the world and then the six months in space. The consensus was that I was more suited to space shuttle missions, typically a week or two long.

I found this answer incredibly frustrating. Frankly, I was pissed. Wouldn't my fifteen-year track record of maintaining a commuting relationship make me *better* qualified for that aspect of the job than most astronauts, since I was accustomed to living apart from my family? Hadn't I proved that I was capable of balancing my mission and my personal life? And last but certainly not least, would they even be asking this question if I weren't a woman?

No one seemed to hesitate to assign the male astronauts because they had families at home, or even asked them how they felt about leaving their families behind, for that matter. And yet there was a tacit assumption that as a woman I was less able to manage those two worlds at once. The higher-ups, all men at that time, didn't even ask me how or whether I could manage these situations, they just made decisions on my behalf, which included assuming *they* knew when *I* would be ready for another mission after having a baby.

My friend didn't just pass on this frustrating intel. As an ally, he also helped me strategize how to improve my chances of selection. He suggested accepting a job assignment within the ISS branch, so that my capabilities would be more visible to ISS management. I agreed, because it seemed like a good idea and because I wanted to learn more about working on the space station.

Luckily, over the course of my career, I had other male allies as well who didn't harbor such outdated double standards. Chris Hadfield, my classmate, bandmate, and friend, is more than an accomplished astronaut and a talented musician. He has a rare aptitude and reputation for recognizing the skills people bring to the table, even when those people, or their skills, don't conform to traditional expectations. Importantly, he helped others to strip away bias and see potential where they might have missed it. As a test pilot, he was highly respected by the Astronaut Office management, most of whom were also test pilots. That gave him a platform to advocate for a number of other astronauts, including me, in a way that was pivotal to our careers.

Chris was Chief of Robotics while I was working in the ISS branch, but his tenure was coming to an end. He knew that I'd just gotten the highest grade on the robotics exam, and felt my talents were being wasted as assistant to the crew support astronaut for the current ISS mission. He made sure management knew that in addition to my robotics skills, I had the capability to knit the robotics community together at a critical time in space station construction, and he strongly recommended that I replace him. And so I became head of Robotics—another important step toward being seen as a valuable ISS crew member.

I took on that leadership role at an exciting and challenging moment. I quickly realized that astronauts in my branch would be spread thin, and I was concerned about how they would balance the intense project schedules with personal commitments. So I made it clear from the outset that I would never judge if someone was working by whether they were at their desks. As long as we stayed on track, I encouraged them to manage their time and work from home when that made the most sense. I knew that taking care of ourselves and each other was key to accomplishing the branch's mission.

Function over Form

If I've learned anything in my journey as a parent, it's that form matters much less than function when it comes to family. What is the function of a family? Family gives us a foundation on which to build and maintain secure bonds with those we love. When children are in the mix, hopefully this foundation helps them develop a deep sense of trust and confidence as they grow into themselves and go out into the world. None of this requires family to fit a narrow definition—in fact, it would serve us all to embrace an ever-growing sense of what family can be.

Josh and I knew that the form of our family, at least when it came to our lifestyle choices, would never be conventional, and it forced us to think more deliberately about how we could make our family function well for our sons. Josiah lived with his dad during the week, spent most weekends with his mom, and seemed to like living in both places. When Jamey was young, and taking turns living with Josh and me, the three of us spoke almost every night on the phone. The advent of the speakerphone made all the difference, allowing Jamey to play while we talked, and he got to feel like the absent parent was in the room with him.

We wanted Jamey to feel a sense of continuity and connection, even though he moved between two homes and two schools, so we sought the advice of a child psychologist about ways to help our son knit his worlds together. Simple things—like working with his teachers in both places to ensure that he could always come back to the same teacher and the same classroom, even the same desk—made a big difference. When he was with me in Texas, we'd take photos of things he and I did together, many featuring our cats. Then, when he went back to Massachusetts, he would show the photos to his friends and teachers and tell them about his life in Houston. Josh would do the same when Jamey was with him, and he'd come back to my house with pictures of his time with his dad.

Nevertheless, there were always tough trade-offs to commuting. A comical but actually tough one to manage: Jamey was a talented Little League player even as a six-year-old, a left-handed pitcher who could hit any ball, even when his mother threw it. And although Jamey didn't seem to mind, Texas takes baseball pretty seriously, and the coaches were heartbroken that he'd always miss the playoffs because he had to be in Massachusetts for the end of the school year. Grown men, in tears. I occasionally half wonder whether Josh and I denied Jamey a career in professional sports, and ourselves good seats in the nation's ballparks.

I also wanted Jamey to feel that his world was connected to mine, and that I was thinking about him when I went to work and even when my job took me far away. I didn't want him to feel like I just disappeared, so I tried to give him a sense of where I'd be going. We'd drop by the simulators in Houston on the weekend and I'd explain what I'd be learning in the coming week so he had a picture in his mind. When I was on the road, I'd call Jamey from wherever I happened to be and we'd read stories together before he went to bed. I also continued our Antarctic tradition of bringing one of his stuffed animals with me on training trips so I could feature his furry friend in the photos I sent home. He didn't always care about what his mom was doing when she was out of town, but he paid close attention to the adventures of "Underwater Doggy" during my eleven-day stay in the Aquarius habitat, sixty feet below the surface of the water. And he loved hearing about his little stuffed monkey, who had to go to astronaut school in Japan to get ready to fly in space.

Family doesn't have to look any particular way to function beautifully. But it takes courage to write and stand up for your own family playbook when the people around you can't imagine how a family could work if it looks different from theirs. In the end, I like to think that despite its unconventional form, our family did what it needed to do—providing a foundation on which both our sons felt loved, secure, and confident. After all, isn't that what we hope for as parents: to give our children a secure base from which to venture out into the world? One day, when Jamey was about five or six, he packed up his little backpack, grabbed an apple and his stuffed tiger, and set out across the fields by our house. When Josh caught up with him, Jamey explained that he was going on an adventure, like Calvin and Hobbes. I was so proud of our fearless little explorer.

We've Come a Long Way—and We've Got a Long Way to Go

"Come on," I said to my son. "It's about to start." Jamey and I were attending a NASA event in Houston, and of course, I was running a little late. But Jamey, then four, had stopped outside the convention center doors, and was staring up at a life-size cardboard cutout of an astronaut wearing a spacesuit.

"Is that you, Mommy?"

I shook my head, smiling. "No, sweetie, that's not me."

"Then whose mommy is it?"

Lateness forgotten, I hugged my son close. It was not lost on me how much it means for a little boy to automatically assume that an astronaut is, by default, someone's mother—a woman, not a man. It certainly was not a default for much of my career—far from it. Being a woman in this field presented challenges, but being a mother and being an astronaut was even tougher to fit in the same sentence.

The space program has come a long way since 1962, when astronaut John Glenn testified before Congress that the absence of women in the program was "just a fact of our social order." He spoke those words while the brave women of the Mercury 13, who had already proven their fitness and willingness to serve, sat and listened in the gallery. How must they have felt?

I wish I could say that our social order is no longer defined by people like Glenn, who believed that it should automatically fall to women to stay home (or stay on Earth!). And there's no doubt that we've made progress. But there are still many fields that are assumed to be the realm of men. The barriers for women are often invisible. Gender inequities— lower pay, fewer opportunities, and greater responsibility when it comes to the care of children and aging parents, to name three—are still widespread. During the COVID-19 pandemic, those inequities were highlighted.

Given what we've learned about the greater effectiveness of diverse teams, in space and on Earth, these disadvantages for women come at a great cost to our society as a whole. With all the global challenges we face, from poverty to climate change, we can't afford to lose the perspectives and contributions of *any* segment of the world's population.

Bottom line, I believe that it's incumbent upon all of us to stand up for what family and closeness means to each of us, no matter what form our family takes. Rewriting the playbook of family life is a cultural project with a long way to go. Of course, each of us has different circumstances and resources that may constrain us. But perhaps we also have more choices than we realize—ones that may make other people uncomfortable but nevertheless may be right for our families and our lives. Hopefully, by finding new ways we also expand the possibilities for others, so they can follow our path or more important, make their own. And if we find ourselves in a role where we can make the culture more flexible, we should seize those opportunities to create ripples into the future.

There's no perfect division of labor or shift in attitudes that will erase the tension between pursuing a demanding career and being a parent. There will always be hard choices to make on one side or another. You can't take a baby with you to space (at least, not yet!), so my career involved many difficult goodbyes—for me and for my loved ones. But we were always there for each other, even when I wasn't on this planet. Jamey grew up knowing that his mom sometimes left, but he also knew that she always came back.

Chapter 6

We'll See You on the Other Side

The Legacy of a Loss and the Limits of Repair

"**L**ost?"

The word made no sense to me. It was 3:00 a.m., and the shrill ring of the phone had woken me from a deep sleep. Gently, my friend Bob Young repeated what he'd just said:

"Cady, they lost *Columbia*."

For a few moments, I couldn't process what he was telling me. *How could they lose the space shuttle?* And then it hit me so hard I couldn't breathe.

STS-107. My friends. Laurel, KC, Rick, Dave, Willie, Michael, and Ilan. Today was their landing day. Their faces filled my mind as Bob's voice told me that Mission Control had lost contact with *Columbia* after reentry and the shuttle had broken apart. All seven crew members had been lost.

It was February 1, 2003. In just hours, the disaster was all over the news. Millions of people had watched in horror as fiery debris rained down from California to Louisiana. But I had seen nothing. On my way back from Antarctica, I was taking a break with Josh at a borrowed house in a remote part of New Zealand. Cut off from television or news at our pilot friend Bob's home, we wouldn't have known about the accident for days if Bob hadn't thought to call me.

We left right away. I just needed to be home. Home to help. Home to grieve. Home to be there for the families, even if that meant giving them space. Home to people who could truly understand what it felt like to lose a crew—our friends, our colleagues. It was such a long trip home, and yet it happened in a blur. Changing planes in Los Angeles, I remember seeing a picture on the front page of the paper, a battered helmet sitting in a Texas field. To this day sometimes a glimpse of newspapers in an airport kiosk brings back that moment in all its agonizing clarity.

STS-107 was a sixteen-day laboratory flight, similar to my first mission, STS-73. I'd been thrilled to be assigned as the Lead CAPCOM for their mission. I knew what it felt like to be the steward of all those precious experiments, to wake up each morning on orbit and tend to a locker full of seedling potatoes or a test tube of crystals. I had trained with them in simulations for almost a year, until at the last minute I was reassigned to go to Antarctica. I'd followed their progress whenever I could get news, felt their frustration with every one of the thirteen slips they went through before finally launching, and celebrated when they made it to orbit. Just a week ago in Antarctica, I had organized a teleconference between all the women at McMurdo Station and Laurel Clark and Kalpana Chawla (whom we called KC) up in space on the shuttle.

On that call, I could hear the wonder of being in space in Laurel's voice as she told us what fun she and KC were having, and added—"and Cady, we look so good in our colorful shirts!" That had been a favorite piece of advice I gave them as they prepared for the mission, her first time in space: bring fun shirts. Laurel loved color; in fact, she was nicknamed Floral because of her love of floral dresses. At her funeral, her women classmates threw off their black coats to reveal dresses Laurel would have adored. I will always picture her in space: big smile, curly hair floating in every direction, and wearing a bright red shirt. I'll also remember how she lent me her maternity gear when I got pregnant, and how, as a medical doctor, friend, and fellow astronaut, she helped me with everything from medical advice to new mom questions.

KC had been my flight instructor when I was trying to stay proficient at flying small planes, when most of my flight time was in the NASA T-38 jet trainers. I remember being nervous, and appreciating her calm, compassionate, methodical presence in the cockpit beside me. Brilliant at robotics, she was always generous with her advice and brought that same steadiness and clarity to helping me train to use the robotic arm, often staying after hours to do so.

I'd also been close to Dave Brown and Rick Husband, both of whom had spent many hours training with me in the T-38. I'll never forget the time that Dave and I flew to Dayton, Ohio, for a meeting, not long after Josh and I had gotten engaged. We had a few hours to kill before we could fly home, so I formulated a plan. Dave could hang out at the air museum near Wright-Patterson Air Force Base while the plane refueled. And I could go wedding dress shopping with my sister, Cari, who lived near the base.

I explained my plan to Dave, but he objected—not to the shopping excursion, but to the idea that he would miss all the fun! Which is how I found myself in a bridal boutique modeling an array of white dresses and being critiqued not just by my sister but also by a tall guy in a flight suit and boots, slouched on a chaise. "Well, for that dress, it would really depend on what kind of head-thingie you decided to wear." We called it the Dresscapade.

Another unforgettable flight with Dave happened back in 1999 when I was in quarantine for the Chandra mission. I liked to fly acrobatics in the T-38 in the days leading up to the launch as a way of getting my inner ear and brain ready to be weightless. Performing barrel rolls and loops, almost to the point of being nauseous, was great preparation for arriving in space a few days later. (Plus, it was amazing fun!) But I accidentally went supersonic right over the Kennedy Space Center—something we are *not* supposed to do. "Shit!" I said. "Sorry, Dave!" But laughter boomed through the intercom between our cockpits.

"You know, Cady, all the Apollo guys are down there celebrating the thirtieth anniversary of the moon landing. They just heard a sonic boom overhead—do you think they're complaining about their ears hurting, or are they saying 'GO, CADY!'?"

Rick, too, was always great to fly with and a wonderful instructor pilot, although I never subjected him to a parade of dresses. Soft-spoken and kind, he was from Amarillo, Texas, a common flight-training destination for all of us. We'd often fly to the airport there to practice landing approaches, and we'd grab lunch afterward at the diner near the control tower, a place that made fabulous pies. Before we flew home, Rick and I would buy whole pies to bring to the maintenance folks back at Ellington, our home base.

At first I didn't know the other three crew members as well—Willie McCool, Michael Anderson, and Ilan Ramon—but we quickly developed a rapport once we started doing simulations with me as their CAPCOM. And I knew Loni, Willie's wife, a professional photographer who had a lot in common with Josh, as well as Laurel's husband, Jon, who was one of our flight surgeons.

I also got to know the STS-107 crew during a nine-day National Outdoor Leadership School (NOLS) hiking trip in the Wind River mountains in Wyoming. NOLS collaborated with NASA to help astronauts build their leadership and teamwork skills. The seven STS-107 crew members were training together for their upcoming mission, and I was part of a second group of astronauts at various stages of our training.

I got the impression that the STS-107 astronauts were still finding their identity as a crew. Six Americans and one Israeli. Two were women. Two were people of color. A mix of rookies and veterans, their crew was made up of highly skilled doctors, engineers, scientists, and pilots. These elements were all in play as they worked to mesh their seven distinct and very different personalities together and trust one another in the way that a crew has to learn how to do.

We set out as two separate groups, but on the last day, we planned to meet the other crew at the summit of Wind River Peak. I remember worrying about whether I'd be able to keep up, still feeling out of shape after having had Jamey. In the end, though, I wasn't the one who held us back. As we made our way up the mountain, one of our guys struggled with altitude sickness, and we fell behind. At a certain point, we realized that we would miss meeting up with the other group. But we agreed as a team that reaching the summit together was more important to us, so we continued at a slower pace. When we got there, the sun was low in the sky, and the STS-107 crew had already come and gone. They'd left us notes saying they'd see us on the other side, and snacks to sustain us on the long hike back down.

Later that night, when we finally made it back to our starting point, tired and footsore, our friends were gathered together, cleaning and packing their gear. I noticed a different quality between them—a deeper ease and connection. The experiences they'd shared, the challenges they'd faced, and the goal they'd achieved together had changed them somehow, as a crew. Their fabric was tighter. In some subtle but unmistakable way, they were more ready for their mission than they had been when we set out for the mountain the week before.

All of this came back to me in the aftermath of the disaster, on the flight home from New Zealand. It was hard to grasp the fact that my friends wouldn't be there in Houston when I arrived, just as they'd been waiting at camp that night. I'd never get to hear the stories from their mission. There was only a grieving community struggling to come to terms with a devastating loss and to figure out how we might better protect future crews so that we could safely return to flight.

The wreckage of the *Columbia* was slowly gathered and reassembled in a hangar at the Kennedy Space Center in Florida. It contained essential clues for investigators seeking to understand the accident. It also contained memories for so many of us. I'd flown on that very shuttle twice, and loved flying on her. But those twisted pieces of fuselage—every inch familiar to me—weren't what we'd lost. We could build other space vehicles. But we could never bring back the people who had sat in those seats, now cordoned off in a special part of the hangar dedicated to the crew cabin.

There's no way to fundamentally lessen the impact of a loss like the one we experienced as a community. But it's a natural human response to throw yourself into any task that makes you feel like you are doing something useful. We couldn't bring back our friends, but maybe we could prevent another such loss.

When I got back to Houston, I was anxious to contribute to these efforts. I was excited when one of the branch chiefs called me into his office to ask me to join a tile repair team made up of engineers, scientists, and spacewalking specialists. The accident had shown us that foam from the tank could damage the shuttle tiles, and we needed to be able to repair this damage from space, so the team was working to develop an adhesive as a repair material. The branch chief explained that my excellent communication skills would be helpful because the lead astronaut assigned to the team was having trouble conveying his ideas without alienating the team. At this point, those excellent communication skills failed me. I was literally speechless. But after a moment, I found my voice: "So you're not asking me to help because I have a PhD in material science and worked specifically with materials like these?"

His blank look said it all, followed by an expression of sudden recollection and a hasty assurance that of course that was part of the rationale. Hoping that at least a small lesson had been learned, I gave myself a mental shake and shifted focus to what was really important: helping with the repair efforts. In the end, I needed both my material science expertise and my communication skills to serve this particular mission.

It quickly became apparent to me that dozens of assumptions and opinions were being voiced but little concrete information had been established. I felt like there was a serious lack of scientific and engineering rigor being brought to some of the materials aspects of the project. We were working to come up with a special kind of adhesive "goo" that would fill in pits or gouges in damaged tiles and also act as an ablative material that would protect the shuttle during reentry. It could be applied with something that resembled an ordinary caulk gun during a spacewalk. However, we had trouble making the goo consistently, and it wasn't simple to determine if it would stick well enough to the damaged tiles to protect them.

I arranged to meet with George Gafka, a legendary trouble-shooter, who had been brought in to lead the team and bring some big-picture clarity. I spoke frankly, explaining that important questions were being missed in a cacophony of arguments about theoretical details and a rush to practice applying the goo during exciting zero-g airplane flights— something tangible that felt like progress. He and I agreed that, without making anyone feel like they'd failed, we needed help. He took me up on my offer to recruit a tiger team of scientists and engineers from academia and industry to join the effort. I used everything at my disposal to bring the project out of the realm of theory and into the realm of data and actual materials. Including a giant slab of cake.

That's right, cake. You see, the goo would need to be spread onto the tiles with something resembling a spatula. And the tiles in question would definitely crumble easily. It struck me that the scientists and engineers who were debating the ways the goo might be applied and the shape of the spatula and all kinds of other details weren't being realistic about the nature of the task at hand—which was likely to be a messy and dangerous affair, and could make the situation worse, not better. These guys had probably never tried to spread thick goo over something crumbling. But I had—and so has anyone who has ever tried to frost a cake. You put a big blob of frosting on your cake and you smooth it over and it looks great! But then you see a little part that's not quite perfect and you try to fix it. And it pulls up a bunch of crumbs and suddenly your frosting won't stick to your cake, and the more you try to fix it, the worse it gets. I wanted them to realize that the problem was more tricky than we had understood as a group. I also wanted the team to relate to one another better, and I thought we could all use a little morale break. So I called my neighbor, a fabulous baker, and asked her to bake me a white sheet cake, enough for thirty people.

I showed up at the next meeting with the cake, a huge vat of pink frosting that looked a lot like our goo, and every spatula and wildly shaped tool I could find in my kitchen. Everyone got a slab of cake, their choice of cake-destroying weapon, and some frosting, and they had to damage their cake and then repair it using the frosting. I could hear people around the conference table laughing and talking and giving one another a hard time about their repairs. It wasn't that frosting a cake was the perfect way to simulate repairing the space shuttle. But doing this together led to conversations that we needed to have. Working with crumbly cake and thick frosting got everyone to slow down and realize that our task of repairing the shuttle was incredibly complex. Emotionally, we all wanted to find a solution that worked, but we shouldn't feel compelled to act as if we had it all figured out when we were still trying to understand the dimensions of the problem. By acknowledging that we didn't have the answers and working together to find them, we were able to get the project on a better footing.

We ended up with goo and a goo dispenser that was kind of like a Home Depot caulk gun on steroids. But still, our repair technique had a lot of uncertainties associated with the reliability of both the goo and the gun. Worried that the gun would fail, the group proposed that shuttle crews would need to take three of them on their missions. I realized that their decision had serious mission consequences, and I quickly arranged to meet with Ken Rominger, our STS-73 pilot who was now the chief astronaut, to explain the situation before the vote came up later that week. I explained the lack of testing data and that taking three units would require a lot of space—a full twenty-three of the forty-four stowage lockers on the middeck. More than half the total storage space on the shuttle would be taken up by a repair kit that we probably wouldn't use and that might not work anyway.

Rommel understood immediately. And at the Mission Management meeting that week, he spoke frankly: "I would rather have two of those guns than three of them on board. I would rather have one of them than two. And right now, without further testing, I would rather have none of them than one." His call to action resulted in more extensive testing of both the repair goo and the gun. Eventually, with the additional data, as a community we agreed that the repair capability, one unit, was ready to be used on future shuttle missions.

I learned a lot about leadership from my involvement with the tile repair efforts. Often, the most important way to serve your mission is just to speak the truth from your perspective. And showing up with cake never hurts.

Leaving a Legacy

The *Columbia* disaster rocked the NASA community to its core and grounded the shuttle for two and a half years. And yet even as we grieved, even as we grappled with the causes and consequences of the accident, even as we tried everything we could to minimize the risks for future crews, we knew that together we would eventually find a way to return to space flight.

NASA began launches again in July 2005 with the STS-114 mission, commanded by Eileen Collins. Her crew also included my friend and 1992 classmate Wendy Lawrence. I was working down at the Cape for the launch, as were many of us, including some of my bandmates in the astronaut band Bandella. It was an emotion-filled time for our whole community, and we sensed that people might need a way to gather on the eve of our return to space. So the band arranged to play at a bar called Shuttles, close to the Space Center. People knew that if they came to hear Bandella, they'd find other folks from the NASA community. We played a long set of old favorites, including an original by Chris Hadfield's brother, Dave, called "Big Smoke." It had been written as a joyful song about a rocket launch carrying a "precious cargo" of brothers and sisters into space, capturing the bravery and bold dreams of space flight. But now we couldn't help but see those brothers and sisters with the faces of our lost crewmates. And one line—"Big smoke, no one says it's easy, big smoke, more fragile than you seem . . ."—rang so much more true. That night, I don't know if any of us in the band or in the crowd got through the song with dry eyes. But perhaps that's what we needed most before we once more took to the skies in a cloud of big smoke: to cry together, to make music together, and to laugh together.

The launch went well, but once they reached orbit, video analysis showed that debris had broken off from the fuel tank. As the Robotics Branch chief, I headed back to Houston via T-38 to oversee the complex robotic arm inspections we had designed to identify damage to the shuttle tiles. The arm surveys revealed that two thin strips of insulation called gap fillers were sticking out into what would become the airstream for landing. Their location on the belly of the shuttle was a long reach for the robotic arm, and it took the coordinated efforts of robotics engineers and instructors, plus astronauts from my branch as advisers, to create a way to get the arm into place so that an astronaut, in a foot restraint at the end of the arm, could remove them. Steve Robinson was able to use pliers to cleanly remove the strips that had worked themselves loose. Fortunately, there was no damage to the nearby tiles, and repairs using the goo were not required. The shuttle was cleared for entry, but I couldn't help holding my breath as it landed, safely, at Edwards Air Force Base in California. I'm sure I was not alone.

I thought a lot about Dave, KC, Laurel, Willie, Ilan, Mike, and Rick that day, as I watched Eileen and her crew walking away from the shuttle after landing. Based on my own relationship with the 107 crew, I thought they would be glad we were flying again. They'd want us to continue their mission and honor their legacy. Because of them, space flight became safer for every astronaut who has left Earth in the years since. But even after many months of working to ensure this important legacy, it was hard to accept that they were truly gone. It still is. Some part of me thinks of them as if they were just still on orbit, wearing their brightly colored shirts and doing the job they loved most in the world.

Chapter 7

If the Spacesuit Doesn't Fit . . .
Wear It Anyway (and Wear It Well)

Knowing When to Make the Best of Things—
and When to Press for Change

Four and a half hours into a spacewalk, I'm busy disconnecting the failed cooling pump when an alarming update from Mission Control comes through my headset.

"Cady, we need you to proceed immediately to Paolo's last known location—ESP3. As you know, we were troubleshooting what we thought was a CO_2 sensor issue in his suit. Now he's not responding to our calls."

Paolo and I are crewmates. This morning he and I are performing an EVA, or Extravehicular Activity, more commonly known as a spacewalk. Spacewalking looks like something astronauts do for fun. And don't get me wrong, it's a task most astronauts live for—the chance to truly be *out in space*, just you in your spacesuit in the midst of that vastness. But because it is high risk and takes time and resources, it's also a task we only do when absolutely necessary—for instance, when we need to repair a critical piece of equipment on the outside of the space station. Today we're replacing the starboard pump module, which is the heart of our cooling system, essential to our survival.

EVA isn't something you ever do alone. Astronauts always spacewalk in pairs. It's a rule, a buddy system of sorts. That's so that if you or your crewmate need help or run into problems, you can come to each other's aid, as I'm about to do now.

Paolo is drifting back and forth at the end of his three-foot-long waist tether maybe fifty feet away from me. For the past two hours, as I've been working to unbolt and disconnect the failed cooling pump, Paolo has been unpacking the spare one over on the stowage platform on the port side of the truss—an elongated cagelike structure the length of a football field that sits on top of the space station and contains attachment points for our solar arrays, thermal control radiators, external payloads, and scientific instruments for research. The field of view from my helmet makes it hard to see anything that's not directly in front of me, but once or twice I caught sight of Paolo working away in the distance, and it was strangely comforting.

"Copy that," I say into my headset.

Privately, I think, *Shit, Paolo is a long way away.*

With Paolo in trouble, speed is important, but caution and deliberation are critical too. *Slow is fast.* At NASA, that's a mantra we all learn, a counterintuitive truth that's imperative when you spacewalk. You stand a better chance of succeeding if you slow down and proceed step by careful step. Act impulsively, or rush through things, and you'll cost yourself time if you make a mistake. It's true for everything we do in space, and in many other situations too. You almost always have more time than you think.

I keep this principle in mind as I begin making my way toward Paolo. Spacewalkers in movies always seem to be bopping around with carefree abandon, powered by jetpacks. Actual spacewalking is more constrained. Inside the space station, we fly around gracefully like Cirque du Soleil performers, but when spacewalking outside you're more like an inflatable cartoon animal in a parade, attached to tethers and bumping into things. My most important tether is called a safety tether. It is ninety feet long, connects to my waist, attaches back at the airlock where we exited the station, and functions like a very long retractable dog leash. We also keep ourselves in place at a worksite with a waist tether, usually a three-foot-long strap that is attached securely to a D ring at our hip and has a large hook that is easy to slap onto a handrail so that we are tethered locally as well.

Ironically, we don't use our feet to move around the outside of the ISS during space "walks." We use our hands! In fact, the exterior of the ISS is covered with handrails that form paths around the station. The number one rule: don't release your grip on one handrail without confirming that you have a firm grasp on another. The same applies to tethers. Don't detach one tether until you've attached a new one. That's what's behind another space axiom: *Make before you break.* You make one connection, release another, hand over hand, and soon you're building up momentum and gliding along, a process known as translating. You can be doing this while you are upside down, right side up, or on your side—but translating safely always comes back to *make before you break.*

The size and bulk of my spacesuit, and the fact that I can only see what's in front of me unless I turn the whole suit, make progress slow. As I glide along with my cloddish boots, bulky arms, and oversize helmet, I pay close attention to keeping my safety tether under control, often by looping it up over my arm like a bride carrying the train of her wedding dress. The last thing you want is for it to get snagged on something, because that means you have to go back and free yourself. This would cause delays Paolo and I can't afford, or force me to perform a high-risk operation to cut the snagged tether.

I've arrived and I'm now a foot away from Paolo. His visor is down, so I can't see his face. I raise it. His eyes twitch a few times, but mostly remain closed. I report what I'm seeing to Mission Control, while running through possible causes in my head. He couldn't have run out of air, that much I know. His suit is still inflated, the pressure looks good on his gauge, and our suits are equipped with seven hours of oxygen, plus another thirty minutes stored in our emergency tanks. Maybe the sensor gave out and he has a CO_2 buildup in his suit? That can lead to dizziness, fainting, and loss of consciousness. Could it even be a heart attack? Whatever it is, I'm betting that we need to get Paolo back inside the station ASAP—that's where we'll be able to figure out what to do.

"Cady, we copy all. Proceed with rescue," I hear from Mission Control over my headset.

Time to move. *Slow is fast.* Paolo is still unresponsive. The first thing I do is tether myself to him, before detaching his own tether from the truss. *Make before you break.* Now comes the hard part. At six foot two, Paolo is nearly a foot taller and has seventy pounds on me. Escorting him back to the airlock is like flying an extremely bulky kite. A minefield of possible tether snags stretches out between the two of us and the airlock. One mistake, and we're both in trouble. It's an awful feeling—the tug, the line getting taut, the knowledge that now I'll have to work my way back and untangle it. With Paolo. The worst, sneakiest way a tether snag can happen is when your tether slides between your oxygen backpack and your suit. You can't see it and you have no idea anything is wrong until you feel the tug. Usually, the only person who can free your tether in this situation is your buddy. But Paolo—my buddy, my crewmate, my friend—is unconscious.

Get to the airlock. We're making slow, methodical progress. I know that I will need every one of the EVA skills that I have learned over my years of training to get us safely back inside. I remind myself to trust my training. I've honed these skills. I know what the next steps are. Despite the stress of the moment, I'm also extremely good at compartmentalizing my emotions. My hands ache from the effort of repeatedly squeezing the inflated gloves for the past four hours. I try not to think about how many more times I need to reach out and grab before we are both safe inside the airlock. Hand fatigue is a very real thing in spacewalking. I've trained my hands for years—doing push-ups on my fingertips, carrying a ball of putty I can squeeze, and exercising my hands in a bucket of rice.

It is hard to know how much time has gone by. "How are we doing?" I say into my headset.

The response comes: "It's been twenty minutes."

It feels like a year. *Too long*, I think, and try to pick up my pace, knowing that I still have to navigate the tricky section that connects the truss to the station, which is going to be even tougher with Paolo in tow. Finally, we reach the airlock and I shove Paolo up inside, feet first, bumping him up to the ceiling, so I can slither into the airlock myself, tuck in my legs, and shut the hatch beneath me. This last maneuver is one of the few situations where it really pays to be on the small side. Our crewmates inside the ISS repressurize the airlock and then open the hatch.

If this were a movie, I imagine this would be the moment when Paolo wakes up, none the worse for his adventure, and he and I are mobbed by our cheering, backslapping crew. Someone would break out a bottle of champagne. The foam would cascade in zany ways in the zero-gravity atmosphere. "Awesome job, Cady," crewmates would say. "That was fast!"

Instead, I ask, "How fast?"

The reply: "Twenty-seven minutes."

My answer, intentionally nonchalant: "Sounds good to me—three minutes to spare."

What just happened isn't a scene from a movie, but it was just as staged and artificial. I have a confession to make: Paolo was never actually in danger. He and I were participating in a rescue training simulation that is a key part of our EVA qualification. Known as "the Incapacitated Crew

Rescue," its goal is to show our instructors that we have what it takes to rescue a fellow crew member within thirty minutes. Not only is it a tricky and strenuous procedure; the rescue takes place several hours into a training session because the instructors want you to be tired and at the end of your mental and physical rope. Which you might well be, in a real emergency. Of course, we all want to be at our best in moments like that, but the truth is we often aren't.

Here's another confession: we're not even close to space. Instead, we are in a cavernous, industrial-looking building a few miles from NASA's Johnson Space Center complex in Houston. Inside is a giant swimming pool, two hundred feet long and a hundred feet wide—about half the size of a football field—and forty feet deep. Submerged in its 6.2 million gallons of water is a full-size mock-up of the International Space Station (in pieces). This pool—officially known as the Neutral Buoyancy Laboratory (NBL)—is where astronauts practice spacewalking. Neutral buoyancy means that in the pool, our suits are carefully weighted so that they don't float or sink, simulating the weightless environment. For all the intricate procedures that we perform during a spacewalk, the practice that we get in the NBL is incredibly valuable. It's the closest you can get on Earth to replicating what it is like to perform spacewalking tasks when we are weightless.

Exercises like the rescue I just described are also the closest we can get to reproducing the extreme difficulty and heightened emotions of an actual space emergency. A lot was riding on that moment—not Paolo's life, thankfully, but certainly my hopes and dreams for living in space. My every move was being scrutinized. I'd been training to do this for almost fifteen years, confronting some of the most challenging obstacles I would ever face in my career as an astronaut. Some were mental, and some were physical: difficult tasks I needed to practice and master and continue to perform even when I was tired, discouraged, or in pain. Others were cultural: deeply entrenched biases about who should be walking in space, and who should not. And there was a physical aspect to that as well: biases and assumptions were built into the very equipment I was using and the environments in which I was working.

Thinking like a Spacewalker

I had begun my EVA training back in 1993, about a year after my selection. For many astronauts, spacewalking is the ultimate aspiration, but we don't all qualify to do it. And even if we do qualify, qualifying doesn't guarantee we'll ever get assigned as an EVA crew member or be able to use those skills on a mission. I was determined to qualify from the outset, but once plans got under way for the ISS, it became even more critical to me, because NASA decided that every ISS astronaut must be EVA qualified. In other words, if I didn't succeed as a spacewalker, I could not be selected for a long-duration ISS mission.

The very first time I showed up at the pool for EVA training, in 1993, Josh was as excited as I was. He was staying with me in Houston at the time, and as I left the house, he asked, "Aren't you forgetting something?"

Yes—pool toys! Loving that Josh shared my quirky sense of humor, I grabbed them and stuffed them into the back seat: my red plastic lobster, a beach umbrella, and my shark bathing cap, the one that makes me look like a not-very-nice great white. I got to the pool by 6:00 a.m., in plenty of time to start suiting up, but feeling a little nervous about the challenge ahead. The pool toys were popular and helped break the tension. In fact, they never made it home. For years afterward, I'd show up at pool runs and find one of the divers wearing the shark cap, or we would open the toolbox underwater to find the lobster peering out at us.

Every astronaut has to prove they have the skills to spacewalk. But the reality is, we're often judged before we've had the chance to learn the skills and demonstrate our aptitude. Some astronauts are immediately pegged as being especially promising spacewalkers before they've even gotten into the pool. Those who pass the invisible prejudgment tend to get trained first. That group tended to be tall, long-armed, athletic, and male.

In the minds of the experienced spacewalkers, I'm not sure I was ever in the "promising" category. But I was determined to rise to the challenge. And it really was a challenge. EVA training was the most physically difficult thing I did as an astronaut. The suits are unwieldy; the tools are heavy and don't work all that well in the water (not a problem we'd have in space, but simulations can only go so far). The sheer amount of work, practice, and training involved is daunting. I spent hundreds of hours in the pool, learning how to replace critical equipment and perform rescues. I also learned lessons I never expected, like how to adapt to circumstances and equipment that didn't fit me, making already difficult tasks even harder. Why? Because spacewalking tools and gear really weren't designed for people my size.

When I first started EVA training, there were four different EVA spacesuit sizes: small, medium, large, and extra-large. EVA suits are different from the orange spacesuits we wear for launching and landing. They are like the much bigger white suits you've probably seen in the historic photos of the first men on the moon. It's more accurate to think of EVA suits not as clothing but as the world's smallest spacecraft—the shape of a human!—with eleven highly engineered layers that create a barrier between you and the vacuum of space. The small suit was a reasonably good fit for me, though like the orange suit, it was clearly designed for a guy, without much thought given to female anatomical realities like boobs. The basic design of these suits had been around since the Gemini, Mercury, and Apollo guys had worn them in the sixties and seventies, and they were incredibly expensive to make or to change. And most important, from NASA's point of view, they *worked*. They'd been tested and proven to be safe and effective in space.

One day, just before my first mission, in 1995, I was in the mailroom when Tom Akers, an astronaut with extensive spacewalk experience, stopped to talk with me. "Cady," he said, "I've been watching you in the pool, and I can see that you have a real aptitude for spacewalking and also a head that thinks like a spacewalker."

I was flattered and encouraged that someone was paying attention to my performance and the way I thought rather than my physical stature. I *did* think like a spacewalker. I had what's known as good "situational awareness"; it came naturally to me to see not only my own part but the entire complex choreography of each task or assignment. Plus, I had an intuitive sense of how the suit and I were located in a three-dimensional space, and I understood how the tools worked. Conveniently, I also have a high tolerance for being extremely uncomfortable for long periods of time.

But then Tom continued, "There's something you need to know. There's been a programmatic decision that the small suit won't be used on the space station. NASA is eliminating the sizes small and extra-large to cut costs. You need to be ready for that day. People are going to look at you and think you're too small, but I think someone like you could learn to function inside a medium suit. So my advice is this: if you are interested in flying on the space station, then when someone asks you what size suit you wear, you tell them a medium will be no problem."

My happiness at his compliment evaporated. I may have had a head that thinks like a spacewalker, but the NASA higher-ups had just categorically decided that people like me did not have the body of a spacewalker. Anyone on the smaller side—which certainly meant a lot of the women—who wanted to be assigned to the ISS had no choice but to figure out how to function inside a medium suit. Otherwise, the implication was that those of us who didn't fit were not a priority to contribute as crew members on the ISS. That slow burn, deep inside me, ignited. Once again, someone was underestimating me (and a bunch of other smart-as-shit, tough-as-nails astronauts, many of them women). Could I prove them—and my own self-doubts—wrong?

Kathy Thornton, my friend and STS-73 crewmate, grabbed me in the hallway. "Cady, the minute you get told you have to wear that medium suit, call me. I'll help you figure it out." I was grateful for her support and determined to give it my best shot. Her advice turned out to be pivotal for my success.

To be clear, at five four, I'm not dramatically small, and my arms are short only in comparison to those of male astronauts. But I had little choice other than to adapt to the equipment that was available—and like so many things, even in that day and age, the equipment was basically designed to accommodate men. One-size-fits-all typically meant one-size-fits-all-the-dudes. This kind of bias isn't necessarily malicious, but it is unthinking. And it does have consequences—like keeping women on the ground and excluding them from taking on mission-critical tasks that could in turn be stepping stones to leadership positions.

Eliminating the small suit was a hugely significant decision in this regard. As a result, eight women—almost one third of the women astronauts at the time—were eliminated from EVA and therefore from eligibility for station missions. Several of them were as tough and skilled as they come, but just too petite to safely operate in a medium suit. The most galling part of the story is that when it became apparent that some men couldn't wear the large suit, the same NASA decision-makers reversed the decision to eliminate the extra-large. But they saw no reason to bring back size small.

Suiting Up

Tom was right about my head for spacewalking, and while the small suit was still around, I qualified for EVA on both of my shuttle missions in the nineties. This meant that I was one of two crew members who were ready to spacewalk if a situation arose that required it. In the end, none did, but I was proud to have been assigned as EVA and considered ready to do so. After STS-93, I ended up taking an extended break from pool training due to being pregnant with Jamey and my Antarctica trip. It was late 2003 by the time I finally got back in the pool, and by now there was no choice but to train in the medium suit.

In order to understand why this was such a big deal for me and even more so for other, smaller people, you need to realize that an EVA space-suit isn't like any other set of clothing. It's challenging to operate inside one even if it does fit perfectly, let alone if it's too big. And don't forget, your ability to perform while inside that suit is literally a matter of life and death. To help make this clearer, let me take you with me as I suit up for a typical "pool run."

The process of putting on an EVA suit takes about an hour. Like spacewalking itself, it can't be done alone—which is where the spacesuit technicians, or suit techs, the NASA equivalent of a team of Broadway dressers, come in.

First comes the adult diaper. For the next six hours, you'll be under-water, performing anywhere from two to four assigned spacewalking tasks. You may not need the diaper, but like an insurance policy or a generator in your garage, it's nice knowing it's there. Next comes the regulation-issue sports bra, almost always shrunken beyond recognition in NASA's industrial dryers. Then the long underwear, to absorb sweat and give you an extra layer of protection from the hard edges of the suit.

Now comes a critically important piece of clothing—the LCVG, short for Liquid Cooling and Ventilation Garment. The LCVG looks like a jumpsuit designed by a performance artist. Tubes of water were woven through the fabric in all directions, like oversize veins. When you're glid-ing around inside three hundred pounds of spacesuit, your body heats up quickly, and your LCVG lets you regulate your body temperature thanks to an adjustable but hard-to-reach knob on the front of your suit.

Extra padding is now added: elbow pads, knee pads, in my case, three-inch-thick hip pads, and finally, a chic four-inch-thick crotch pad. In the pool, it's less about protecting myself against getting banged up, and more about stabilizing myself within the middle of the pressurized suit. You see, there's room inside the medium suit to fit two of me, which means I'll be sharing that space with a large air bubble. The suit itself has been weighted down to seem weightless, neither sinking nor floating. But within it I'm still subject to gravity, as is that shifting air bubble. Wherever the bubble is, it pulls that part of the suit toward the surface of the pool. I battle that buoyancy constantly as I position myself to perform tasks. This is not a problem I'd actually have in space, but it is a significant training complication that has to be negotiated on Earth. The padding helps me take up more room in the suit and keeps the air bubble evenly distributed, as if I were a medium-sized man rather than a small-sized woman. Kathy Thornton was the inspiration for the extra padding. She suggested that I show up with a waterskiing vest to wear inside the suit, and while this was met with horror by the suit techs, the fact that the idea came from Kathy, an experienced EVA crew member who had been on the Hubble team, catalyzed the engineering team to come up with this new regime of extra padding. It turned out to be a surprisingly useful technique for other crew members as well.

Finally, I slip a girdle over the hip pads, and waddle-run stiffly out onto the pool deck. I look nothing like Sandra Bullock in *Gravity* slipping into her spacesuit in her little black shorts and tank top before jetting out into the stars; rather, in the LCVG, I resemble an ungainly Egyptian mummy who just emerged from the tomb after several thousand years.

It's finally time for the formal donning of the spacesuit. The bottom half comes first. With my dexterity already restricted by stiff water tubes, I plunk down on my butt, and shimmy forward into the spacesuit bottom until my feet are inside the boots. Then, with a giant one-two-three, heave-ho, the techs swing me up onto my feet. At this point, the suit techs add even more padding inside the bottom half of my suit, stuffing it inside the girdle. "Don't be shy!" I'd tell them. "The more padding the better!"

Held steady by the valiant suit techs, I waddle-shuffle a few feet and step up onto a platform, where the top half of my spacesuit is clamped to the top of a stand. Ducking down and angling my head and shoulders backward, I slither up and inside the torso, poking my arms out first, followed by my head—like a turtle. The techs attach the spacesuit top to the spacesuit bottom. They also place a communications cap over my head. It has a leathery Rocky-and-Bullwinkle-meets-Amelia-Earhart look and lets me talk to the simulated Mission Control and hear them underwater.

It's now time for the ritual of the gloves. Every astronaut has his or her own protocol involving moleskin padding and Band-Aids. I slip my fingers inside the glove liners, making sure the seams are facing out, and weave each finger into the appropriate slot. The big gloves come next, locking into place.

The helmet comes last. It seals the deal. Literally. If my nose itches during the next six hours, that's too bad. I am now sealed off from the outside world and completely dependent on the suit for breathing. Our suit techs know what a disconcerting experience this is, even when we've done it dozens of times, and they make sure we feel the airflow before they lower the helmet. They pressurize the suit slowly, and we maintain eye contact as the pressure increases. I nod my head up and down to show that I'm doing okay as I focus on clearing my ears to keep up with the pressure. Once the helmet is in place, I'm fully dressed, and after attaching my rack of tools to the chest of the suit, it's time to enter the pool. There are no swan dives or cannonballs involved here. Instead, astronauts are deposited into the water by a crane. Picture two spacewalkers with their backs to each other. Each of us hangs by the top half of our suit from the platform stand. The crane now hoists us up and lowers us into the water.

As my helmet submerges, I am suddenly in a different world. But it's not until the divers have detached me from the platform stand that I become aware of the buoyancy of the suit. Apart from the drag of the water, it seems weightless.

The clarity of the water accentuates the equipment at the bottom of the pool. The replica of the space station looks like a large shipwreck or a toppled oil derrick down there, upon which for no good reason someone has stacked portions of a jungle gym.

We're never alone in the pool. My fellow spacewalker and I are each assigned two utility divers and two safety divers. The utility divers' job is to supply us with tools, and while the safety rescue divers may look like they are just escorting us from task to task and keeping a sharp eye on everything, in fact, our lives are in their hands as soon as we are lowered into the pool. They are amazingly skilled and can respond to an emergency with cheetah speed. They can get an astronaut wearing a three-hundred-pound spacesuit out of the water and onto the pool deck in sixty seconds. And I've seen them do it during a drill that only I, the other astronaut in the pool (who was asked to pretend to be unconscious), and the supervisor knew was not a true emergency.

Everywhere I look underwater there are cameras—more than twenty of them, plus a gaggle of camera-divers who follow the action. Everything we say and do is being recorded, transmitted to the instructors in the control room, and even piped over to the NASA Visitor Center, as well as to the desks of most of the NASA bigwigs. You learn quickly to watch your language, even when things go wrong. The cameras look on as I reach down to engage the toolbar—known as a mini workstation—that's attached to my chest. None of the tools are lightweight, some are corroded by age and water, and all require—you guessed it—their own separate retractable tethers made of fishing line. Those tethers make them difficult to work with, but without them, one careless movement, like forgetting to grip a tool, means it would be lost forever in space.

There is no question that the *make before you break* mantra applies to tools too.

During a pool run, our training focuses on equipment that is likely to break on the ISS. Swapping out a pump. Repairing a cooling system. Rerouting power. Installing new solar array batteries. We'll practice several of these during each six-hour training session. Six hours sounds like a long time—and it is—but EVA is one of those experiences that requires so much focus, you don't really notice the time.

I also don't notice the discomfort of my suit once I'm submerged. I'm focused intently on the task at hand. I'm reminding myself to relax every muscle that doesn't need to be tensed, in order to preserve energy. The *wiggle your toes* trick comes in handy here as well. And for the benefit of those evaluating me during the run, I prioritize maintaining the demeanor of someone who was born to spacewalk. I am patient. I don't ever lose my cool. I act as though, if it were up to me, I would work underwater in this pool until the end of time. Another task? Sure, no problem, but I'd like to work in an extra tether swap for practice along the way, if that's okay.

By the time they hoist us out of the pool at the end of the day, I'm wiped out, but you won't ever see me show it. I will come across as cheerful, competent, and at home in my suit from the minute I enter the pool until the crane deposits me back onto the pool deck. I know that this is essential—especially for someone like me, who wasn't pegged as a "promising" spacewalker from the start, because of my size and gender. It's not really fair that I feel like I'm held to a higher standard than others who have different physical attributes, but it's often true. I can't afford to give the powers that be even the slightest reason to double down on their preconceived ideas and dismiss me.

After being extricated from the suit—a reversal of the process I described earlier—and sprinting to the bathroom, I'm always surprised to see myself in the mirror. My arms and legs are covered with red and purple bruises and abrasions. Sometimes I'm bleeding from where the suit and I battled to get into an especially tricky position. My fingers are raw from being mashed inside the gloves, and the nail beds are often bruised, occasionally leading to the loss of a nail. I've been so focused on the task at hand that I didn't even notice until now.

The bumps and bruises are a daily reminder that the medium suit really doesn't fit me. Even with all that extra padding, I could still do a hula dance in that suit. I have to strain to position myself at the front of my suit to grip anything, which makes it harder to reach for the tools on my mini workstation, and harder in general to do EVA tasks. I crush my arms and torso against the sides and armholes whenever I try to reach things. Even with the padding, I'm a mess when I take it off.

Cheerful and Overprepared

Throughout my career, navigating around my smaller size in the EVA suit required imagination, supreme negotiating skills, a sense of humor, and showing up cheerfully, even to meetings where I wasn't invited. A steady supply of baked goods never hurt either. It might have been an unfair situation, but I knew that complaining was not going to get me anything but a higher profile on the "not cut out for spacewalking" list. Blaming the equipment was not an option. But more important, most of the astronauts and engineers who were evaluating me had never experienced the same types of challenges that I had using the equipment, and therefore they could not imagine how it might be different for me. They seemed unable to put themselves in my clumsy, ill-fitting shoes.

Case in point: The very first time I was in the pool, under intense scrutiny, I had to maneuver my spacesuit boots into a foot restraint, the device astronauts use to remain in a fixed position while working. In order to accomplish this, we need to use a handrail in front of us to align and stabilize ourselves so that we don't float away. But because the foot restraint was in a "standard" position (read: appropriate for average-sized men), the handrail was too far away for me to reach it without tilting forward, making it impossible to keep the heels of my boots flat enough to slide them into the thin slots on the boot plate. But none of this was acknowledged when the instructors commented: "Boy, Cady had a hard time today with that foot restraint." And of course, they didn't really mean just "today." The unspoken assumption was that if I had this much trouble doing a basic thing like sliding my boots into a foot restraint, I'd probably struggle with everything else. If that was the case, I probably didn't have what it took to be a spacewalker.

In the same way, if the larger-than-normal air bubble inside my suit pulled me toward the surface and kept me from being at the right angle and position to accomplish a task, the instructors would unthinkingly and unanimously concur that it was my fault. *Not strong enough. Not trying hard enough.* Mostly, I kept my frustrations with the equipment to myself, and learned not just to manage but to excel at spacewalking, despite the too-big suit, achieving consistent above-average grades.

But on one particular day, not long after I'd returned to the pool after my extended break, the always difficult tasks of operating in that too-large suit seemed even harder. I was partnered with another astronaut who was being graded that day, and my task was just to be helpful, under the watchful eye of a very senior astronaut. But I couldn't seem to get anything right. Even tasks I'd mastered years before seemed impossible. I couldn't reach things. Everything felt wrong. When I finally finished the run, having performed extremely poorly, my confidence and self-esteem were as battered and bruised as my body. We gathered for the debrief, and I tentatively suggested that maybe something was wrong with my suit fit.

The senior astronaut gave me a withering look. "Cady, really, after today's performance, I'd say you should *never* be in an EVA suit again."

I was angry but opted for a matter-of-fact tone. "There's no question I had a bad run today. But I have a ten-year history of above-average performance in the suit, and I think the first step is to look into the accuracy of my suit build for today's run."

His willingness to dismiss me on the basis of that one performance was a harsh reminder that EVA qualification is never something to be taken for granted—especially when you're someone whose competence people secretly doubt. Put one foot—or hand, or tool—wrong, and you prove what they already thought they knew. It doesn't seem to matter how many times you outperformed their expectations before.

This is a situation that women and people of color face in all kinds of circumstances. When we do well—better than people assumed we would—it often doesn't register. But the moment we make a mistake, they seize on it as proof of our inherent inadequacy. As a woman astronaut, I often felt like I was held to a different standard than my male counterparts, who could get away with occasional mediocre performances that would have diminished my career, or that of any of the women.

In that particular instance, thankfully we did check with the suit engineers to understand whether my suit had been configured correctly. There isn't a lot of variability, but arm and leg lengths can be adjusted to some extent. And it turned out that the techs had set my suit arm lengths too short by a whole inch on each arm. For a person with shorter arms, that inch can make all the difference when trying to reach tools that were within my reach but just barely.

The senior astronaut, when he learned the outcome, seemed suitably chagrined. I saw an opportunity to help an astronaut of his experience level to better understand the challenges that people like me face in the EVA suit. I asked if he'd come to my suit fittings and help brainstorm about how to optimize my ability to work in the suit, including things like getting the arm length right. He did, and we both learned some new things. He became a great supporter, proud when I did well in the pool. But none of the small adjustments we made could change the fact that the suit simply didn't fit me. And that regardless of that fact, if I wanted to be selected for the ISS, I'd need to excel in spacewalking, in that suit, and keep excelling right up to the day I launched. If I didn't, they might just decide to take me out of the running for EVA. I might never find out about it directly, but at some point, I would realize I hadn't been scheduled for a pool run for a long time.

So was the equipment designed incorrectly for someone my size, or did I simply need to work harder and smarter to adapt? From the point of view of those watching and evaluating, the gear is seldom at fault, and you just need to get used to it, understand it better, or practice more. What is to blame, in my mind, is the standardization of equipment, and the role it plays in performance. The result is that some people blame themselves rather than blaming the design of the world around them. The world is right; the individual is wrong. But I know—it's not always easy to make that distinction. By saying, "It's not me, it's my gear, it's the air bubble in my suit," you sound like a tennis player who blames the sun or the height of the net for the fact she just double-faulted. But by staying silent, are you being complicit in perpetuating a system that is rife with inequities, and that affects not just you but others like you? It's a difficult conundrum that I've wrestled with throughout my career.

The fact is that how my equipment fit me was an issue that dogged me for decades, and not just in EVA training. When I did water survival training in the Black Sea, the Russian launch suits we used for training had feet like children's footie pajamas. Unfortunately they were twice as big as my actual feet. It was a dangerous situation, unsafe for climbing ladders and walking on wet ship decks. In this case, I came up with a simple fix: I folded the excess fabric onto the top of my foot and used a bunch of hair elastics to secure it in place. On the second day of training,

I found a package of new hair elastics resting on my spacesuit. An older Russian sailor met my eyes, smiled, and gave me a thumbs-up. If only all equipment compromises were that easy!

Most of the time, I took the approach that if the suit didn't fit, I would simply wear it anyway—and wear it well. Wear it better than anyone expected. This meant that I set a personal goal to be completely prepared for every EVA training event. I'd always worked hard to keep in top physical shape, but the bigger suit demanded even more strength. The gym became one of my top priorities. I made a point of learning how to do pull-ups (men, for some reason, have a thing for pull-ups), and would toss off a set of five or six nonchalantly when I noticed any of the experienced EVA folks at the astronaut gym. There was no such thing as too much foresight or practice. My strategy was to maximize the skills that I brought to the task, so that I could focus my energy on the skills that were harder for me. Before doing a pool run, I prerehearsed everything I might be doing underwater. I went to the tool shop the night before and practiced using all the intricately designed tools I knew I'd be using the next day. I made drawings of how I wanted to configure all the tools on the mini workstation attached to my spacesuit. I watched and rewatched footage of underwater spacewalkers doing the same tasks I would be doing. I identified situations where I might be vulnerable to making mistakes. The night before a pool run, I always tried to get a good night's sleep. And even if I was at the end of my rope—my internal tether, so to speak—I stayed cheerful. Well, cheerful-ish. Being considered "easy to work with" was a key requirement for spacewalking. Then, when it was over, I always requested feedback from both the diving team and my instructors. What should I do differently? How can I do it better?

The divers, who gathered at the side of the pool next to the crane after our training runs, often had the most valuable advice, and they knew I was open to it. They'd been right next to me in the pool, as opposed to the instructors, who had to rely on the blurry camera views from their control room high above the pool. The female divers, in particular, were experienced in finding creative ways to work with the heavy tools underwater to compensate for having less strength than some of the male divers. They knew what it was like balancing on the seesaw of Blaming Your Equipment versus Looking Objectively at Your Own Performance and would share what they'd learned when we saw one another in the women's locker room. They knew how tricky it is when you feel you don't quite fit in. Tricky, because the whole time you are trying to make sense of your environment and figuring out how to make it work best for you and others, you are usually busy doing something, as well as being judged and graded by your colleagues, instructors, and superiors.

My advice to anyone who finds themselves in such a situation is to start by asking: Why am I not fitting in here? What's really going on? Is it just a vibe, or am I justified? And can I push for change or do I need to make the best of the way things are? Some situations, like being a small-framed woman who finds herself inside a cavernous, medium-sized spacesuit, may appear to be intractable. You can't really design your own spacesuit, at least not yet. Sometimes there's nothing you can do about the constraints of the situation, and you just have to adapt yourself. But other times, you may have more control than you realize. Sometimes you can make the world adapt to you (within reason), and not the other way around. Sometimes you can redesign the parameters of your environment to better accommodate the people who come after you. It's up to you to determine when to try to change things, and when to let them go.

I would love to inhabit a world where instead of saying, "Cady is probably too short to be a spacewalker," someone said, "Cady brings essential contributions to our team. Knowing that, what can we do to help her excel so that people like her can be on space station crews?" In many other aspects of my career, male allies did just that. But for all those years when I was hoping to get selected for spacewalking, I had to accept fact that I didn't live in that world and do my best to outperform

everyone's expectations anyway. "Do you really fit in that suit?" male astronauts would sometimes ask when they passed me in the halls, even during my last years at NASA. I'd just smile and remind them that I'd been
"fitting" in that suit for years, with above-average grades in spacewalking.

Waiting for the World to Change

The "Incapacitated Crew Rescue" that I described at the beginning of this
chapter was my final test. If I'd flunked that assignment—if my tether had
snagged, if I'd forgotten to connect Paolo to me before untethering him, if
I'd been too slow getting him back to the airlock—my dreams of going to
the ISS would have been dashed. But I passed—with no big mistakes and
three extra minutes. At the time, I became the smallest person ever to
have been assigned to a spacewalking team for the ISS.

Finally, I felt able to drop the "cheerful and effortless" act and speak
my mind. In fact, knowing that my mission and my crewmates' lives
might depend on it, I felt I *had* to. I sat down with my instructors and
told them that I had spent years acting as if EVA was easy for me in order
to avoid triggering people's biased views. "Now it's time for me to tell you
all the things I can't do as well or as easily as I'd like," I said, "and you
need to share with me every doubt that you have about my spacewalking
skills, so that we can work together to mitigate all these things and make
sure we are sending the best possible spacewalker to the station."

Did I wish we could have started the process that way, fifteen years
earlier? Sure. But that wasn't the world I was training and working in.
From where I stand now, I can say without hesitation that it was unac-
ceptable that NASA would deny astronauts the opportunity to fulfill the
missions they'd trained for—not through any failing of their own but
simply because something about their physical appearance didn't fit an
institutional template that hadn't been redesigned, or reimagined, in half

a century. But if I'd tried to speak that truth from day one, I'd never have made it to the day when I was taken seriously enough to begin to have those conversations from a place of strength—a place where I could be heard and make a difference not just for myself but for astronauts who came after me. Systemic inequality is tough to change. Sometimes you have to master the ill-fitting equipment before you get a chance to redesign it. Sometimes you have to play by the unfair rules in order to get to a point where you can change those rules. And again—do I wish it wasn't that way? Of course.

And thankfully, things are changing. My friend and fellow astronaut Tracy Caldwell Dyson, after her role in a real-life emergency spacewalk to replace the cooling pump, led an effort at NASA to revamp the EVA training program, redesigning it to help new astronauts develop their skills, as opposed to eliminating them from consideration based on assumptions. It was a novel, brilliant approach to teaching and objective grading, and when combined with the latest astronaut class's stated motto not to leave anyone behind, it led to all five women in that class of twelve becoming qualified for EVA. The suits themselves may have been hard to change, but changing the cultural environment in which people were using them made a big difference. Tracy told me someone hung a picture of me in the hallway outside the women's locker room inside the Neutral Buoyancy Lab. It meant a lot to me to hear that, and I'm proud to be one of the people who helped make it possible for a wider range of people to excel as spacewalkers. Over the past few years, we've seen multiple women perform spacewalks and witnessed Christina Koch and Jessica Meir performing the first all-female spacewalk. I'm not a big souvenir person, but I loved seeing a T-shirt at a shop in the Houston airport celebrating that awesome event. And finally, efforts are under way to redesign the spacesuits to better fit the diversity of astronauts. When NASA's Artemis takes the first woman to walk on the moon, she will do so in a redesigned spacesuit. I hope it fits her like a glove.

Chapter 8

Who's Your Ground Crew?

Asking for the Help You Need
to Succeed—and Paying It Forward

The long-awaited call came in 2007. Finally, I was going to get to *live* in space! When Steve Lindsey, then chief of the office, told me I'd been assigned to an ISS mission, I could hardly contain my excitement. But before I could reply, he added, "I don't need an answer today. This is a big decision and I know you'll need to think about it. You're looking at a multiyear commitment."

I knew he was right. I'd dreamed of flying a long-duration mission on the ISS for years, ever since I'd first heard we were building a real "home" in space. But the chief astronaut before him had told me that the chances were slim, and I should expect a shuttle mission instead. Now that it was a real possibility, I did want to think it through carefully, with my family. In accepting the mission, I wasn't just committing to six months in space; I was also committing to several years of training—first as a backup for my friend Nicole Stott, the first step for any station astronaut, and then as a crew member myself. Much of this training would take place in Russia, as well as Japan, Canada, and Europe, meaning I'd be leaving Josh and Jamey behind for long stretches.

I'd hoped to go when Jamey was young enough not to remember such an extended absence (in hindsight, I'd rethink that rationale). Now, he was seven. Josh and I talked through what the training and the mission might look like for us and for Jamey, and how we would make it all work. I also talked through the decision with my close friends Mary and Stacey and made a few phone calls to my siblings. The question that pulled at me the most was, "How can I do this and still be a good mom to Jamey?" But by the end of our conversations, I had come to the realization: *This is who Jamey's mom is. Part of my identity is that I'm an astronaut. And one of the best examples I can set for my son is to show him the importance of carrying out a mission I am passionate about, one to which I know I can bring unique contributions.* For all these reasons, and grateful for the enthusiastic support of the people who meant the most to me, I said yes.

Even though the flight itself was still a few years off, Josh and I sat down with Jamey right away, realizing that once people started to talk about my assignment, he might think that the flight was soon. We told him, "It won't be when you're in first grade, or second grade, or third grade. But when you're in fourth grade, I'm going to go and live on the space station." Not only did we prepare our son well; we inadvertently prepared the whole town. Jamey told his friends at Buckland Shelburne Elementary School, and finally, in the fall of 2010, those fourth graders reminded their parents: "Jamey's mom is going to space at Christmas!"

Part of what helped me to make the decision to fly on the ISS was the knowledge that Josh and Jamey would not be alone during all the times when I was in space. And neither would I, throughout the months and years of intensive training that lay ahead. Our little family had so much support—both practical and emotional—from our families, our friends, and the communities we both lived and worked in. Without all those people having our backs, I'd never have gotten off the ground.

One of the things I figured out early is that just as a space mission needs a ground crew—engineers, flight controllers, trainers, medical staff, schedulers, crew secretaries, food scientists, maintenance staff, and more—so do many of us in our personal and family lives. I have no doubt that I need other people to help me make the practical side of my life work, supporting me with everything from childcare to travel planning. Equally important and maybe less celebrated are those who help in less tangible ways: people who encourage me and make me feel valued; people who make me laugh; people who can listen and help me process challenging decisions; people who can just be there when things are tough. We all need people to lift us up and people to catch us. We need people who know our weaknesses but don't judge them, and maybe even help us improve on them, and people who know our strengths and remind us that we shouldn't hesitate to use them. My ground crew—my community— means everything to me, and I'm grateful for the wealth of support I have, knowing that many people are not so fortunate. For every story I share about the things I experienced and accomplished in space, there were dozens of people on the ground who made it possible.

Know Your Strengths and Weaknesses

One of the reasons we need community is the simple fact that we all have different strengths and weaknesses. When we work together, we complement one another, and the overall effort gets stronger. But that kind of team building starts with knowing your own strengths and weaknesses. You can't afford to be shy about either when you have a mission to fulfill in the midst of a complicated life. You have a responsibility to bring your very best self to the table when it counts, which means doing your best to have a clear-eyed view of your *whole* self. I knew that I had talents and qualities that would serve the NASA mission. But I also knew I had shortcomings that might not. And while I was clear about some of those, I wanted to take a deeper look before embarking on my six-month ISS stay. When there's a lot riding on your success, and the mission is so much bigger than you are, you want to be sure you're seeing clearly.

Now that I'd been assigned, I decided that a good starting place would be understanding any hesitations management might have had about assigning me to the ISS. After my second mission, circumstances conspired to keep me grounded for a while—being pregnant and then the delays in returning to flight after the *Columbia* disaster. Also, there had been the hurdle of EVA qualification, but that was now behind me. I knew that some people had been initially hesitant about assigning me due to my family situation. Now, I assumed that people understood that I was skilled at managing my commuting life as well as demonstrating mission-critical skills in robotics. Still, I wanted to find out if the people in charge of assignments had other, unspoken reservations. If so, I needed to understand what those were. Maybe some would come down to bias, to people's inability to grasp that the same person who was funny and good at PR and the instigator of happy hours could also be smart as shit, good at understanding space station systems, and a logistical wiz at organizing a complex family life, and could perform well under high pressure. But other concerns might point to real weaknesses that I should try to improve upon.

Flight assignments, as I've shared, are always a bit of a black box. But one thing I could say with confidence was that Peggy Whitson, who had been the chief of the Space Station Operations Branch of the Astronaut Office, would have been part of those conversations. I'd known Peggy for years, and she was someone I liked and respected. She'd clocked more hours in space than any U.S. astronaut, having completed two six-month tours on the space station, the second one as station commander. At the time, no one compared to Peggy, whose early ISS mission was legendary in terms of how much work she had accomplished. Despite being somewhat reserved, Peggy was approachable, and I knew I could count on her to be honest, so I asked to meet with her. I was eager to hear her perspective and learn how to do my job better.

When the day came, I was also a bit nervous. Peggy is not a chatty type, whereas I am a filler of silences. I didn't want to end up blabbering, so I'd prepared a list of questions and points I wanted to touch on. I told her I knew that initially, some people had reservations about assigning me, and I imagined that either she was one of those people, or she was aware of any issues that might have been raised. I mentioned a few that I knew had been cause for concern in the past, including my family logistics and whether I would be able to qualify in the larger EVA suit. "Now that I'm assigned," I concluded, "I'd like to understand if any of these are still of concern, or if there were other hesitations about my readiness, so that I can work on mitigating any issues."

Peggy looked a little taken aback by my frankness. I'm not one to tiptoe around elephants in rooms.

"Well, Cady." She paused for a moment, as if trying to come up with the right words. "What I would say is that most people we select for the space station, and most people who do well there, are . . . well organized. And that's not the first phrase I would use to describe you."

Of course, this wasn't a surprise. No one who knows me—and least of all myself—would disagree with that characterization. And yet—it stung. Certain types of organization did not come easily to me, especially those involving paperwork and timeliness, but I'd worked hard to counter this weakness and not let it interfere with my ability to carry out my role in our NASA mission. An image flashed into my head of a favorite cartoon that I keep in my office. It shows a person working at their desk. But closer examination shows chaos in the background, to-do lists scattered everywhere. The caption reads, "Life is difficult for the organizationally impaired." I was discouraged that my efforts to counter my shortcomings in that area didn't seem to be enough. Hearing Peggy's blunt assessment did serve as a healthy kick in the butt. I appreciated her directness and knew that the mission was more important than my feelings. I reminded myself that I'd come to her for information and I'd gotten exactly what I asked for. Now I needed to recalibrate and reprioritize.

"You're absolutely right," I told her. "I recognize that. I'm working quite hard on being better organized, and clearly I need to keep that as one of my highest priorities. I started working with a coach about a year ago, and I've also hired some personal admin support. I know we have really great administrative people here in the office as well, so I will make sure to ask for the help I need to keep my paperwork up to date."

Peggy frowned. "Well, no," she said. "Asking for more help from our office staff is not on the list of solutions. You are someone who asks for a lot. Not anything big, but a lot of little things. I don't want you to burden our administrative staff any more than you already do."

This was not easy to hear. To be honest, even now I find it difficult to write, and I still worry, as I did in that moment, about how to be honest and forthright in my response without coming across as defensive. Peggy was right—I did ask for a lot, and my requests were not always timely. But—but, but, but! Like any working mom with a demanding job, I had a complicated life that wasn't always acknowledged or accommodated. It required endless logistical contortions to make it work while staying within the constraints of government regulations, which definitely weren't designed with families like mine in mind. A common example when it came to travel involved making a stop in Massachusetts on my way to Russia. While it was legal to do, it was not convenient from a paperwork point of view. But not making the request meant an additional two weeks away from my family on each trip.

I had enormous respect for the administrative staff and made an effort to understand their needs and limit my impact. But the reality was that the amount of intricate paperwork generated by my "alternative" lifestyle did get the better of me on numerous occasions. At one point, when I was traveling constantly, I was even audited for poorly documenting my travel expenses. Pretending I didn't need help, or being too proud to ask for it, would not have served my mission.

There were, no doubt, moments when I overstepped, and I didn't always put a high enough priority on timeliness with regard to filing deadlines when my time already felt overstretched. But I was also operating in a culture where asking for help was subtly frowned upon—a culture that celebrates people for being highly capable, self-reliant, and—well—*organized*.

The last thing an astronaut wants (especially a female one, or one who seems not to fit the mold in some way) is to get a reputation for being high maintenance or burdensome. Just as I'd learned in EVA training, those who are different from the norm are already more visible and subject to more scrutiny. We don't want to betray weakness or look like we're asking for special dispensation. You'd rarely hear one of the women astronauts calmly say she needed to leave early or couldn't fill her CAP-COM shift because she had the kids that week. She'd have already figured out how to cover it. One guy would just say, "Single parent this week, so no CAPCOM shifts for me!" Julie Payette and I, both moms, both with husbands living outside of Texas, would roll our eyes. Others would declare, "I'm the day-care pickup today, so I'll have to leave our class early." They didn't worry that their fundamental competence might be called into question if they revealed that they couldn't do everything perfectly all at once. And indeed, it wasn't. But every woman knew that the same standard did not apply to her, and I know that I always had plans A–F ready to put in place.

Some of this came down to outright sexism. Some of it pointed to the fact that the Astronaut Office needed to take a new look at how missions and mission training affected astronauts and their families, regardless of sex. And a lot of it, more broadly, reflects a broader societal failure to truly consider the needs of modern families in the way our workplace cultures are set up.

Clearly, I didn't always succeed in managing my own complicated life without burdening others—as that meeting with Peggy confirmed. I knew I had things to work on. But I firmly believed then, as I still do today, that needing and asking for help doesn't automatically make me any less capable as an astronaut, a crewmate, a mother, or a person, for that matter. I'm not ashamed to admit that I'd never have gone to space, or raised our kid, without an incalculable amount of help and support.

In fact, I've come to embrace the ways in which I'm embedded in a cycle of community support, both giving and receiving help. My fellow astronaut Scott Kelly recently told me, "Cady, I always say to people that you're the kind of person who might ask for things other people would never think of asking. But if I were to ask you to mow my lawn, I'd find you out there the very next day pushing the mower."

Celebrate the People Who Make Everything Work

Do you know what one of the hardest jobs in the Astronaut Office is? It's not (pardon the cliché) rocket science. It's scheduling. Which brings me back to those goddesses, otherwise known as the ladies in the scheduling office (and Arthur, an honorary goddess). They were responsible for the incredibly complex, bordering-on-mystical three-dimensional jigsaw puzzle of fitting dozens of astronauts into hundreds of hours of pool runs, simulations, language classes, T-38 flights, robotics training, business trips, emergency training, medical training, medical testing, and the multitude of other procedures that lead up to an actual flight. All of this while launches are constantly being rescheduled, foreign space agencies are involved, crew assignments are changing, and every individual astronaut has particular needs or preferences.

In my early years at NASA, the scheduling was all done on paper (in pencil, of course, to allow for the inevitable changes). Even when computers arrived, the task was wildly complex. It was awe-inspiring that despite the constant rearranging, those goddesses exuded a calm, nonjudgmental energy. Incredibly, even the schedulers responsible for space station training remained unflappable, despite the added challenge of scheduling international crews for training all over the world. Goddesses Alicia Simpson and Karen Floyd can take 100 percent of the credit for getting me trained for my ISS mission—and keeping me married!

The scheduler I worked with most, especially during the first half of my career, was a charming and extremely well-organized Texan named Erlinda Stevenson. She had one of those cute hairdos that flipped up at the sides, and she wrote out the schedule in her neat, precise cursive on extra-wide sheets of computer paper. Another memorable scheduling goddess was the equally charming and formidable Kandy Thomas (famous for her rollicking laugh and showing up at parties with that cardboard cutout of Fabio). Besides a bigger-than-life personality, Kandy's superpower was seeing the potential order in the maze of airplanes and astronauts and getting everyone where they needed to go for their mission training. Kandy's sister Beth Turner also worked in the office, as the most capable—and hilarious—crew secretary on the planet. She wrangled our crew on STS-73, and I was incredibly lucky that I could also hire her to work with me outside of NASA, with the added bonus that her wonderful teenage boys often agreed to babysit Jamey.

Erlinda had many, many priorities, and we both knew that helping me juggle my complicated family life could not be one of them. But I never felt judged by her and therefore never felt bad about asking. If she could give me information that helped me plan, she would, but if she couldn't, she'd just say, "Cady, I can't predict that." If she could accommodate any specific requests, she would, but if she couldn't, she'd let me know clearly and candidly.

From my side, I tried to make her life easier whenever I could. I'd let her know my travel plans, and we also had a clear understanding that I was happy to change any plane ticket, anytime it was necessary, at my own expense. So if she said, "Cady, I'm putting you in the pool next Friday," I'd just say, "Thanks for the heads-up," and reschedule my plans to travel home that weekend. For safety reasons, you weren't allowed to fly for twenty-four hours after being in the NBL, so a Friday pool run meant the weekend was essentially a write-off as far as travel was concerned. But being in the pool was important and tough to schedule, and an invaluable opportunity to hone my EVA skills, so I never argued. I learned to pick the really important family events—like the time Josh was one of only a few artists being honored by President and Mrs. Clinton—and be firm about my commitment to those but flexible about almost everything else.

One thing I always tried to remember is that it's okay to ask someone for help, but it's also important to make the effort to understand their world. We all know what it's like when someone comes running in with "just a small request," oblivious to the trickle-down effects in your world. The change may seem small to them but could cost you hours of extra work. I know that you can never fully understand another person's world, but I did my best to be sensitive to which requests were putting people in a difficult position. I also reminded myself to always be ready to be told no and to accept that response gracefully.

The astronaut schedule was an enormously complex beast. Curveballs like travelers stranded by weather, crew members who became ill, and broken simulators were a constant. I let Erlinda know that during the times when I was in Houston, especially when Jamey was with Josh, I was happy to take the shifts no one else wanted. If she needed to fill a night shift, or schedule someone on a holiday, or plug a gap at the last minute, she could call me. When I look back on my years at NASA, Erlinda is one of the people I remember with the greatest affection. I wouldn't say I got special treatment; it is clear that she genuinely tried to help everyone. But without her, it would have been infinitely harder to be an astronaut and also be there for my family.

The Wisdom of Girlfriends

I met my wives, Mary and Stacey, not long after Jamey was born. Okay, technically they are each other's wives, but they are both my best friends. But after they heard me joke more than once that I needed a wife, especially in the years leading up to my ISS mission, they told me I could consider them my spouses, at least in the practical sense, since I was geographically single. Mary is a pioneering pediatric surgeon who was recommended to me when Jamey needed surgery as a baby. Stacey is a leading pediatric oncologist and also a science fiction author. They live in Houston, and during my many years there, I relied on them more than anyone—for support, for home-cooked meals, and for adult conversation. They both shared invaluably wise counsel on how to conduct myself in what was still a man's world. Mary was a seasoned navigator of this terrain, having become a pediatric surgeon back when there were so few women surgeons that they had no locker rooms and had to change in the nurses' lounge.

It was Mary, for example, who taught me to recognize—and graciously accept—the "boy apology." At one point, I'd been doing a lot of telework (a new concept and option for us at the time), and there were apparently questions about whether I was actually working, even though I was submitting detailed weekly reports. I was both nervous and angry to be summoned to a very serious-sounding review meeting with the leadership of the Astronaut Office.

The night before, I was having dinner with Mary and Stacey. "Cady," Mary said, "I know it's hurtful and offensive that anyone would doubt your work ethic. But in my experience, this is something that you won't get closure on. My suggestion is to sail in there like Grace Kelly tomorrow, knowing your truth. Answer every question gracefully, just like Grace would do."

The meeting came, and I was asked: "Why didn't you submit telework reports that detailed your work?"

I'd been prepared to defend and justify my productivity while teleworking to a room full of people who didn't understand my world. But this was a much easier question. Taking a deep breath and channeling Grace, I replied, "I did submit my telework reports." It turns out my supervisor, a fellow astronaut, had simply not passed them on. Everyone, including my supervisor, shuffled their papers in embarrassment, and then the meeting was over.

I was insulted and furious. It felt like yet another instance of people jumping to confirm their own assumptions: because I operated differently, my productivity must be inferior. And here was the proof! The next day, my supervisor sent me a note informing me that empty T-38 seats had unexpectedly opened up later that week, and I should get my name on the schedule quickly if I needed the flight time. It was the end of the quarter, and I did need to fly to make my T-38 minimums—and those opportunities were hard to come by. I appreciated him giving me the early heads-up before other people got those slots. But wasn't he going to mention the unsubmitted reports? Or the embarrassing meeting? Or why it had been so easy to be critical of my work ethic?

That night, I went to dinner with Mary and Stacey again. I showed them the note, still fuming.

"That's it!" Mary exclaimed. "Cady, don't you get it? That's the boy apology."

"The what?" I asked.

By way of an explanation, she told me a story about a surgeon she had once worked with. One night, they'd disagreed strongly over something to do with a patient, and as events unfolded, it became very clear that Mary had been right. The next morning, she returned to work, feeling vindicated. She and the surgeon were scrubbing in together, and he turned to her and said, "How about them Red Sox?"

Mary paused, to see if I was catching on. "That was it. I realized that was as close as he was going to get to saying 'I'm sorry.' It's the boy apology. You have to listen real closely or you'll miss it." I laughed out loud, but I realized it was a serious lesson as well. She went on: "Your boss is not going to come and say, 'I'm sorry I got you in trouble, and we were jerks for jumping so quickly to unfair conclusions.' You might want him to, but it's not going to happen. That was his apology. So accept it." It was the hard-won wisdom of someone who'd gracefully accepted a lot of boy apologies in her career.

Of course, I'm not defending guys who can't apologize or suggesting that we should all tolerate a world in which that's acceptable. Far from it. In the big picture, it serves none of us to continue to gloss over blatant injustices or coddle fragile egos. One could argue that graciously navigating around such issues only serves to keep them in place, and further disenfranchises those who do not understand the unspoken rules yet or know how to play the game. Wherever I felt I could make a difference, I fought for transparency within the Astronaut Office and on the teams and crews that I was a part of. But you just can't be angry and fighting all the time, or you exhaust yourself and drain your stamina for the long haul. That's really what Mary was teaching me: how to preserve my own emotional energy for the moments that mattered.

In the real world, you have to learn to pick your battles. Change happens slowly, and some worlds change faster than others. Just as girls of certain generations grew up learning that asking for help is a sign of weakness, boys of certain generations grew up learning that admitting their mistakes and apologizing is a sign of weakness. I hope this is changing. We're all still figuring out how to shed these outdated, sexist, and limiting cultural norms. Along the way, sometimes we have to make a choice about which situations are worth getting worked up about, and which are not. Mary and Stacey often helped me to remember what was big and what was small. There are times when demanding a proper apology makes sense—especially when that fight has the potential to encourage new behavior patterns that could benefit everyone. And there are times when you decide to accept a boy apology with the poise of Grace Kelly, because you have bigger things to achieve in life.

My friendship with Mary and Stacey made me realize how invaluable it was to have girlfriends who weren't in my professional world but understood it—and more important, understood me. They made me feel seen and acknowledged. They let me know that who I am is okay, even if I have work to do on certain skills. Hearing that they had experienced similar treatment in their worlds helped me realize that when it happened to me, it was seldom the result of what I had personally said or done. Knowing this helped me move on to more effective ways of responding.

I soon introduced them to some of the other women astronauts, and we evolved into a close circle of friends. I thought of Mary and Stacey (who exist as one word for us) as the steady center of the group, the hub of our wheel. It was often hard for us astronauts to find one another, being assigned to missions and training all over the world, but I think it meant a lot to each of us to find our friendship with Mary and Stacey waiting for us on our return. For me, those friendships have endured for decades, and to this day I know they'll always be there for me—to advise, to listen, to commiserate, or to watch wonderfully silly movies about a futuristic world, with costumes optional, but appreciated.

What a Village Can Do

My friends often say, not even half jokingly, "It takes a village to raise a Cady." It's true. I function better as part of a community—and not just logistically but emotionally as well. Indeed, my village is so extensive that it would take a whole book to truly do it justice. I'm someone who thrives best when working with others, and I tend to create community wherever I go. I think about the crew team in college, my lab group in graduate school, and my ASCAN class when we joined NASA. Even if I'm just showing up at a conference for a few days, I try to make it a home. The people who become part of my circle in a particular place often remain lifelong friends, even when I've moved on and made my home somewhere else.

Case in point: my dear friends Catlin Donnelly and Hampton Watkins, who were the married "tutors" who lived in our dorm at MIT and acted as surrogate parents for many of us. One day, Catlin found out that, as she delicately put it, my flexibility with time had gotten the better of me, and I was in danger of getting an "incomplete" in French. Not wanting to see me fail, she told me, "Cady, we'll be expecting you at our apartment every night to spend twenty minutes on that French paper." And I showed up. Catlin and Hampton have been part of my village ever since (meaning that I still call them at the last minute, needing a place to stay or some grown-up advice). I'm one of many wayward students they adopted. They have taught me a lot about the value of that kind of generosity to people who just need a little support to thrive.

My village often steps in to help in those areas of life where I'm, well, challenged. Anyone who's close to me has helped me pack, including my crewmates, my friends, and of course my husband and now Jamey. As in, I'm leaving tomorrow for a trip back home or a ten-week training session overseas or even a mission to space, and my bag is still empty and a million piles are scattered all over my room. Yep, that's me. Of course, it's not just the putting things in the suitcase that's tricky; it's the fact that packing shines a glaring light on all the things I'd intended to be done with by this hard deadline of a looming departure.

Trips to Star City in Russia were particularly challenging because they usually involved taking various food items to share with the folks I'd be working with, since it was logistically hard to get to a grocery store. Many of us would also help our Russian friends at NASA who wanted to send things back home to their families. No kidding: I once flew to Russia with a purple satin ball gown for a colleague's five-year-old daughter's kindergarten graduation. Unfortunately, it was in the same bag as a box of cocoa powder I was taking for another colleague, which exploded in flight. I was terrified to open up the duffel bag when it showed up on the baggage carousel smelling like a mug of hot chocolate. Fortunately, the gown was wrapped in plastic. On that same trip, I packed high heels (which I never do) for a black-tie embassy function and one of those heels pierced a half-gallon can of maple syrup in my suitcase. Unbelievable! On the bright side, it was an excellent opportunity to practice swearing in Russian.

I also have friends who dress me. As in, can I really wear *this* to *that* event? When a few of us shared a house together, my buddy Mark Polansky would always ask, "Do you want me to answer as a guy or as your roommate?" Sometimes, help went beyond just giving advice. Mary literally went to the ladies' room and took off her sports bra to send it to my landing site in Russia after my flight surgeon mentioned that somehow the bag I had packed for landing had shown up without this important item. Pam Melroy was often my go-to for any kind of formal wear. Shopping in her closet is fascinating and so much more fun than any department store. And neither of us will ever forget the first time we dressed each other, back when we were both aspiring astronauts anxiously preparing for our NASA interviews. Mine came up first, and I realized that in addition to a business suit for the formal interview, I'd need "business and nice casual" clothes for the other six days I'd be at NASA. I didn't possess such clothes, and neither, it turned out, did Pam. We had only military uniforms or casual clothes, but nothing in between. So we each found a few decent outfits, and then Pam boxed hers up and sent them to me. After my interview, I boxed up hers, added mine, and sent them to her. I'm sure no one at NASA noticed that two of their women candidates wore the same clothes! I thought this was a uniquely female story, but I recently heard Scott Kelly tell an interviewer that he and his twin brother, Mark, actually wore the same suit to their interviews!

I have mental and emotional health professionals in my village as well. I'm a talker (in case you hadn't noticed), and I like to verbally process most of my decisions. My friends and family are wonderful in this regard, but I'm also a great believer in the value of professional coaching and counseling. NASA always encouraged, supported, and even at times required counseling for all astronauts, and I've sought it out myself as well. Throughout my career I've seen counselors and therapists who have helped me personally and also guided Josh and me as parents. I sought out counseling to prepare for the isolation I'd experience on the ISS and worked with a productivity coach and now friend, Meg Edwards, who helped me to develop strategies to maximize my performance in our highly scheduled training environment. All this was enormously helpful in training for the ISS and even while I was onboard.

Mental and emotional health is another of those areas in life where there's an unspoken expectation that we should be able to manage by ourselves. There's still some stigma attached to asking for help—we'll do it if we're going through a crisis like the loss of a loved one or a marital breakdown, but structured support and expert guidance can be just as helpful in everyday life. I like to talk openly about how helpful counseling has been for me because I think it's important to normalize the fact that almost everyone needs help at some point in their lives. Even astronauts.

My village also included all the people I'd call on to take care of Jamey, or pick him up from school, or keep him until I could get there, or perform a carefully timed airport handoff. All the astronaut spouses and women astronauts with kids supported one another in this regard—we'd help out and share childcare, and the single women astronauts would be the first to volunteer to show up at my house at all hours when needed. But as is true for so many quasi-single parents, there never seemed to be enough people to call. I'd get a last-minute schedule change and find myself calling the thirteenth person on my list of twelve potential baby-sitters.

And it wasn't just in Houston. We'd never have survived without our Massachusetts village as well, including Josh's amazing mom, who moved into an apartment in our town in order to help with Jamey when I went to the ISS. Our dear friends Bill Gibson and Diane Flaherty, both economics professors, always seemed to know just what was needed without being asked, which was incredibly reassuring when I wasn't there. They'd show up when Josh had had a particularly hard week and say, "Hey, we're going to the movies. Maybe Jamey wants to come." Or they'd arrive with dinner—"meals on wheels," as they called it. Our neighbor Debbie Lane orchestrated and ran the after-school program at the local elementary school. Even the kids who went home after school would want to play there; it was one big family. And if I couldn't be home with Jamey, it was an amazing gift to have Jamey be there with Debbie. Her husband, Rick, helped Jamey with math for years as well.

Speaking of Jamey, he's part of the village too. When we were late leaving the house, he used to stand there by the door, pleading, "Mom, when are we going? Are you ready?" Finally, I said to him, "We could get in the car faster if you would ask me, in a kind way, 'Mom, what can I do to help?'" To this day, when we're getting ready to leave the house and I am running around doing last-minute things, he'll say, "Mom, what can I do to help?"

In the end, I know that while I may always need to improve my paperwork and punctuality, I have many other skills that are valuable contributions to any mission and to the teams that accomplish those missions. I may be challenged by the myriad small tasks involved in being an organized person, but when it came to performing highly technical maneuvers in space, such as launching a ten-thousand-pound telescope into orbit or capturing a supply ship using a robotic arm, I was focused, precise, and dependable, and I earned the trust of my crewmates. I've learned to hold both those truths in my mind at once; to take on board fair criticisms without allowing them to define me or undermine my overall confidence that I'm worthy of the mission and the opportunities that I trained so hard for. Peggy was right—I did ask for a lot. But I contributed a lot as well. And I wouldn't have been able to do any of it without my ground crew.

The Best Birthday Present Ever

In December 2010, after my three years of training around the world were complete, Jamey, Josiah, and Josh flew to Baikonur, Russia, for my launch. Jamey, then ten, got a furry Russian hat to keep his ears warm in the bitter cold. He loved the hat but found all the waiting around pretty challenging. And it was hard for him (and me) that the quarantine rules limited our contact to walking outside in the frigid weather at arm's length behind the "Cosmonaut Hotel." After an unspoken nod from the doctor in charge of quarantine, who we affectionately referred to as "Dr. No," we did sneak a couple of hugs behind a tree.

The morning before launch, I was washing my hair and getting ready for the day, when my crewmates came and banged on my door.

"Cady, come to breakfast!"

"I'll be down in a few minutes!" I replied.

"No, you have to come now!" they insisted.

"Okay, okay," I said.

I headed down to the breakfast room, looking disheveled with my wet hair and hastily thrown-on clothes, only to find a sea of smiling faces watching through the glass wall. There must have been fifty people out there, and Jamey, Josiah, and Josh were in the middle. On the table was a cake. It was my fiftieth birthday. I waved at everyone through the glass as my crew and I cut my cake and thought to myself that I was about to get the best birthday present ever: six whole months in space.

Chapter 9

Friendship Is Optional, Trust Is Essential

Building a Strong Team across Personalities, Beliefs, and Cultures

My crewmate Paolo and I are floating, shoulder to shoulder, under the dome-like interior of the International Space Station's Cupola, surrounded by computer screens, control panels, and cue cards, all securely Velcroed in place. It's as if we've set up our own private cockpit in here for the day. I've been up on the station for a month now, but this view never gets old. Two hundred and twenty miles below us is the luminous blue curve of the Indian Ocean, contrasting sharply with the red-brown desert. Today, however, we're looking at the view differently. We've just gotten a call from Mission Control to tell us that the thing we've been waiting for should be coming into sight—and there it is!

A tiny blip appears against the steadily moving background of the Earth. It's so far away it looks like nothing more than a bug, but it is in fact our Japanese H-II Transfer Vehicle (HTV) supply ship, moving slowly toward us to rendezvous in about four hours. There are no astronauts on board, but the ship is carrying eighty-five hundred pounds of supplies, food, experiments, spare parts, and our long-awaited care pack-ages containing letters and chocolates and—I could already smell it—good coffee.

The vessel's name, Kounotori, means White Stork. Today, I will be operating the space station's Canadian-designed robotic arm, Cana-darm2, to capture Kounotori and guide it safely to the docking port—all while both vessels are speeding around the Earth together at 17,500 miles an hour.

Capturing a free-flying vessel using a robotic arm on the space station has only been done once before, by my friend Nicole Stott. I was Nicole's backup and had trained with her; now it was my turn. On space shuttle missions, Canadarm1, a smaller six-jointed arm, was used regularly to capture and repair small satellites or telescopes like the Hubble. But on these missions, if something didn't look right, the commander could quickly fly the shuttle away from the target. The space station, however, is a very different beast. It's the size of a large factory, and the supply ship is the size of a tractor trailer. The ISS can't move away, so you need to be much more precise with the capture. You can't risk a collision. Imagine you're on a high-speed train, conveniently equipped with a robotic arm on the roof, and you're reaching out with that arm to grab a flying, remote-controlled car that's traveling alongside at equally high speed. We can tell the supply ship to retreat, if needed, but a poorly executed capture could still result in a collision and severe damage to the robotic arm and the station.

For the next hour, as Paolo and I go about our preparations for the capture, we keep an eye on the approaching vessel. Soon, it no longer looks like a distant bug; and as it grows larger and larger in our view, we can see that it is shaped like a giant floating soda can. Even though capture is still a few hours away, the whole crew eventually migrates to the Cupola and we position ourselves: Paolo and me in the Cupola with Scott, our commander, and the other three hovering just below us. This is a big day for all of us. I rest my hands on the joysticks beside the computer screen, mentally reviewing the procedures and simulating the moves I'll be making. *You've practiced and you've got this.*

My job, as the prime robotics operator (R1), is to operate the arm and perform the actual capture, so I have to pay attention to the cameras that will allow me to guide the arm to the grapple fixture, the exact spot where it can connect. Paolo's job, as the primary visiting vehicle operator (VV1), is to control the HTV supply ship from our onboard control panel, as well as to communicate with Mission Control and with me. He has several screens to monitor, but he also looks out the window—to confirm that what the computers are telling us matches up with what we can see outside. If they indicate that the vessel is ten meters away, but we look and it's clearly closer or farther, we need to respond to the reality, not the computer calculations.

The supply ship is now about 250 meters from the space station. It approaches what we call the Keep Out Sphere, the point at which we put the visiting vehicle through its paces, so to speak, to ensure that it's behaving well before we allow it any closer. It's been through multiple tests as it approached, but now we need to verify that it can respond to the commands we send from our onboard control panel, confirming that we can send it safely away from the station, if needed. We tell it to stop, to retreat, and to advance—like a dog performing an obedience test before being allowed off leash. *Sit. Stay. Shake a paw.* Satisfied that we have good control, Mission Control informs us that the HTV is now allowed inside the Keep Out Sphere, to a point just thirty meters away from the ISS.

Paolo is giving the ground a detailed status of the HTV as it approaches, repeating phrases I've heard him say hundreds of times over the past few years. We've practiced this maneuver in simulators that range from desktop computer displays to virtual reality in a huge dome. But this is one of those moments when you realize that even the very best simulators fall woefully short. The cartoonish VR images I trained with bear little resemblance to the reality I'm now confronting. They didn't prepare me for Kounotori being *this* big and *this* close—a giant hunk of metal that I have to grab with perfect precision. I can hear a slight edge in Paolo's voice that even his lilting Italian accent can't disguise. Still, the familiar sequence of our carefully scripted conversation keeps me focused on the routine we have performed together over and over again. *We're a team. We've got this.*

One monitor shows me the view from a camera at the end of the arm. The grapple fixture on the side of the HTV that I will be aiming for looks like a target, and at the center is the pin that will plug into the end of the arm. The supply ship is moving toward us in an invisible corridor that gets narrower as it gets closer. It has sensors that tell it where it is within that corridor, almost like modern cars can sense when they're within the lane on a highway. And just as your car might correct you if you drift, the supply ship uses its thrusters to correct its course and stay within its corridor. When the HTV gets to the Capture Point, ten meters from the station, it pauses, just five short meters—a car's length—from the tip of Canadarm2.

This is it. The moment I've spent countless hours training for. The supply ship looms large in the Cupola windows, the size of a school bus. The robotic arm, extending toward it, looks like a giant crane on a construction site. This is the trickiest part. The HTV has been using tiny thrusters to bounce slowly back and forth in its invisible, virtual cage, directly in front of the robotic arm. In order to capture it, I have to follow the HTV's movements and try to have Paolo disable the thrusters when it's headed for the middle of the corridor. When we disable the thrusters (a state known as Free Drift), we'll know if this puppy will sit still enough for us to put its leash on, or whether we will have to chase it. That's why we call it "Track and Capture."

Mission Control tells us we are "GO for HTV Capture."

Paolo and I study the motion of the HTV together, and when the alignment looks good, I give a nod and Paolo announces, "Starting in." I push in on the controller to start moving the robotic arm toward the target, and then I tell Paolo, "Ready for Free Drift."

"In free drift and GO for approach," Paolo responds. "Ninety-nine-second clock has started."

Now I continue moving the arm toward the target, adjusting if it drifts a little in one direction, coming back if I've corrected too far, and keeping the target lined up. Our HTV "puppy" is relatively well behaved, but sailing slowly to the left while rotating around just a little left as well. It still takes constant vigilance to ensure that the end of the arm stays right over the target.

I expect to hear Paolo say the words he always says at this point: "Good rate." Rate refers to the speed at which the arm is moving toward the HTV, and so Paolo would be confirming that he sees me flying inbound fast enough to capture it successfully before it gets too far away. But then I realize Paolo hasn't said a word. Later, he'll tell me that the view out of the actual window, so different from the computer simulations, threw him off, and he was unable to accurately judge our speed for a moment. I check the calculated rate on my display. *Too fast!* Between excitement and nerves, I'm moving the arm toward the HTV too quickly. Gently, gently, I slow my capture rate, knowing that the change in speed will cause the arm to swing back and forth a little as the software processes the adjustment I'm asking it to make. It's a known behavior of the arm, and not a problem now, when it is still a few meters away from the HTV, but the broad motions are still unnerving for everyone watching in Mission Control (and for me). The arm steadies, now inbound at a good rate for capture. *All good*, I reassure myself, toes wiggling. *Fly the arm.*

Paolo's voice returns, calmer now, reciting the distance between the arm and the supply ship as I close in, measured by the length of the pin that the arm will grapple.

"Four pins."

"Two pins. Thirty seconds left."

Plenty of time. Looking good, I tell myself.

"One pin."

I'm lined up over the target, and the pin is now entering the canister at the end of the arm. "Inside grapple envelope," I report as the arm covers the pin. Paolo concurs. "Capture!" I announce as I pull the trigger and the wire snares inside the end of the arm lock around the ball-shaped end so that it will be securely held. As the snares tighten, I feel almost as if it were my own hand that reached out through space to grab the incoming vessel.

"Capture confirmed," Paolo says, and I check my monitors for the required indications that Canadarm2 has Kounotori firmly in her grasp.

Houston confirms a good capture. Throughout the delicate procedure, I've been intensely focused on the monitors, but now I can finally turn my head and look out the window, seeing the supply ship firmly attached to the end of the arm. And behind it, on Earth, I notice a series of long, thin lakes that look like a row of claw marks between the wooded green hills. The Finger Lakes! I immediately recognize the distinctive area of New York State where my grandparents lived and I'd spent many happy summers swimming and picking berries. I reach for the camera and snap a picture. It seems fitting that as I completed one of the most demanding tasks on my mission—one that had only ever been accomplished twice, both times by women astronauts—I was right above the site of the historic 1848 Women's Rights Convention.

"Great job, you guys," the voice of Megan McArthur, our CAPCOM in Houston, comes through our headsets, and I can hear clapping in the background as the U.S. and Japanese Mission Control teams celebrate. "Congratulations to all of you and to the entire HTV flight team."

I reply with the little speech I've prepared for this moment: "We have Kounotori in our grasp. This demonstrates what humans and robots can do when we work together."

Paolo and I grin at each other, feeling equal parts pride and relief. *We did it.* Or, as Paolo likes to joke, *Houston, we 'ave no problem.*

Learning to Trust

Paolo and I were a great team. In the case of robotics, we were each good at our roles, but we also each knew the other's job well enough that we could have stepped into the other's shoes if needed. Through our years of training, I had learned that we both liked to work with other people and didn't hesitate to ask for help when needed, although we usually asked for it in different ways. We also both appreciated having a buddy to vent to at the end of a long day, one who would listen and make us feel heard.

We shared a love of good food, and I quickly learned during our training that the only way to truly get to know at least this Italian was to eat lunch with him. It took me a while to understand that lunch meant an actual sit-down meal involving real food eaten at a real table, rather than the granola bars and bottles of water I kept in my car to eat on the run between training sessions. I also learned (with the help of Paolo's wife, Sasha) how to calibrate the "Italian factor"; large gestures and loud exclamations were not necessarily indicative of tragedy or disaster. Sasha, who is Russian, would later help me calibrate the Russian factor, too, when training in Star City, her hometown. Paolo is very tall and I am relatively short, so we made a funny pair. We developed a mutual respect for each other's capabilities and dedication to the mission, and we achieved an easy camaraderie that made the extensive travel and training a lot more fun. But above all, we trusted each other. And that was the key.

It takes an enormous amount of trust to perform a complex aerial ballet involving a robotic arm, a space station, and tens of thousands of pounds of flying metal, all while coordinating with control teams on five different continents and knowing that even a tiny mistake could be catastrophic. In the same way, it takes trust to venture out together on a spacewalk, or to allow yourself to be strapped into a rocket and blasted into space. People often think space travel would require bravery, and it does. But trust is just as critical—trusting your crewmates, the ground team, the people who built and designed the spacecraft to have done their best.

Interestingly, while trust is essential on a space mission, friendship is not. Indeed, over the course of my career I've learned a lot about what it takes to turn a diverse crew of astronauts with different nationalities, backgrounds, beliefs, and, of course, personalities into a tight team. Sure, it's nice when you get along well with the people you work with—and most of the time, I did, as with Paolo. But personal compatibility is not a necessity for the mission, and certainly not something the higher powers at NASA spend any time trying to engineer.

Although I'm sure that the Astronaut Office leadership is aware of the range of personalities across the astronaut corps, when picking crews they don't have the luxury of saying, "Oh, these people will get along nicely together." It is just logistically impossible: NASA starts out with a limited number of people who have the training, skills, or flight experience necessary to go into space. When it comes to assigning combinations of those people to missions, there are far too many urgent variables already under consideration—like getting the requisite mix of skill sets for spacewalking, robotics, and experiments; ensuring that astronauts are getting the right experience at the right time for their career progression; coordinating schedules and training; and the always mysterious question of whose turn it is to go next.

On the shuttle, we occasionally had international crew members, like my French colleague Michel Tognini, who helped launch Chandra. But the ISS is truly a collaborative endeavor between the U.S., Russia, Europe, Canada, and Japan. At the time I was assigned, only twelve astronauts a year got to fly on the station, and of those, six would be Russian and the other six would be some combination of American, Canadian, European, and Japanese.

Oftentimes, crew members meet for the first time once they are assigned and begin mission-specific training. Every astronaut has to accept that part of the job is living and working in close quarters with a group of people you may not know ahead of time and didn't get to choose—and learning to trust those people with the success of the mission and with your life. It's like one of those reality shows in which a group of total strangers get stranded on an island and have to depend on one another to survive. Or going camping with a bunch of folks you don't know very well. Or any number of situations you might encounter in your workplace or extended family. We don't always get to choose the people we must work with or live with.

On a shuttle mission, you're working and living in a space the size of a tiny two-story apartment, but you don't spend more than a week or two on orbit together. Relatively speaking, the station is more like a palace, but you will be up there with your crew for months at a time. The three-person crew you launch with has been training together intensely for three years at that point, so you know them well, but that's not always true of the three-person crew that will be onboard when you arrive, or the second crew that will trade places with them halfway through your mission.

Over the years, I've worked alongside some people who were challenging for me to get along with, and I'd guarantee that some of them felt the same way about me. Learning to trust and collaborate well with those people was one of the most critical skills I learned in space, and one that has served me well on Earth.

An Italian guy, a Russian guy, and an American woman—our crew was, as our National Outdoor Leadership School (NOLS) trainer John Kanengieter liked to say, like the beginning of one of those "walked into a bar" jokes. Paolo, myself, and Russian cosmonaut Dmitri Kondratyev

were an unlikely trio, to say the least. I was short and female, with a reputation for being chatty. Paolo was tall and ebullient, with a reputation
for being a little headstrong. And Dmitri (known as Dima) was formal,
efficient, and had a reputation for being, well, old-fashioned in his thinking. The three of us would launch from Baikonur, Russia, in a Soyuz (pronounced *saw-yooz*) capsule to the space station, where we would join
American commander Scott Kelly and two Russians, Aleksandr (Sasha)
Kaleri and Oleg Skripochka. Together we made up the Expedition 26 crew.

The six of us would spend four months living and working together,
and then Dima would take over as commander and Scott, Sasha, and
Oleg would be replaced by three new crew members, Russians Andrei
Borisenko and Aleksandr (Sasha) Samokutyayev, and American Ron
Garan. At that point, we'd transition to be part of ISS crew 27 (one space
flight on the ISS spans two different expeditions). For the entire six
months I'd spend aboard the station, I'd be the only woman. I'd also be
the only Cady, which may have been more consequential!

Paolo and I had bonded quickly once our training began, but Dima
was a different matter. It quickly became apparent that he found it hard
to listen to me or to hear me. It wasn't a language barrier—he was fluent
in English, and my Russian was excellent. It wasn't a cultural barrier in a
general sense—I'd been working and training with Russians for years
and we had gotten along fine. I'd successfully completed winter survival
training with Alexander Misurkin and Nikolai Tikhonov at a time when
we were all beginners in learning one another's languages, and laughter
became our shared language. Even after three days of being cold, tired,
and hungry, they'd been eager to hear my ideas. And Dima's issue wasn't
my specific questions or suggestions—if they were voiced by one of our
male colleagues, he'd have no trouble acknowledging and responding ap-
propriately. No, clearly it was me. Not me personally, I hoped, but me as
a woman. I don't think he'd had much experience working with women
during his military career, and there hadn't been a woman in the cosmo-

naut corps for a decade. He was a skilled pilot and extremely good at his job, but he didn't seem to trust that I could be competent at mine. This was frustrating to me—I'd flown on two space missions while this was his first. Yet he seemed to require me to prove that I was worthy of being anything more than a passenger.

One day, early in our training, we were together in the capsule doing a landing simulation. There is a critical stage of the Soyuz landing process where you fire, or "burn," the engines for a precise amount of time in order to slow down, reenter the Earth's atmosphere, and reach your intended landing point. Too long or too short, and you might not make it to landing at all. In our prep session the day before, I'd asked how I could help. Dima, who clearly didn't think he needed my help, suggested that I be ready to calculate "burn times" in case of engine trouble. Calculating burn times is an advanced skill that Dima, as commander, and Paolo, as the copilot, had trained for but I had not, and Dima knew that.

Given my role on the Soyuz crew as the flight engineer, no one expected me to learn the intricacies of those calculations, let alone in a single evening, but I reached out to the other astronauts studying in Star City and just the right person volunteered to teach me. The next day, the instructor team simulated an engine failure at a tricky point in the deorbit burn. I quickly calculated the remaining burn time, wrote it on a piece of paper, and held it up where Dima could see it.

Looking irritated, he brushed it out of the way, as if to say, "I've already calculated this." So we continued—and our Soyuz capsule (virtually) crashed. It turns out that Dima and Paolo had miscalculated. In the debrief, Dmitri reached over and grabbed my piece of paper, which showed the correct time. He looked at me intently and said, "You'll do the calculating." *Boy apology accepted*, I thought. *I will indeed do the calculating—along with a dozen other mission-critical tasks you don't even notice or imagine I could be capable of.* But I just nodded and said nothing. It wasn't the time to say "I told you so." Dima may not have been entirely comfortable with a woman astronaut on his team, but in that moment I think I began to earn his trust.

Was it fair that I had to work harder than my male crewmate to earn our leader's trust and be allowed to do my job? No, it wasn't. Should I have challenged Dima more, or demanded his respect? Perhaps. I worried that I wasn't standing up for my feminist values when Paolo and I decided it was best that he ask questions or make suggestions so they would be heard. We'd exchange a quick look and the question would be asked, and answered. In some situations, a more direct approach might have been appropriate, but in this case I suspect it would not have served the mission. Plus, while my gender no doubt exacerbated certain tendencies, I knew it wasn't the only factor at play, and the issues were not limited to me. As a fighter pilot accustomed to working alone, Dima never seemed to lose that mentality. One day, I requested a meeting with a senior cosmonaut who was a good friend and asked him for advice on how I could be a better crewmate to Dima. He just put his head down on the table.

I recognized that I needed to move carefully—as carefully as I moved that robotic arm reaching through space to capture the supply ship—because confronting and risking humiliating Dima would only have further damaged the trust between us as a crew. Confrontation is great if your goal is to be right; it's tricky if your goal is to be trusted.

In the end, the mission is what mattered, so I tried not to take his attitude personally. I looked for opportunities to prove my competence and show that I respected his. I also sought small ways to connect with Dima on a more human level, based on the advice of a friend who specialized in bridging cultural divides in the workplace. It was a major breakthrough when I decided to ask him about his son, several years younger than Jamey. His eyes lit up and he became a different person, showing me photos and telling me about his boy. It often helped me to remember that this person was Dima too.

We made progress, but as our launch date got closer, as the senior person with the most flight experience I worried about our crew coordination in a real emergency. Would the gaps in trust between us fragment our crew? Would Dima just try to do everything himself, as he had a tendency to do—a potential recipe for poor team performance and even disaster? Assuming he wouldn't listen, would I then not speak up? I was working hard to trust him and to understand how I could be a better crewmate, though I believed he didn't really trust me.

The folks at NASA know how important it is that a crew develops deep trust. And they know that we're not going to develop trust just by having a few barbecues or karaoke contests. Building trust is serious business, and it's best done in serious situations. Trust is forged—and tested—when you spend time with others in a stressful or challenging environment. Navigating situations where actual risk is involved can catalyze a crew to dig deep and find a way to work together. Making those situations also physically uncomfortable and mentally challenging helps bring you to a more vulnerable state, in which you make the most mistakes and have the most to lose—and the most to gain.

This is why NASA sends crews into the wilderness with NOLS. Basically, you travel to a remote and rugged area like Wyoming's Wind River mountains (as I had done some years earlier with the STS-107 crew) or Utah's Canyonlands for a week or more with the NOLS instructors, putting new leadership skills into action in adverse weather conditions, sleeping in shelters you build together. You're out there for long enough that you really have to put your differences aside and rely on one another to survive. Typically, each day of the trip, the crew decides together on a goal and works out a detailed strategy to achieve it. Then the real work begins as the friction of everyday life in difficult conditions changes people's capabilities and attitudes. You learn from your mistakes and celebrate your successes. I knew how powerful these trips could be.

When Paolo, Dima, and I were training, NOLS was seldom scheduled for space station crews, mostly because some of the ISS partner countries would not pay for the training. Plus, there often wasn't time in the schedule. But as our launch date drew closer, my concerns were borne out when we performed poorly in a key crew emergency training exercise. Dima raced through the procedure and was off to fight the simulated fire by himself, while Paolo and I were left standing there. Another such training exercise was already scheduled with the other three members of the crew who would be joining us on the ISS, and I doubted that our team would perform any better. We needed some help.

I asked the Astronaut Office management if we could have another experienced astronaut observe our training and give us feedback—someone senior enough that the hierarchically minded Dima would respect them. At first, there was not much support for this idea, based on availability, but as the more experienced crew member and the only U.S. astronaut on the crew, I insisted. Chris Hadfield, who had trained with Dima and me for almost a year when we were a backup crew, volunteered to observe the training. I shared my concerns with him, and he spoke privately with Dima afterward. Chris didn't share what they discussed, but it seemed to help, and Dima became more inclusive. We also managed to schedule a brief leadership training retreat—twenty-four hours, to be precise. It wasn't enough time to go into the wilderness, but our NOLS trainer, John Kanengieter, agreed to come and work with us in crew quarters, the place we typically use for prelaunch quarantines.

Even spending a day and a night together, isolated as a crew and working with an accomplished coach like John, seemed like a good investment. John had us do very simple group activities, like cooking meals, and he guided us into conversations designed to forge connection—for example, sharing why we each decided to become an astronaut and what it had taken for us to get here. I opened with my story about meeting Sally Ride and daring to consider, for the first time, that maybe I could have that job. I hoped that being vulnerable about the sexism I had to overcome to even imagine myself in this job and the way that made me feel would invite vulnerability from my crewmates too. Plus, it was a nonconfrontational way of bringing up the elephant in the room: the sexism that informed Dima's and sometimes the Russian management's attitudes toward me. Dima's responses were telling—he was sympathetic, but it was clear he'd had little experience working with women, or for that matter, with minority groups. When Dima talked about his childhood, I was able to appreciate how very different it had been from mine, how geographically and culturally isolated he'd been in his youth. Recognizing what had made each of us the people we were brought us closer.

Many years after our mission was complete, Paolo and I were interviewed on the *WorkLife* podcast by leadership expert Adam Grant about our experience being part of that crew and the themes of trust, cooperation, and teamwork. And Adam said something that stopped me in my tracks—one of those aha moments when someone puts something into words that you knew intuitively but hadn't voiced before. "What comes first," he asked, "trust or vulnerability? Most of us assume that you have to build trust in order to be vulnerable. But actually, the opposite is true." That's what I'd sensed when I requested the leadership training: that being vulnerable is what builds trust, not the other way around. And it's hard, because when you feel that trust is lacking, your instinct is not to be vulnerable. But sometimes simple acts of self-revelation, like the storytelling exercise we did, can go a long way.

Another important lesson came out of that training experience: don't forget to let people surprise you. Prior to our session, I'd drawn my own conclusions about Dima, and looking back, I'm not sure that I went into the session thinking there was more to learn. But our discussions changed my ideas about who he was and who he could be. At the end of the all-too-short time we spent at crew quarters, I did feel that we got closer to being on the same team. Were we prepared to put our lives and the success of our mission in each other's hands? I think all of us were ready to find out.

Homecoming

Home. That's the word that came to mind when I saw the Space Station for the very first time. I'll never forget the moment. Paolo, Dmitri, and I had launched two days before in our little Soyuz capsule and spent forty-two hours in orbit before attempting the rendezvous. We changed out of our spacesuits and into our comfortable coveralls and enjoyed gliding back and forth between the two small modules of the Soyuz, reveling in the feeling of weightlessness. We had intermittent communication issues (nothing to worry about) that left us out of contact with the ground for many hours, so it was just the three of us, in our tiny spacecraft the size of a Smart car, out there alone in the vastness and silence.

It was a magical time. It made me think about the early missions when the Gemini and Mercury astronauts flew in tiny capsules. We took turns sleeping, so there were times when I'd be the only one awake, looking out the window. I thought about Valentina Tereshkova, the very first woman in space, who had made her historic flight alone in a Vostok capsule in 1962. Was this how she had felt, sailing through space all by herself? I'd had the privilege of meeting Valentina not long before my flight. We sat together over coffee in a glassed-in office after she had shooed everyone else out, including the translators, so that she could share her experience and advice. The crowd watching and filming us through the glass seemed to retreat into the distance. It was clear from that conversation that our dedication to exploration transcended borders and languages. I'd loved meeting her, and now I treasured the feeling that I was following her path on orbit.

And then, as we got closer, I saw our station for the first time—like a city floating in space. It took my breath away. I'd spent years training on the replica that sits in the NBL pool, so I was accustomed to it all looking a little green and scummy and waterlogged. The real thing was so beautiful and pristine. I couldn't believe that I had finally arrived at my home in space. All the stresses of the years of training leading up to launch fell away. It didn't matter who I had to get along with, so long as I got to do it up here.

Docking requires complete focus from the entire crew. And after the Soyuz is firmly attached to the station, the pressure checks (to make sure that we've achieved a good seal) can drag on for what seems like forever. Finally, both the Soyuz and the station got a "GO" to open hatches, and we were greeted by Scott Kelly's enormous smile. Oleg was close behind, young and jolly. Our third crewmate, Sasha, a veteran cosmonaut, was quieter and more reserved, but seemed equally happy to welcome us. We exchanged comical zero-gravity hugs and then Scott led off the grand tour, our crew following him like a pack of overexcited puppies, bouncing off the walls. He showed us where things lived, how to prevent things from floating away, how to conserve wet wipes, how to use the bathroom, and he even explained how to successfully capture a urine sample ("the hardest thing we do up here," he said). He was eager to show us the U.S. module, but I also loved going through the Russian module and seeing all those labels we'd worked so hard on in their natural habitat.

I felt giddy being back in space, and liked that my body and brain seemed to recognize it as a place I had been before. And there was so much space! Zero gravity had felt amazing when I'd been on orbit in the shuttle, but the station, by comparison, is huge. Its corridors and modules were familiar from our training mock-up, but now we weren't walking through it; we were flying. And when you fly, you experience the space around you differently. Somehow, on Earth your brain knows it can ignore how much space there is above your head in a high-ceilinged room. You can't really use it. But then in zero-g it becomes viscerally clear that there are entire highways—with an emphasis on the *high*—that are now yours to zoom along. Three-dimensional space opens up to you, and it quickly feels normal to fly up and over an obstacle in your path— including your crewmates.

Down on Earth, our families had flown from Baikonur back to Moscow and were invited to Mission Control to watch the docking. Now they were eagerly awaiting a videoconference, and I couldn't wait to see Jamey. I kept thinking about what it must have been like for him to watch the rocket blast off the launchpad, knowing his mom was inside. I'd tried my best to prepare him, explaining when we'd watched launches together that there would be a big cloud of smoke and and that it was normal that the rocket would disappear for a moment, and then reappear. Still, I hoped he hadn't been scared.

When the video call connected, my little boy looked so grown-up in his plaid shirt, sitting there at the desk alongside his dad and all the serious Roscosmos Space Agency guys. He said he hoped I'd had a good trip. He'd been waiting a long time while we docked. He laughed at my big "whoopy" hair. "You should have gotten a better haircut, Mom!" he said, but I told him I liked it this way. He told me that when we reached orbit, all the grown-ups had celebrated with a toast and they had given him a thimbleful of whiskey, which was not to his liking at all. So they gave him some candy instead. Dima's little boy, Vlad, asked his dad to bring him home a toy. And then they all waved goodbye, and we were alone in space, just the six of us.

Borscht Diplomacy and Other Unexpected Points of Connection

Confronting challenges can bring a team or crew closer together. But after arriving on the station I discovered other powerful bonding agents: awe and wonder. When you're looking out of the Cupola windows at the magnificent view of the Earth lit up by the aurora borealis, and you turn to look at the person beside you and see your own emotions reflected on their face, you feel the vibration of shared humanity more strongly than any differences. When you're flying through a module, reveling in the experience of weightlessness, and a crewmate flies past looking equally childlike and joyful, you connect wordlessly.

There were other moments of childlike delight. You know that feeling when you wake up on Christmas morning, or another eagerly anticipated holiday that you celebrate? I felt like that almost every single day I woke up in space, but about two weeks into my mission, I woke up and realized it actually was Christmas morning. I went through my morning guessing game (Which way is up? Where in my sleeping compartment am I?), unzipped my sleeping bag, floated out to go brush my teeth, and found a bag of chocolates tied to the outside of my door. Looking over at Paolo's and Scott's doors, I saw the same thing. Our Russian crewmates, who celebrate Orthodox Christmas later in January, had left us presents! They also had special holiday shirts for us with snowmen on the front. Those presents were a surprise that I treasured as much as anything Santa had delivered to my stocking as a child.

Meanwhile, back on Earth, Jamey and Josh were celebrating with Josh's mom and his brothers. It was really fun to talk to them, although I almost hadn't been gone long enough for them to miss me! All of us on the ISS loved bringing our tiny artificial Christmas tree to our family conferences. It was about two feet tall, and we had wrapped it in a string of Josh's small glass planets that I'd brought up with me. On Earth, the solid glass spheres would have weighed down every branch. But in space, they danced weightlessly around the tree, majestic and beautiful.

Even more exciting than Christmas morning was the night when a Master Caution alarm blared loudly out of the speakers in our cabins. Whipping out of our sleeping compartments, Paolo, Scott, and I flew down to the lab to join our crewmates at the main computer. Of course, we hoped it wasn't anything serious. But I confess, we also hoped it wasn't nothing. All of us would have welcomed a small, non-life-threatening issue, one that would require . . . spacewalking!

Mission Control quickly informed us we had a power issue. Half the power on the space station was affected. Scott had a huge grin on his face, and a funny little eyebrow raise that I'd learn meant he was ready to rumble. We had a reason to do one, or maybe several, EVAs.

And then—we didn't. Mission Control told us they could reroute power and data from the spare unit, and we could go back to bed. And that was the closest I ever came—after all that training, all that padding, all those bruises and battles with huge, recalcitrant tools—to spacewalking in actual space. I was disappointed, of course, but still proud that I'd qualified. And it had all been worth it, because without that qualification I would not have been eligible to fly on the ISS until 2021, when NASA finally lifted the EVA constraint.

As the days and weeks passed, we settled into a rhythm of life and work in space. One of the keys to building trust among a diverse, multilingual team, I've learned, is finding languages that go beyond words. Food is one such universal language, and in space it was extremely important for morale. It became my favorite means of diplomacy. The Russians had their own food, and we had our menu in the U.S. segment, which rotated every nine days, but there was no rule against trading meals. I quickly learned that the Russians loved steak, which was a regular option on our menu. Every nine days, one of our steaks was mine. Luckily, I liked the Russian borscht, and, seeing their wistful glances toward my steak, I'd offer to trade. All of us seemed to love the coffee and tea with cream and sugar. There was a limited amount of that, and so I proactively divided them equally between all six of us every time I opened a new box. When it came to our favorite foods, we each got to choose a few snacks to bring along with us, and later our families would send care packages up on the supply ships. Mine were Gummi Bears and Swedish Fish. Mary, Stacey, and my girlfriends sent wonderful chocolate spheres that looked like tiny Earths in their foil wrappers. Like everything in space that's not bolted down or Velcroed to a wall, they'll sail off if you don't keep an eye on them. Sometimes I took a Gummi

Bear out of its package, waited for it to float into range, then leaned out and snapped it up, like a frog swallowing a fly. Other times, I would set a school of Swedish Fish loose in the module (off camera, of course), and we'd all chase them around the cabin, like fearsome sharks, jaws open.

Connectivity between the ISS and Earth is surprisingly good, so I got to talk to my family by phone almost every day. Just as I had done during my training, Jamey and I often did math homework together, an idea I'd gotten from Mike Barratt, also an astronaut, while training in Russia. I had taken photos of Jamey's math textbook to bring with me, along with some favorite books that we were reading together. Once a week, we were allowed to have videoconferences, and Jamey would haul our very large and tolerant Maine coon cat, Fang, over to join in. Like most ten-year-olds, Jamey was sometimes upset or cranky and once or twice even refused to join the video call. It was hard not to be there to comfort him in those moments, and hard to see Josh looking tired and frustrated and be unable to fully share the burden. It was heartbreaking to watch those videos after I got home, to see how frustrating it was for Jamey to act like the distance between us didn't matter, in those moments when my physical presence might have made a difference.

Sometimes we didn't need words to connect. Josh had an app that would tell him when we were passing over Massachusetts, and often we'd time our calls for that moment. I'd go to the Cupola window and wave. I couldn't actually see the house, but I knew that right below me, the people I loved most in the world were looking up and waving as the brightest star they could see sailed across the sky.

The Cost of Cockroach Thinking

For the most part, I'm proud to say that during my time on the ISS I was able to rise above the interpersonal challenges our crew had encountered in training. We can't control how others behave, and we can't necessarily change how that makes us feel, but we can control how much we let them dominate our experience. It's a choice to obsess over those feelings and to let that obsession color our ability to be truly present. One of my coaches used to call focusing on the negative in this way "cockroach thinking." I'd learned not to let frustrations with people take up too much mental and emotional space in this way. At least, most of the time.

There was one notable exception, however. We were scheduled for a routine emergency drill with Mission Control—a fire scenario. We had a script, and just like actors in a play, we'd perform the simulation, allowing Mission Control to problem-solve while also evaluating our skills. It was always useful to do these practices on the actual station, because even though we'd practiced a lot on the ground, things weren't exactly the same, and having accurate physical and mental muscle memory was important when dealing with emergency scenarios. A fire extinguisher might be overhead on the station, where it was easy to reach in zero-g, but in Houston it was more practical to have it on the floor. On this particular day, anticipating the fire alarm drill that was happening right after lunch, I approached Dima and asked if he wanted to spend a little time running over our crew's part in the scenario together. I thought reviewing the steps would be useful for us.

He looked up from his lunch, clearly irritated. "Cady, just follow the procedure," he said, and went back to eating, as if that were the end of that conversation. Paolo looked at me over his head and shrugged as if to say, "Well, you tried."

I bristled at Dima's dismissive response. "Fine," I said, turning and giving myself a push back toward my cabin in Node 2. One downside of zero-g: you can't stomp out of a room to make a point. And once I got in my cabin, I didn't let it go; I stewed in my annoyance, letting the cockroaches have their way, and was still quietly fuming by the time the simulation began.

I had the opening line, and I positioned myself in the middle of Node 2. "Houston, I am simulating that I smell smoke in Node 2." Note that we are very careful to use the word *simulate* in our calls, so that no one will get confused between the drill and an actual emergency. And then I flew over to the Caution and Warning panel in the upper corner of Node 2, near my cabin. "And now I am simulating pressing the fire alarm button."

And then, I lifted the plastic cover that protected the panel and *actually pressed the button.*

The moment I did it, I knew I'd made a huge mistake. When we practice on the ground, we actually do push that button. But on the station, for a simulation, I was *not* supposed to do so. The alarm was sounding, but everything else in the module was eerily quiet because the system had turned the ventilation fans off, just as it should to keep an actual fire from spreading. Every one of my crewmates was converging on Node 2, looking concerned.

"Houston," I stammered, "that was me. There is no fire. I repeat, there is no fire. That was me. I accidentally pushed the button."

The CAPCOM made it clear that my message had been understood, and that we should take a short break while they regrouped. For the first time since I'd arrived at the station, I wanted to retreat into my cabin and cry, but this wasn't the moment for that. Indeed, it was my inability to put my emotions aside that had caused this problem in the first place.

As we waited for instructions, I inwardly berated myself. What was I thinking? I knew not to activate the alarm during a sim. But I'd let Dima's dismissal and the feelings it had provoked get under my skin, and in the moment, I was focused on them instead of our drill. Sure, those feelings might have been justified, but what was inexcusable was that I'd put them above our mission. As a result, I'd made a serious mistake, and certainly one that could have been avoided.

When everything was back up and running, we restarted the

simulation and performed the drill. The flight director wrote me a note and asked me to give him a call after our dinner that night.

"Listen, Cady," he said, "I know that you're embarrassed. And nobody likes to make a mistake. At the same time, it might make you feel better to know that pushing that button gave us some pretty valuable data on our ISS systems and how they work together, or don't. We've been trying to plan an exercise like that for literally years, and it's never convenient. Someone always has a reason why it's not a good time to shut things down. We learned some really valuable things today, and we'll be making some significant changes to our ground procedures based on the data that we were able to collect. It's always a good day when you learn something. We did, and knowing you, I'm sure that you did as well."

It was nice of him to share all that, and I certainly did learn a valuable lesson: when you let your feelings about someone get under your skin, you put your mission, whatever that mission is, at risk. I think the reverse can be true as well. Focusing on the mission makes it easier to ignore those disruptive feelings, and easier to be fully present wherever you are. Luckily, there weren't any lasting consequences of my mistake (other than being the butt of a few fire alarm jokes over the years). But in a real emergency, there could have been.

Being Present, from Afar

People often ask astronauts if they worry about something happening to them while they're in space. And we do. But honestly, most astronaut friends that I talk to worry more about what it would be like if something happens to someone we love back on Earth, or some major tragedy strikes and we're not there. The risks to ourselves are part and parcel of the job, and we, along with our families, each have our own ways of dealing with that reality. But it's hard to imagine being so far away if a family member or friend were to get sick or even pass away, or if a natural disaster struck your hometown. It's hard to really reconcile that you can't just drop everything and go home, even in an emergency. Those moments when you just need to *be there*, you can't.

Interestingly, I think most people will now be able to relate to this in a way none of us could have before the COVID-19 pandemic. So many of us had to suddenly come to terms with not being physically present for our loved ones through major life events like births, weddings, sickness, and even death. I think that most of us learned that phone calls and videoconferences can do more to span those gaps than we would have thought, but it's not the same as reaching out to gently touch an arm or receive a silent hug.

For each of my missions, I was asked how I would want to be informed if something happened to Jamey, to Josh, or to my parents or siblings. Thankfully, those plans never had to be activated. But during my time on the ISS, I watched people I cared about deal with loss and disaster, both in space and on Earth. And as much as we all wish we could have avoided such moments, they did bring us closer as a crew.

One Saturday morning in January, just a few weeks after my arrival on the ISS, Scott and I were in the middle of a very important task: fixing the toilet. That might not sound so consequential, but a nonfunctioning toilet is a high-profile situation that can lead to serious health and logistical consequences. Not to mention that a crew of six sharing one bathroom is going to get ugly pretty quickly. This repair was not simple, because it involved a leak around a cannister of concentrated acid that buffered our urine for storage. Just as Scott and I were about to disconnect the canister, we got a message from the flight director that Scott needed to give the ground a call. When he came back, his normally stoic face looked shell-shocked. He told us that his sister-in-law, congresswoman Gabby Giffords, had been shot at a rally in Arizona. He didn't yet know if she was going to make it, and he'd need to be on the phone with his family down on the ground for a while.

"Of course," I told him. "We're here for you. We'll complete the WCS repair and cover your events on the time line until the ground tells us otherwise." He asked me to show Paolo what I'd been learning about the toilet repairs, so that we could do it together. Then he reminded us more than a few times that if we needed any help, we shouldn't hesitate to knock on his door. (Later, he'd joke that it really took an emergency for him to hand off such a mission-critical task.)

Scott had asked the folks on the ground to send the CNN feed up to the station through our channels, as we often did on the weekends when the data load was lower. We gathered around, listening to the breaking news, and were horrified to hear the reporter confirm that Gabby had died. That was followed by a scheduled loss of signal, and it was about thirty long minutes later that we got comm back and the flight director was able to tell Scott it had been an error. Gabby was alive and on her way to the hospital. It was a tough few days for Scott, and we all did our best to support him. He's not a natural talker, so all of us appreciated his willingness to keep us informed and let us know what was happening for him.

In the midst of his own challenges, he made it easier for all of us—an example I never forgot. Sometimes being a good teammate simply means letting people know how you're doing. Sharing is an act of generosity, especially when what you're sharing is hard. Thankfully, Gabby recovered, and has gone on to be a powerful voice in the fight for sensible gun control. Her husband, Scott's twin brother, Mark Kelly, was also an astronaut and flew to the ISS on one of the last space shuttle missions, arriving just five days before our crew departed. Mark is now a U.S. senator from Arizona.

Another tragic event back on Earth took place just six weeks after our successful supply ship capture: the deadly tsunami that struck Japan on March 11, 2011. During our HTV training, I'd grown close to our Japanese colleagues in Mission Control. I remembered the day that Nicole and I had been introduced to them as the first two astronauts who would capture their HTV supply ships with the robotic arm. The entire room rose as one and bowed. It was an emotional moment filled with mutual trust and respect. I'd worked with some of them years earlier when I was the Chief of Robotics, in the early days of planning these supply ship operations. So when we woke up that morning and heard the news, it felt really close to home. The Japanese Mission Control center had been damaged, and people on the HTV team had lost family members.

What can you do when you're so far away? My first thought was, we can simply be there, be present when we fly over Japan. So we asked Mission Control for a list of the times and set our watches to remind us. Whenever we could, we gathered in the Cupola and took photos of the island nation to provide useful data for the Japanese government. In the nighttime shots, I was shocked to see how few lights were shining across the country compared to the way it had looked before the tsunami hit. And in the daytime shots, we could see the terrible extent of the flooding. The coastline we'd seen so many times just looked out of focus and . . . wrong.

Wanting to do more for our friends, I reached out to Shu Ichimura, who had often been our Japanese CAPCOM and had become a friend. He told us that for the Japanese people, the white crane was a symbol of hope and rebuilding, and he thought that it would give people joy to see us make those birds up in space in the Japanese module, using the traditional art of origami. And so we did. We created a flock of small white paper birds, live on Japanese television, and floated them in the space station. We posed them in front of the HTV, and taped them to places where we often gathered, including the Cupola. I later learned that the videos were displayed on billboards in Japan for months afterward. It was a small gesture, but it meant a lot to us to be more closely connected to our Japanese space family during this difficult time for their nation.

The first four months of our mission went by so quickly that I kept feeling as if it were just last week that Scott had welcomed us onto the space station and given us that whirlwind tour. But suddenly it was time to say goodbye to the three crewmates who had been up there before us. I thought about how I'd felt before my arrival, wondering if I'd get along with them. Scott and I, in particular, were so different from each other, and I'd worried we might not easily connect. Later, I learned that many people on the ground had shared that worry, and they'd asked Scott, "How are you and Cady not going to kill each other?" He is a man of very few words, and I am, as you have probably gathered, a woman of many words. We were both a little surprised at how much we came to like and respect each other.

He came out of his cabin that last morning with all his belongings tied up in a bag and hanging on a stick, like a small boy getting ready to run away from home. I knew he was excited to go back to his family, but I also realized that our gruff, businesslike commander was actually going to miss us. So when he gave me one of those side-by-side hugs that isn't really a hug, I said, "I'll miss you," and from the look in his eyes I knew he really meant it when he said, "I'll miss you too." Watching Scott, Oleg, and Sasha fly into their Soyuz and close the hatches, I knew that even if we never spent much time together in the future, we'd always share a special connection because of those months we'd spent in space together—both the magical moments and the most heartrending ones.

After Scott and his crew left, Dmitri, Paolo, and I were joined by Ron, Andrei, and Sasha. We were getting to know one another and adjusting to the new crew configuration when Paolo got the unexpected news that his mother had passed away. It was not entirely a shock—he and his family learned that she was sick after launch and knew that this might happen—but nevertheless the loss was heartbreaking. I tried to imagine how it must feel to be so far away at a moment like this.

When I asked Paolo how he was doing, he told me he was okay, but that it was hard for him that some of his family were upset that he would not be present at the funeral. I asked Paolo if there was anything I could do to help. He responded, "Maybe you can help me figure out how to be present from up here." So I talked with Emily Nelson, our flight director, and she was immediately on board. "Just let us know whatever we can do," she told me.

As I was calculating time zones and the position of the space station, I realized that we were actually going to be flying right over Italy at the time of the funeral. We gathered the whole crew, all six of us, in the Cupola. We floated in a circle and looked out the window at the unmistakable boot-like shape of Italy. I glanced around at my crewmates, feeling connected to all of them, even the new guys who had recently arrived. On Paolo's face, I saw grief and loss but also gratitude for having this moment of ritual to connect and honor his mother. I saw an expression on Dima's face that I hadn't seen before. It looked to me like a sense of pride, as if he, now our commander after Scott's departure, were proud of his crew coming together to support one of our own. On the faces of our new crew members, I saw more openness.

I can't speak for the others, but it seemed to me like that moment brought us all closer. Our reason for gathering was to support Paolo in his loss, but I think in some way it also served as an acknowledgment of the temporary losses we were all experiencing being so far from our families, and the unspoken fears we each had about what could happen to our own loved ones while we were so far away. It's something each astronaut deals with in his or her own way, but it's a common currency among us all. We've all committed to being "here" and not "there" for the duration of our mission. We all have someone we leave behind, someone we love. We all grieve—not just the big losses, but the loss of so many ordinary moments with family and friends. In the end, we're all human beings, despite our differences. We bond in rising to the challenge of our shared mission; we bond in the awe and wonder of being in space; and we bond in the painful moments of loss that remind us of our capacity for love and connection.

Toward the end of my stay on the ISS, one of my crewmates joked (half seriously) that he'd like to go home sooner than planned. Without even thinking, I said, "I'll stay! I would spend another six months here in a minute." What I didn't say—but I truly felt—was that I would spend another six months here *with these same people.* Because despite the interpersonal challenges we faced, every day up there was magical. Yes, I missed my family and couldn't wait to see them again. But my crew were family too. I think that's a testament to the fact that when the mission is more important than the way you feel about one another, you can make the team work. What we were doing together was so much bigger than our individual differences, and to let those differences get in the way of the mission, or of enjoying that unique experience, would have been a tragedy.

I'll always feel a special bond with each of the people I went to space with. There are so few people who have shared that experience, in all of its incomparable highs and unique challenges. I remember the small moments of connection, like trading meals, sharing coveted snacks, or simply looking out the window together, with as much pride as I remember the big milestones, like capturing that supply ship. In the end, when I look back on those six months, what stands out to me is the trust we shared—a trust that meant all the more for having been hard won.

Chapter 10

There Is an *I* in Team

Celebrating Individuality in Collaboration

I loved nighttime on the ISS, when all my crewmates were asleep, zipped into their sleeping bags and tethered to the padded walls of their tiny cabins. I knew I needed my rest, too, but I couldn't resist lingering a little later, enjoying those moments when I got to be the only one awake. I welcomed the break from both the joys and challenges of living and working together. And where better to be alone with my thoughts than the Cupola, with the best view in the universe? Sometimes I'd just float around, gently bobbing back and forth the way you might in the ocean. Sometimes, I'd take my computer there while the moon was in view and call Josh on the phone. "Do you see the moon?" I'd ask him. And he'd go outside and look up, and it was always comforting to know that we were looking at the same moon, just as we had done through all our years of living in different places.

The Cupola was also my favorite place to play my flute, thanks to its bright-sounding acoustics and its distance from all my sleeping crewmates (the Russian and U.S. crew quarters are at either end of the station, with the Cupola in the middle). I've been an enthusiastic amateur musician most of my life, ever since I first picked up a flute in sixth grade, and when I was assigned to my long-duration ISS mission, I knew that my flute would be coming with me. Playing music allows me to feed another side of myself that I didn't want to leave behind on Earth for six whole months. And thank goodness I picked wisely on that fateful day when twelve-year-old Cady was asked what instrument she'd like to play in the school band. I thanked my younger self for not picking the trombone, the drums, or the tuba. But I love the fact that my fellow space travelers have made their own marks on the music world by bringing instruments that mattered to them, including a trumpet, a saxophone, a full-size keyboard, a guitar, and astonishingly (and perhaps unfortunately), a set of bagpipes. At one point, Don Pettit even made a didgeridoo using parts scavenged from the ISS trash.

On a typical night, I'd fly through the lab and hook a right into Node 3, and then launch myself up into the cupola. I'd crank open the window covers so I could see the view. I'd tuck my toes under a foot restraint and settle into a comfortable position, then take out my flute, which was bundled up in a red T-shirt secured by a hair tie. On Earth, the instrument would be packed in its case in three pieces, but in space I kept it assembled, since I had a great fear of one piece floating off and getting lost somewhere in the infinite recesses of the space station. I imagined a future astronaut coming upon it, puzzled, as I had been when I found myself suddenly staring at a treasured family pocketknife someone had lost a couple of years earlier.

I'd start out by playing a phrase of an Irish folk tune I knew by ear, or just a few low and haunting notes. As the sound filled the dome, I'd smile at the incongruity of me floating up here in space playing music. A couple of times, in the early days, Scott's bald head would poke up into the Cupola on his way to the bathroom and give me a stern, parental, "you should be in bed" look. But he soon accepted that this was how I needed to end my day.

My favorite way to play up there was to put on my headset and listen to a recording of Bandella, our astronaut band. I'd play like I did on

Earth, noodling in the spaces that needed to be filled, giving our marvelous vocalist, Micki Pettit, room to soar, and then taking a solo as if Chris Hadfield, the bandleader, had given me the nod. For me, playing music has always been something that means the most to me when I play with other people, and I loved making music together with our band and other friends even while I was circling the Earth, more than 250 miles above them. I also loved feeling connected to myself—remembering who I was beyond the day-to-day stresses of my work on the ISS. I'd watch different countries pass by below and feel as if I were playing for each of them. I never felt lonely. I did, however, believe that I was, in fact, alone. It was only when I returned to Earth and stopped by Mission Control late one night that I realized there's a huge screen showing the view from a camera that's trained on the Cupola any time the shades are open. All that time, I hadn't known I had an audience!

What Would You Take to Space?

My flute wasn't the only very personal object I took to space. When I was first assigned to go up on the Soyuz, we were given a minuscule baggage allowance—about three pounds, which is basically nothing. But then, at the very last minute, we found out that there would be two shuttle flights to the ISS during our mission, so we were given a bit more space—about the equivalent of two shoeboxes. I gave a great deal of thought to what I would bring, and I'm sure my crewmates did too. It can be an interesting exercise to try for yourself—what would you take to space?

Of course, what I really wanted to take with me were the people I loved. But barring that, I chose to take objects that meant something to each of them. How could I fill my limited space with things that would connect me more closely to people back on Earth? And what could I take that could become a meaningful gift for someone on my return—a thank-you to the people who are part of my village? "Flown objects," as they are known, are instruments of outreach and sharing. They can be used to create ripples in the world long after you return.

My items included Jamey's stuffed tiger Hobbes, as in Calvin and Hobbes (but pronounced *Ho-Bays* thanks to Josh, who loves to come up with funny pronunciations), and also a bracelet Jamey had made for me, which I wore sometimes when I was on video so he'd know I was thinking of him. I took some of Josh's smallest glass planets—a tangible reminder of the man I love and his unique creative vision. Floating around with the view of the Earth in the background, they offered a whole different perspective, worlds within worlds. And afterward, they made perfect, meaningful gifts for my extended family. I confess, I came home with one fewer than I had packed. I doubt it will be found anytime soon, as duct tape was involved, but I love that as the ISS continues its mission, that little planet is along for the ride.

I chose earrings and necklaces made by artist friends that I would wear onboard, and then give back to the artists or pass on to my friends and family when I returned. I particularly liked wearing dangly earrings, ones that would dance in zero-g. I also took T-shirts from various organizations I wanted to support and books that felt special to me.

Besides taking my own flute, I wanted to use the flight as an opportunity to connect with and honor one of my all-time musical heroes: Jethro Tull's Ian Anderson, the musician who brought the flute to rock music. I enlisted the help of Dayna Steele, a friend and famous Houston DJ, who knew how to reach out to Ian and his team. She explained who I was and asked if I could bring one of Ian's flutes with me to space. Emphasizing the tight time line, she requested a single reliable point of contact who could help get everything arranged.

Ian, who I would learn has a wonderful sense of humor, wrote back himself, saying he believed himself to be fairly reliable, took a shower and brushed his teeth most days, and he'd be happy to provide his flute in service to space history. There wasn't time before launch to figure out exactly what I planned to do with Ian's flute, but we agreed to connect by email once I was on board the ISS. Alongside Ian's flute and mine, I also took a tin whistle for Paddy Moloney and a hundred-year-old Irish flute for Matt Molloy, both of them members of the Irish band the Chieftains, known for their eclectic collaborations with artists from around the world. We had become friends over the years, and when our paths cross, it's always an honor to play with this extraordinary group of musicians and dancers.

Brave and Open

At a certain point, my nightly musical interludes in the Cupola took on a more serious tone. I was no longer just playing for fun; I was *rehearsing* to play on a global stage. Ian Anderson and I had exchanged emails, and I'd proposed the perfect way to use his flute: in a space-Earth duet (the first of its kind!) to celebrate the fiftieth anniversary of the first human to fly in space.

Among space enthusiasts, April 12 is known as "Yuri's Night," after Russian cosmonaut Yuri Gagarin, who strapped himself into a small capsule known as Vostok 1 on that day in 1961. Just before the rocket engines fired, he shouted, "Poyekhali!" (a phrase that sounds like *Pa-yeh-xha-lee* and translates as "Let's go!" and was still a favorite expression among all the Russians I flew with). And then he launched into space, from the very same pad I would launch from decades later, becoming the first person to leave our planet and orbit the Earth. It is an anniversary that is celebrated globally. Which led to my idea of bridging Earth and space by commemorating Yuri's Night in my favorite language: music. When I researched Ian's schedule and saw that he would in fact be playing in Perm, Russia, on the day of the anniversary, it seemed meant to be.

Ian was game, and suggested that we play "Bourrée," a Bach duet that bridges the old and the new with Ian's improvisational interpretation. Hence those serious rehearsal sessions in the Cupola in the wee hours. I think Ian may have overestimated my musical know-how, sending me instructions that I had a hard time making sense of. After a long night during which I completely failed to figure out what he wanted me to play, I wrote him an email titled "Lost in space." He replied quickly, with good humor and a clarifying explanation, and I had what I needed to learn my part. When the day came, I was almost more nervous than I'd been to capture the supply ship. Dressed in my blue flight suit, with our crew patch proudly displayed on the front, I flew down onto my makeshift stage, my flute floating down ahead of me and my hair ballooning around my head (Eileen Collins would have been proud). I tucked my feet under a handrail and started to play.

That duet was one of my favorite memories from my time in space. It was an incredible privilege to be a part of that fiftieth anniversary and to reflect on and hopefully inspire an appreciation of how far humans have come in just a few decades—and how far we might still go. It's not something I'd have worked up the courage to do alone, so I was grateful to Ian for saying yes and giving me a reason to perform. And it was especially meaningful because the performance was a way to take something that was deeply personal to me and share it around the globe in honor of an occasion that meant something to all of us. Not only was I bridging Earth and space; I was bridging my own worlds—the personal and the professional, the artist and the astronaut, the musician and the adventurer.

It also crystallized an important lesson for me about what it takes to be a good team member, in any kind of collaboration: be brave and be open. You have to be brave enough to say who you are and declare what you bring. And you have to be open to learning what other people bring, without making assumptions. To make that duet with Ian Anderson happen, I had to be brave enough to ask, to tell him who I was and what

I hoped to do, and he had to be open to an unusual opportunity, which included collaborating with an amateur. He didn't know me at all. But I think we both suspected that we were of the same heart.

Celebrating Individuality

I'm sure you've heard the saying "There is no *I* in team." It's the kind of phrase that sports coaches, motivational speakers, and corporate facilitators love to throw around. I think that phrase is not just overused, but actually wrong (except, of course, in the literal sense). People use this expression to encourage team members to set aside individual needs, preferences, and opinions in order to focus on a team's collective purpose. And while that's often necessary to keep the mission in sight, the adage sidesteps one of the most powerful contributions each of us can make to any collaboration: our individuality.

It's been my experience that the most effective teams contain lots of *I*s. Creating a successful team depends on recognizing and appreciating each person's uniqueness and their potential contribution—the distinctive sound of their instrument and the melody they're playing. The best teams find ways for every member to thrive and grow and be their best selves—and the teams become stronger in the process.

We all bring unique gifts to the table, and for a team to truly excel, we can't afford to overlook any of those—even if they're unexpected or unconventional. From my missions in space, on land, and underwater, I learned important lessons, sometimes the hard way, about celebrating what each person brings and not wasting time worrying about what they might lack. The great thing about being a team is that you don't need each person to be the best at everything. You just need to bring out the best in each individual and then see how those pieces fit together, compensate for one another, complement one another, and amplify one another.

I love the example of complementarity that Paolo and I represent. One of the things that made our collaboration so effective was the fact that we were so different. When it comes to getting things done quickly, there is no one more capable than Paolo. He's truly a master at having a vision, figuring out the series of steps to make it happen, and making that project a reality. However, he's sometimes so focused on getting started and achieving his goal that he might not always consider all the ramifications beforehand. I, on the other hand, tend to entertain a world of possibilities. You might say that I'm a master at considering all the potential consequences of any particular path. What if the shuttle launch is delayed and we have now stored all that equipment in front of the CO_2 removal system that we need to fix at the end of the week? And what if this happened—or that went wrong? But that kind of X-ray vision of future consequences can also make it hard for me to actually begin.

You might imagine that Paolo and I would get on each other's nerves—that he'd be frustrated by my need to think things through and impatient to get going, while I'd feel anxious about his blinkered approach and railroaded into action before I was ready. In fact, it was quite the opposite. Okay, we did drive each other crazy sometimes. But mostly we were a great team who accomplished a lot because we each accepted our own strengths and weaknesses and recognized each other's.

Case in point, the day Paolo decided to take apart the space station table that we used for meals and rehang it on a diagonal. It was a brilliant idea—we'd been banging our hips on that thing for months when we flew back and forth between the U.S. and Russian segments, as had dozens of astronauts before us for the past ten years. After Scott and his crew left, there were just three of us up there for a few days, and Paolo was the lead for the U.S. segment, so it was the perfect moment. He jumped right in and started disassembling it. When I saw what he was up to, I showed up with ziplock baggies to keep the nuts and bolts from floating away and extra-long zip ties to keep things connected. Paolo appreciated my scenario-planning capabilities, and I was grateful for his willingness to act on something I'd have never gotten around to doing, despite all the bruises on my hips, and everyone else's too.

How Rowing and Music Taught Me to Be a Better Crewmate

I've learned a lot about collaboration and teamwork from my various missions and expeditions as an astronaut. But I've also learned critical lessons in other areas of life, which I brought with me to my role at NASA.

Back in my MIT days, I rowed on the crew team for four years, three of them varsity, and I served as cocaptain along with my best friend, Laura Kiessling (the one I once thought was too gorgeous to be any good at chemistry). I was amazed to discover that eight people with such different personalities and physical capabilities could thrive together in a single boat. We learned that our very differences were what helped to weave us into a cohesive unit when we rowed together, and eventually we went on to win the Eastern Sprints, essentially the Nationals for rowing at the time.

At five four, I wasn't someone you'd pick as an obvious rower. But I tried to maximize what I did bring to the crew. I could keep the boat set up and balanced; I was ambidextrous, so I could fill in on either side; I was persistent and hardworking, and always showed up. Laura was the physical leader of our crew and inspired the team to be their very best in terms of strength and performance. I tended to be the person who tuned in to the different people in the boat, knowing when someone was struggling, upset, or frustrated and helping to ensure their questions and perspectives were heard.

Another way I learned a lot about collaboration was through playing music in bands, often improvisational. I was at a language camp learning

Norwegian when I discovered the joy of improvisation as a musical language. I was a high school exchange student in Norway at the time, and Olav Njaastad, the lead instructor at our initial two-week language camp, played guitar. He encouraged me to grab my flute and play along with him as he taught the group folk songs. When I protested that I didn't know what to play, he said, "You know how to play in the key of G, right? You know how to listen? That's all you need to know." And he was right.

I soon found that I had a knack for this kind of wordless conversation. I could sense whose turn it was to lead and whose turn it was to follow. I knew when a gap needed to be filled, and I had a sense of where we might end up, even if I didn't know precisely how we might get there. I learned to trust other musicians and take risks rather than just playing it safe. And when I hesitated, my bandmates helped me along. There's nothing like having the bandleader say, "And here's Cady!" and then the rest of the band going silent. In those moments, I'd swallow my nerves and put aside my overthinking. Perhaps most important, I learned to listen and to find ways to use my own melody to weave together the different sounds of the other instruments.

My musical adventures have made me a much more perceptive, courageous, and trustworthy teammate on my space missions. The skills I learned include an ability to listen openly—not just to individual notes or instruments but for patterns that are unfolding; not just to what is being played, but to what's not being played. It turns out this skill is invaluable in conversations and teamwork, as well. When you're in a team meeting, you need to be able to pay attention to who's speaking and who is not; to the pattern, direction, and energy of the discussion; and to what might be missing. You need to consider when to jump in yourself, and when to work to bring in other voices that aren't being heard. Thinking of a conversation as a piece of music that you can contribute to, enrich, or fine-tune can be helpful if you're someone who struggles in meetings or collective decision-making. And that kind of paying attention doesn't just happen with your ears—you can also focus in on body language and other visual clues.

Another skill I learned in music is to move between the big picture and the small details. Sometimes you get captivated by a particular note or harmony; other times you need to think about how the overall piece of music is developing and the pattern that's being created. This is true in any collaboration where the goal is to get something done together. Details matter, but so does keeping that overall picture in sight.

When I've been part of a crew or a team, I've often been the one whose unofficial job it becomes to glue together the disparate parts—just as I do when I play in a band. In fact, I've come to see that members of a crew or team are really not that different from a group of musicians who each play a different instrument. Where do each of the different melodies fit, and what makes them mesh together into harmony? I've had to learn to listen to my crewmates as carefully as I'd listen to the members of my band, trying to hear how each person can strengthen and enhance the overall group. What people bring isn't always immediately apparent. It's easy to make assumptions if you don't really listen, or to drown out the less obvious voices. A great crew or team, like a great band, is made up of unique individuals, and knows how to celebrate those individuals without sacrificing the cohesion of the group.

Of course, I'm aware that the kinds of skills I've just described can sometimes be disparagingly referred to as "soft," and it's often assumed that women will take these roles in a group (whether they are good at them or not). When you demonstrate these so-called soft skills, people may find it hard to see that you could *also* be a gifted leader, and they may not give you the opportunity to take leadership roles.

Despite those assumptions and attitudes, however, the ability to bring a team together is invaluable. Case in point: though we were six talented people who could all perform individually, our ISS crew was not expected to excel. People just didn't feel that we would mesh in a way that would allow our team's performance to emerge as more than the sum of our individual efforts. But in the end, we did excel. And, although everyone contributed in their own way, my ability to bring us together and create an atmosphere where we could thrive was certainly a powerful catalyst for our achievements.

While I've sometimes felt unseen in my team-connecting role, I recently heard a story that made me rethink that assumption. One of my MIT crew teammates, our coxswain Anita Nagem, recalled a conversation she'd had with Doug Clark, our coach, in which he'd asked her who was the most important person in the boat. She'd guessed the woman in the number 8 stroke seat. No. She'd guessed Laura, who inspired everyone with her conviction and her athleticism. No. She'd guessed the strongest women who sat in the middle of the boat, known as "the engine room." No. Finally, he told her, "It's Cady. In the bow. Setting up the boat for balance, and more than that, keeping the team together. She isn't the strongest or the fastest, but she sees everyone on the crew and knows what they need to be their best, and she creates that atmosphere for them. Even though she is often the alternate for the boat, she always shows up, and that inspires them to show up as well. And when they come to the boathouse, they know they will be seen."

It meant a lot to me to hear that story. Sometimes, the glue isn't invisible, and it's anything but soft.

The Power of Perspective

There's another reason individuals matter so much. It's not just our talents or our personalities that can make the difference for a team, but the way we *see* the world. No one else looks at things quite the way we do. Each individual has a unique perspective, as distinct as our personalities. Those perspectives are among the most valuable things we can contribute to a team. To fully solve a complex problem, a team needs multiple perspectives. Learning to respect, value, and be curious about the perspectives of others—*especially* when they're profoundly different from our own—is critical to successful collaboration.

I was often reminded of how different our perspectives are when I would gaze out of the space station window with my crewmates. We were all seeing the same view of the same planet—*our planet, our home.* It's a powerful, life-transforming experience to see the Earth from a distance, as a whole. Even when you've heard it described dozens of times, it's still a surprisingly emotional experience that makes me feel connected to our shared humanity and the beauty and fragility of our home planet. In addition to that holistic perspective, however, each of us also has our own distinctive view of the Earth. As you gaze out the window, you see the places that have meaning in your particular life's story. And the person beside you sees the places that have particular meaning in their life's story.

At night, I liked to follow the lights of I-91 up from the Connecticut coastline, past the big patch of lights that was Hartford (so many airport stories) and then the smaller patch of lights that was Springfield, and then zoom in on that little dark patch in the hills where the people I loved were sleeping. In the daytime, the hand-like shape of the Quabbin Reservoir helped me find my home quickly. Or I might see the islands of Hawaii, glowing like jewels in the blue ocean, and remember how Josh proposed right down there and I didn't know what to answer. If Paolo were standing beside me, he'd point out where he grew up in Italy, and joke about how Italians stay up later than their northern neighbors, as evidenced by the brightly lit "boot" below us with a sharp line into darkness at the border. Scott liked to take close-up pictures so that when he got home it would be almost like a guessing game, trying to figure out where on Earth his camera was pointing.

One night, I was taking a short break in the Cupola and enjoying the view of Europe, when Ron flew in beside me, grinning. I asked him, "Hey, what's up?"

"I'm just having a really good day," he replied.

"Really? What happened?" I asked. I'd been listening to the comm and it had sounded to me like he'd been working on some frustrating procedures. None of it said "great day" to me. But Ron went on to explain that the reason for his great day wasn't up here in space, it was down on Earth. "Right there!" he said, pointing toward Africa passing below us. He told me that today, down in Kenya, the world was a little safer for millions of people because they had cleaner water to drink. Manna Energy, the social enterprise he'd founded with Nicole Stott and others, had just worked with partner organizations to distribute 4.5 million drinking straws that filtered water to rural communities across the country. I was floored. Here I was, thinking I'd achieved something today because I'd made it through everything on my schedule and talked to my family. And meanwhile, Ron had been changing the world.

Each of us saw the world through our own particular lens, shaped by our own life stories. Hearing stories like Ron's helped broaden the world for me—bringing home the message of what a difference one person can make, and how many ways there are to make change in the world. It was a lesson I'd hold close when I went back to Earth and began to think about what impact I might have in the next chapter of my life.

Chapter 11

Landing Is Not the End

Navigating Life's (Sometimes Bumpy) Transitions

It was hard saying goodbye to the space station. I know it sounds strange, but it really felt like home. When I first got assigned and Jamey was seven, he referred to it as "Mommy's Space House," and that's kind of how I saw it too. Of course, I missed Earth. I missed my family and friends. I missed my cats. I missed green things and real food and decent coffee and the smell of fresh air on a windy day. But I truly loved living in space for almost every day of the 159 days I got to live and work on the station. It felt like what we, as humans, *should* be doing.

My friend Don Pettit said it perfectly: "I'd have been quite happy to keep living and working there forever, if I could have had my family up there with me." I sometimes imagined how it would be to fly through the space station with Jamey by my side, showing him how to do all the zero-gravity flips and somersaults I was so proud of. Undoubtedly, he'd be showing me new tricks within moments of arriving. I pondered the potential challenges Josh would face if he were blowing glass in space, envisioning terrifying rivers of molten glass floating around the station's corridors. I think it will be a while before we evolve to practicing the flammable arts in space. Then I even pictured, with a smile, how my Maine coon kitties would look with their long hair and floofy tails liberated from gravity. I knew that they would still find a way to follow me from room to room to supervise my work. It energized me to think that the work I'd been doing for the past six months was preparing the ground for a future when families—maybe not mine, but someone else's—really could live in space.

Even the best of times must come to an end. Change is the only constant in life, whether it be gradual or sudden. Sometimes, our transitions are smooth progressions from one place, job, relationship, or phase of life to another. Other times, they're jarring, disorienting, even painful. Most of us have experienced plenty of each kind. I'm someone who has lived with a lot of change—commuting between two homes and working in a job where schedules, launch dates, and crews can change without warning. As my transition back to Earth approached, I was too busy to give much thought to the changes ahead. But if I had stopped to think about it, I might have anticipated that reentering the Earth's atmosphere, and my own life, would be an adventure of its own.

This would be my first time landing in a Soyuz capsule, and it's quite a different experience from the shuttle. The space shuttle essentially lands like a large plane, except that the final descent is seven times steeper—we call it "diving" toward the ground. Just before landing, the commander pulls the nose up to stop the descent rate. The back wheels touch down first, and then the nose is rotated downward until the front wheels connect with the runway and the careful braking begins. On my second flight, with Eileen Collins in command, I remember bracing for the back wheels to hit the tarmac, not realizing we were already on the ground, smooth as butter. The Soyuz has no wheels, no wings, no brakes, and by the time it gets down, no engines. Paolo, Dmitri, and I would essentially be strapping ourselves into our little capsule and spiraling around the Earth to land somewhere on the desert steppes of Kazakhstan, slowed only by the capsule's parachutes.

I didn't particularly want to leave the ISS, but I was excited about landing. Scott Kelly had enthusiastically described his Soyuz landing as being wilder (and more fun) than any amusement park ride you could imagine. I couldn't wait to see it all unfold from my window seat. And despite our differences, there are few people I'd trust to pilot a spacecraft more than I trust Dima and Paolo. We were well trained, we were a really sharp crew, and we knew all the ways we could save ourselves if things went wrong. In the end, life's just too short not to enjoy every last minute of an adventure—even the bumpy parts.

As the day of our departure approached, I tried not to mourn the fact that there were so many things I still wanted to do, and nowhere near enough time left to do them. Quite apart from my personal never-ending task list, we had been busy for weeks, working around the clock to get ready for the arrival of the space shuttle *Endeavour*, with the STS-134 crew under the command of Scott's brother, Mark Kelly, only five days before we were scheduled to go home.

When a new shuttle crew arrives, it's like having your entire extended family descend on you for the holidays. Once they were aboard, we were even busier, supporting them as well as preparing for our own departure. I was simply too busy to savor those last days, but I insisted on grabbing little moments here and there to be fully present. I tried to remember to cherish those long, graceful flights through the station. I stopped taking pictures of the Earth and focused on searing into my memory the feeling of living in a spaceship where that view of the Earth was always outside my window, waiting for me to look.

A couple of days before departure, Dima, Paolo, and I ran through a series of full-scale practices of our landing procedures. This included suiting up and climbing into our Soyuz seats. The liners for those seats had been made for us back in Russia, where we literally sat in a bathtub wearing old spacesuits as they filled the tub with plaster of Paris. Then, once our personalized molds were made (and we were lifted out with a crane), a sculptor (complete with wild hair and a long gray beard) actually carved them out to accommodate the one to two inches in height that we would gain up in space. Climbing into my seat for the landing practice made me remember how delighted Jamey (then eight) had been that his mom had a mold made of her butt, and that the mold itself was still sitting back in Russia in the Hall of Butts!

I was happy to find that my seat still felt just fine, even though I was at least an inch and a quarter taller in microgravity. Luckily Paolo, who had added over two inches to his more than six-foot frame, also seemed to fit. Since he was one of the tallest people ever to fly in the Soyuz, a sigh of relief was felt around the world.

The day of our scheduled departure was truly frenetic for me. I realized later that I'd opened at least a half dozen packages of food over the course of the day, but not managed to eat any of them, except for the packages of chicken broth I had parked at the Soyuz hatch. We "fluid load" with salty liquids to help us transition back to gravity. Ron and his crew were probably finding my food packages for days! I spent my last few hours with the STS-134 guys doing experiments and collaborating on video projects that were important to folks back on the ground. The capsule was all packed and ready, and thanks to my buddies on the STS-134 crew, so was I. I said goodbye to Ron, Andrei, and Sasha, who would be staying up there for another few months, and reluctantly flew into the Soyuz. Dima closed the hatch, and then it was just the three of us, leaving the way we'd arrived.

Once we were suited up and had settled into our seats, the transition began to feel real. We hadn't even undocked, but already the Earth felt closer. Had it really been only six months ago, I thought to myself, that we'd last sat like this, shoulder to shoulder, sailing around the Earth in our tiny craft and then docking with our city in space? It felt like a lifetime—and also not long enough.

We were a different crew from the one that had docked at the station.

Dima seemed to have come to value Paolo and me as crewmates, and I could see the increased trust reflected in the easier way we'd worked together in the landing practices. This particular Russian, Italian, and American trio might never walk into a bar or fly in a spaceship together again, but as I looked at their familiar, helmeted faces beside me in the capsule, I felt that unmistakable connection that comes with truly being a team.

My musings were washed away by a flood of excitement as our Soyuz pushed off gently from the station and we got to see our beautiful home from the outside in all its glory. There was one big difference from the view we'd seen on arrival. The space shuttle *Endeavour* was docked on the International Space Station—a sight no astronaut or cosmonaut had seen, since no crew had ever undocked from the station during a shuttle mission. It was more than just a cool visual—that image was an iconic representation of what fifteen nations had created. The last task of our mission, before we turned our attention to getting safely home, would be to capture that image to share with all the people down on Earth who had worked so hard to make it a reality.

Since this was the second to last shuttle flight before the program shut down, this might be the last opportunity to capture the image. Knowing it wouldn't be a simple task, Paolo, Dima, and I had proactively figured out lenses and viewing angles, and Paolo was able to take a non-stop series of photos and videos as we pirouetted around the station in an intricate ballet between our Soyuz and the space station, all while we circled the Earth together. After a last look, we fired our engines to maneuver ourselves away and begin the landing process.

Silently, I said goodbye to the ISS. I still hoped to come back, although I knew that the line was long even for experienced crew members like me, and it would be a while before I would possibly be assigned again. And then I turned to catch one last glimpse of the view I'd treasured every day as I brushed my teeth down in Node 3 and looked up through the Cupola windows. The curve of the Earth, the glow of the atmosphere, and a perfect sunrise over an unforgettable horizon.

Down to Earth

The Soyuz has three modules—like three Smart cars joined together. The one in the middle is the capsule where we sit, known as the Descent Module, because that's the only part that's actually going back to Earth. Above us is the living room capsule, known as the Orbital Module. This was the part that had been attached to the space station. Below us is the segment containing our engines, known as the Propulsion Module.

The first thing we do, once we're ready to initiate landing, is to turn the Soyuz so that the engines are firing against the direction of travel, a procedure called the deorbit burn ("burn" sounds alarming, but it's just astronaut lingo for firing the engines). This slows us down, just a little— from 17,900 miles per hour to 17,630 miles per hour, only a 270 miles per hour difference. It doesn't sound like much, I know, but that small decrease in speed is enough that our orbit will degrade, bringing us closer and closer to the ground until eventually we land, hopefully where we intended to. The deorbit burn is an important milestone, because once we burn those engines we're committed to landing. And if our burn goes as expected, it tells us that, barring any malfunctions, in approximately ninety minutes we will touch down at our expected landing spot, about halfway around the Earth from where we started those engines.

Next, the modules above and below the Descent Module where we are sitting are jettisoned explosively, with a loud bang. Once these are gone, we lose our more powerful engines, but until we enter the Earth's atmosphere, we can still fire some smaller jets to control our position.

The detached modules burn up as they enter the Earth's atmosphere. And we're left in our Soyuz capsule (think one Smart car), heading inexorably down to Earth.

I was glad Scott had warned us about the next part, reentry, but it was still pretty wild. The bottom of the Soyuz is a heat shield made of hard, insulating rubber the consistency of a pencil eraser. It is actually designed to burn away (ablate) as we enter the Earth's atmosphere, while still keeping enough of an insulating layer to protect us from the intense heat of reentry. The bottom line is that you see pieces of burning spacecraft literally flying past your window as you descend. If the system is working correctly, there is no need to worry, but even though you know this, it's hard not to feel like you're going down in flames. Luckily, I had Paolo's singsong voice in my ear, narrating the process like a comedic Italian football commentator. "And there eet ees. The burning stuff. And now we are inside the atmosphere. We are headed for home." It was strangely comforting—a reminder that all the things that were happening were the things that *should* be happening—the things we'd been told again and again to expect.

At this point, I started to feel my head and arms getting heavier. We were actually lying on our backs, but I could sense that if I wanted to lift my head, it would be heavy. Even my checklist felt heavy. Pencils that had been floating on their tethers when we undocked now hung down and stayed there.

Next comes the tough part: parachute deploy. Scott had emphasized the need to be ready and braced, with mouths closed to avoid biting our tongues. In fact, I believe his words were, "Cady, I'm looking right at you. You want to make sure you are NOT TALKING at chute deploy." I guess he knew me well. And he also knew what that moment feels like. A big parachute is released from the top of the capsule, fills up like a balloon, and stops the capsule abruptly in midfall. And I mean *abruptly*. It jerks to a halt and starts spinning and swinging wildly. I was glad that I'd taken Scott's advice and set a timer so we'd be prepared, but it was still a shock. Even Paolo paused his narration for a moment.

As the spinning stopped, I saw clouds passing by the windows, so I knew we were still descending, gently, under the main parachute. I could hear the Russian voices on the radio welcoming us back to Earth. "*Варяг, Варяг*, we see you and we see the parachutes." (*Варяг*, pronounced var-ee-ahgk, was our vessel name, meaning Viking in Russian.) The altimeter was counting down. We no longer had engines or jets to help steer, but if everything went to plan, Mission Control at Korolov could already predict pretty accurately where we would land. We'd been in contact with them throughout the descent, and they had confirmed that we had a "good burn," which meant we were on track for a normal landing, and the helicopters would be heading toward the expected landing site.

If things don't go according to plan during a Soyuz landing, the capsule makes what's known, rather dramatically, as a "ballistic landing." This is basically a no-frills, just-get-the-ship-down-safely landing. It's faster and a lot less comfortable, and it's more difficult to predict where the capsule will end up. In the early years, it took the helicopters a long time to find the crew. Luckily we didn't have to experience this, but a few years earlier my friend Don Pettit did, and he reported that it was *not* fun. It was also hard on his family, who had to wait several agonizing hours for news that he was safe.

Right before landing, the seats rise up to allow the shock absorbers room to do their job. Our individually molded seat liners distribute the forces that we experience as well, but because the capsule can land at up to 20gs, those shock absorbers make all the difference. In the background, we hear the communications beacon signaling our location to the helicopters that are hovering nearby, waiting for us to land. Ideally, the capsule lands on its bottom, but depending on the winds and other factors, sometimes it bounces. Moments before you touch down, the jets fire directly at the ground to ease the impact. They're known as the "soft landing jets," but the term *soft* is definitely relative! Hopefully the parachutes separate from the capsule after landing, especially important on a windy day—no one wants to be dragged, bouncing, across the desert right after they land, sometimes leaving a trail of burning grass in one's wake.

Thunk. Our capsule hit the ground with a solid thud, in a huge cloud of dust blown up by the jets. I was sure that we were spinning and tumbling out of control across the desert. But then, as the dust settled, through my tiny window I could see the grass of the Kazakhstan steppes, standing tall, upright, and perfectly still. It was just my confused head that was spinning.

We were home. I love that NASA photographer Bill Ingalls took a marvelous picture of my eye peering through that window, capturing exactly that moment. In minutes, more helicopters would be arriving to transport us back to the base. For now, it was nice to just sit in our capsule and enjoy a quiet moment in our little spot in the desert.

Embracing Gravity

The faces waiting to greet us when they opened the hatch above us were familiar, the same people who'd taught us survival training in Russia. One by one, they pulled us out onto a large metal ring stand that circles the capsule and allows our ground crew to sit above the hatch. The capsule was still hot as we swung our legs around to the outside and slid down the built-in slide. Four people were waiting to catch each of us at the bottom to carry us to seat liners, similar to the ones in the capsule. In my case, one of the guys decided that I didn't weigh very much and he should carry me by himself. I think that he forgot how heavy the spacesuit was! Feeling him struggling with his unexpectedly weighty passenger was a comical reintroduction to gravity. I think I told him that this would be easier for him if we were in space instead of Kazakhstan. Looking back at the capsule, sitting dusty and blackened in the desert like some kind of crashed alien craft from a movie, it was hard to believe we'd just come home in that!

Next, we were taken to a medical tent where I got checked out by my flight surgeon, Dr. Steve Hart, and Peggy Whitson, now chief of the Astronaut Office, came along to help me take off my suit and change into my landing clothes. She laughingly shared that there had been a mix-up with the bag that contained my clothes, and they had to be repacked at the last minute.

"You've got my flight suit, Mark Polansky's T-Shirt, and your friend Mary Brandt donated the bra she was wearing when all this unfolded." A small but important reason why it's convenient to have more women in the Astronaut Office, and girlfriends who would give you the bra off their back when you get back from space.

It took a while for my body to get used to the experience of gravity again. My first thought: Gravity sucks! When I tried to walk to the helicopter, the world seemed to swing wildly back and forth every time I took a step. Luckily, it's standard procedure to have someone support you on each side until your vestibular system recalibrates, likely sometime over the next day or two. Each time I got up to walk, my balance got better, and I could walk a straighter line. Transitioning from space to Earth plays havoc with your inner ear and your head. After being weightless, gravity is simply overwhelming. If the lightest push with your pinky finger can send you flying across the space station, then back on Earth a single step feels thunderous. Truthfully, I landed like a million dollars, but I was still grateful that we had good antinausea meds, and I knew from my first space flight that it works best to take them right after landing. An added bonus, I got a much-needed nap on the two-hour helicopter flight to the airport in Karaganda.

After arriving at Karaganda, a major milestone: we all took showers.

Real ones! It felt unbelievable, even though I had to sit on a stool to avoid falling over, and Peggy helped me wash my hair. Then, feeling human, we sat through a charming series of ceremonial welcome events that U.S. astronauts affectionately referred to as the Funny Hat Ceremony. The guys were presented with the aforementioned hats, which were very grand looking, in black and gold, but apparently women don't get funny hats. Instead, I was given a ceremonial burgundy velvet jacket that I still wear today to black-tie functions. There were dancers, tea, and presents. I received a Russian nesting doll with my picture on the outside and a huge box of chocolates with our crew picture on the lid. I may still have those, too, but I'm a little afraid to open them! What a homecoming!

And then, we separated, Dima flying to Star City and Paolo and I boarding a jet for the twenty-hour flight back to the U.S. I think it felt abrupt to all of us.

It also seemed strange and somehow wrong to me that it took almost twenty-four hours to get halfway around the world, after spending the past six months circling the globe every ninety minutes. We stopped in Scotland and Maine for fuel, before landing in Houston. The plane was stocked with our favorite snacks, but neither of us wanted to eat much until we got to Maine. And then, there it was. Pizza! No meal had ever looked better.

When we landed in Houston, our families came on board for a private reunion before we stepped out to face the NASA and ESA folks who had come to welcome us home. I'd been anticipating that first moment of seeing Jamey and Josh for so long, but it was even more marvelous than I could have imagined. Gravity was suddenly the best sensation in the world as we hugged and hugged and hugged and nobody floated away.

When Paolo and I stepped off the plane, the first face we saw at the bottom of the stairs was the same one that had greeted us when we arrived at the space station: Scott Kelly. "Well, you know, I just had to make sure that you guys made it home," he said gruffly, but I knew that showing up to welcome us was his way of acknowledging that the three of us would always share that special bond from our time in space together.

Pizza, hugs, and being with Josh and Jamey were just a few among many things about life on Earth that I appreciated after being gone for six months. Close behind was the warm weight of our purring cat nudging me off his spot on the couch, and the reunion with Mary, Stacey, and my friends and neighbors. Gravity may have robbed me of a cool extra inch and a quarter of height, and my freedom to fly from place to place with the touch of a finger. But it was a joy to feel physically connected— to those I loved and to the ground beneath my feet.

My brain and body seemed to quickly readjust to being back in a place where everything falls and nobody flies. The faint sensation of the world rushing down when I bent to tie my shoes stayed with me for about a week, but I didn't mind that—it was a little reminder that I'd been somewhere special. But outside of my family and my circle of close friends, a feeling of emotional distance persisted long after I'd mastered walking, unaided, in a straight line. After my time isolated on the ISS with just my crewmates for company, I felt a little removed from the bustling world around me. It was almost like I was still deciding whether I was part of it all; uncertain whether people could actually see me. I was excited about seeing the hallway in Building 4 South where I knew there would be photos of Paolo and Dima and me, with wonderfully funny captions to celebrate our mission, but I waited to go check them out until I knew the place would be almost empty. I just wasn't ready to see a lot of people yet. Feeling fully grounded took a little longer than I thought it might.

The first few weeks were not helped by the fact that home, for me, was two places. And the home in Massachusetts with Jamey and Josh was not the home where I needed to be for a month's worth of medical tests and debriefings. Neither Josh nor I had quite anticipated what it would be like for Jamey (and for us) when Mom came back to Earth—but then didn't come home with them. As someone who always thinks through every possible scenario (and a few impossible ones as well), I felt terrible that I'd missed this, and I worried that I'd lost some trust with our son that would take time to rebuild.

Thankfully, it didn't seem to take too long. I flew home to Massachusetts the very next weekend, and that summer I spent more time than usual up there, reestablishing the routine Jamey had known all his life: that Mom and Dad live in two places; that sometimes one of us leaves, but we always come back. When Jamey and I look back now on his unusual childhood, we can recognize the strength of self-reliance and resilience he built as a result of my absences, while also acknowledging that these were hard lessons to learn so young.

I love that to this day, Jamey still keeps a journal and has become a talented photographer—storytelling skills that he adopted early in his life as a way to knit his worlds together.

I've always been grateful for the important role that Josiah has played in Jamey's life, a bond that I think was solidified during my space station training and the mission itself. Despite the demands of pursuing his career as a landscape architect, Josiah always made time for his younger brother, and their close relationship has helped Jamey grow into the wonderful person he has become.

Finding Your Feet in a Changing World

Change is rarely comfortable, even when it's positive and forward-looking. Sometimes we're thrown into a time of transition by a tragedy or a loss, but we can also face transitions because of something gained—a dream fulfilled. Whenever we mark a major achievement or realize a lifelong ambition, there's huge satisfaction—but then, at some point, there's the question, what next? We have to reorient to a world where the thing that was pulling us forward is now in the rearview mirror.

I'd spent decades dreaming about what it would be like to live in space, hoping I'd get the opportunity to live in space, and training to live in space. Now I'd done it. And it had been everything I'd imagined—more, even. Perhaps I'd get to do it again; I longed to go back. But I knew that with the shuttle program coming to an end, and with only a handful of seats every year available on the Russian Soyuz flights, NASA would be prioritizing the newer astronauts who hadn't had the chance to fly. We needed them to have the experience and credibility of having flown in space so that they would be ready to help design the new vehicles for the upcoming missions to the moon and Mars. This left me pretty far down the invisible list. I would have to find my feet again on the ground.

My transition back to Earth was helped tremendously by the fact that I felt needed and valuable back in the Astronaut Office. Going back to space might or might not be a part of my future, but the importance of the NASA mission was still very clear to me. Rather than being able to take an extended break after my flight, I was thrown into a mission-critical job to help the parties involved with supply ships—companies, crews, trainers, and Mission Controls—improve the process and coordinate better between groups before the next supply ship launch. This was the beginning of our current era, when NASA began working with commercial partners, including SpaceX and Orbital Sciences (now Northrop Grumman). For SpaceX, these supply ship missions were the precursors to building the new vehicles to fly people to the station that we see today. These were uncharted waters at the time and, as only the second person to capture a supply ship with the robotic arm, I had unique insights into how to improve these critical operations.

I was also uniquely qualified to be a bridge between the supply ship companies, the folks at the various Mission Controls around the world, and the astronauts on orbit. The crews trusted me because I was one of them; and the supply ship folks trusted me because I'd successfully grappled one of their precious vessels. Thanks to this role, getting back to work happened naturally, and it also left time for me to spend much of the summer up north with my family. Still, it was beginning to dawn on me that my life after reentry was not going to be quite the same as it had been before my mission. I just didn't yet know what the new life would look like.

As I write these words, it strikes me that many of us have experienced the discomfort of reentry in the recent past, and some are still experiencing it today. The COVID-19 pandemic threw us all into a different way of life. For months or even years, most of us lived in a way that was not so different from my time on the space station (only without the flying and with better food). We stayed isolated in our homes, either alone or with a small group of people. We connected with our family and friends mostly virtually. Then we had to get used to going out into the world again. For some of us, reengaging with large numbers of people felt overwhelming, awkward, and even scary. We didn't quite feel like the same people we'd been before the lockdowns began. Many of us did our best to go back to the lives we were living; others used the forced transition as an opportunity to start something different.

When it comes to life's transitions, big and small, it helps when you know what to expect, as we did during that wild ride in the Soyuz. That's why it can be useful to talk to people who've gone through what you're going through, the way we talked to Scott before our departure, and to other long-duration astronauts about their reentries. I think it's helpful to have some clues and signposts to guide you: The chute deploy was *supposed* to be a sudden stop. Burning bits of spacecraft were *supposed* to be flying past the window. In the same way, when going through a life transition like a change of job, an empty nest, a divorce, a loss, or a big move, you can expect some emotional debris. When facing change I know is coming, I try to remind myself not to be surprised when powerful feelings keep flying around, long after I'd like them to have settled down. All of this is to be expected. (If it helps, try imagining there's an Italian guy in your ear saying, "There eet ees." It's surprisingly comforting!)

Of course, we can't always be prepared for life's transitions. Some-times the biggest changes take us by surprise—like the pandemic did to all of us. These unexpected transitions are the hardest of all, and in the midst of them, sometimes the best we can do is be kind to ourselves and those around us, and look for ways to absorb the shocks and soften the landing, at least a little. When the dust settles and we find our feet in the new world, perhaps we can help others know what to expect the next time around.

It has been said that transitions begin with an end, and end with a be-ginning. I think that's such a helpful insight to remember. When we're in the midst of an ending—whether it's the end of an adventure like my journey to space, or the end of an important relationship, or the end of an era of life—it can feel as final as that *thunk* of the Soyuz hitting the dirt. But there's almost always another horizon ahead of us. For me, landing was not the end, because it brought me back to Earth for a series of new beginnings.

Chapter 12

Making Space for Everyone

Expanding the Possibilities for Others

My name is Cady Coleman, and I'm an astronaut.

I'm always amazed, grateful, and proud to be able to say those words. Even now, years after my retirement, I still find myself speaking about my career in the present tense. Though I'll likely live out most of my remaining days firmly grounded on this planet, I'll always be an astronaut at heart, dedicated to the mission of exploration. To me, being an astronaut means much more than going to space. Under the banner of that single term I've had dozens of jobs, most of them not involving "sailing in space," the literal definition of *astronaut*. Like all my fellow astronauts, cosmonauts, and taikonauts, I'm an explorer, an ambassador, and a person who bridges worlds. We share qualities of courage, curiosity, persistence, patience, and the stomach to handle a wild ride. Those qualities also come into play in my other roles, as a scientist, a communicator, an advocate, a team leader and facilitator, a robotics expert, a musician—the list goes on.

Each of us has our own combination of skills, perspectives, and ways of thinking. And that means we each have unique ways of creating ripples in the world. If you've been trained for one specific job, or spent decades in a particular field, it might not be clear at first how to translate your skills to a different role. What good is an astronaut, on Earth? What good is a teacher outside of a classroom? What good is a mother, when the kids have left home? Of course, the answer to all those kinds of questions is "A lot of good!" But it can take some creativity and courage to look beneath the specifics of a role and recognize the truly unique set of qualities that you carry with you into every new context. That time of transition and discovery can be exciting, even when it's also daunting.

Several years after my ISS mission was completed, I accepted an invitation to transfer to NASA headquarters in Washington, D.C., to work in the Office of the Chief Technologist on their programs around innovation, education, and sustainability. I was excited about being closer to Josh and Jamey, and to be pursuing a new role and a new purpose.

During my time in D.C., I discovered so much about who I could be here on Earth. I realized that all that time training with my crews had made me an expert at bringing people together—a skill that was helpful not just within NASA, but between NASA and other key players in academia, industry, entertainment, and business. I learned that my willingness to have hard conversations was a valuable asset that helped clear the air and move diverse groups forward toward common goals. And I confirmed that growing sense that my ability to tell stories—to "share space the way Cady shares space," as the Hollywood director once put it—was perhaps my most formidable tool for making change.

The Power of Story

Storytelling is another of those things that sounds like a "soft" skill, but in fact it's extraordinarily powerful. Humans, by our nature, are storytelling creatures. We think, and make sense of our world and ourselves, through narrative. If there's something important we want to convey, story is our best means of doing so. A good story can transport people to a different world, open minds, dislodge assumptions, and reveal possibilities that weren't obvious before.

Being a storyteller wasn't a new job for me. Throughout my NASA career, I was often picked for PR activities because I excelled at them. I willingly accepted those assignments, despite the presence of a culture at NASA that went all the way back to the 1960s: as an astronaut, you never shared, unless you were made to—and you certainly never let anyone know if you enjoyed that role. But I knew how important it was that we share space with everyone, and I had a knack for explaining the work we did and its importance in a way that felt approachable and human; including relatable, and sometimes funny, anecdotes from my own life that subverted the stereotype of the hero-astronaut in a way that inspired audiences to reexamine their own potential. I also knew that storytelling wasn't just about sharing my experiences. It was about asking important questions and creating space in which other people's stories could be heard as well.

Sometimes my storytelling meant doing run-of-the-mill press interviews or commentary on launches. But occasionally it had a touch of Hollywood glamour. One of my favorite instances happened in 2011, while I was aboard the ISS. It started with an email from my brother Kip.

"Hey Cate," he wrote, "I met this guy at a wine industry event and when I mentioned that my sister was an astronaut, he said that his sister-in-law, Sandy, is about to play an astronaut in a movie, and he asked if you would mind giving her some pointers. I assured him that you'd been up there with five guys for four months and you'd talk to anybody."

Sandy, it turned out, was none other than Sandra Bullock, and the movie was *Gravity*. I was, of course, thrilled, although the guys grumbled a bit that I got to talk with Sandra. In the end, all of us helped her understand what it was like moving in a weightless environment and how it felt to be so far away from everyone you loved. It was fun—and a little surreal—to be picking up the ISS phone and calling up a Hollywood movie star on her cell phone to try to convey how it feels to fly.

A couple of years after I came home from the space station, NASA asked me to look at an early screening of the film and strategize about how the movie could be used to highlight the important work we did on the ISS. I loved the movie. Okay, Hollywood had taken some fairly creative liberties with the subject matter, including the moment when Sandy shimmies gracefully out of her spacesuit in shorts and a tank top, no padding in sight. And don't get me started on long, tether-free spacewalks propelled by fire extinguishers! But these small inaccuracies paled alongside the fact that the movie gave millions of people not just the breathtaking views of Earth I'd seen every day of my mission, but the *feeling* of witnessing those views. And it showed something else as well: a woman having that experience, looking through the visor of a spacesuit helmet.

As I write these words, early in the third decade of the twenty-first century, NASA is preparing to send the first woman and the first person of color to the moon as part of the Artemis mission (named for Apollo's sister, whose existence I only recently discovered, which is telling in and of itself). It means the world to me that little girls born in this decade will get to stay up past their bedtimes and watch a woman take a giant step for humankind.

True, in this day and age, kids are more likely to be able to see fictional depictions of astronauts in a diversity of shapes and colors. But while I'm a strong believer in the importance of diversity in fictional representations, the impact is exponentially greater when the figure you're watching on the screen isn't an actor playing a role, but a real, live person who looks like you, launching on a rocket, flying through the space station, or even walking on the moon.

I can't tell you how many of my male colleagues, when asked about the first time they knew they wanted to be an astronaut, will tell the story of being woken up and tucked under a blanket in front of a crackling, fuzzy television to watch Neil Armstrong take those historic first steps. Sure, some of my female colleagues will tell the same story. But how many little girls never even saw that momentous event as it happened, because their parents, like mine, never thought to wake them up?

How might our world be different today if a woman had taken those steps in 1969? Imagine it for a moment, all those kids tucked up in front of the TV, witnessing a woman astronaut taking those very first steps on the moon. How many life stories could have unfolded differently because of that moment of inspiration? And how many assumptions about a woman's potential in all areas might have been overturned? Even the slightest change in a vehicle's trajectory can send it to a vastly different landscape; why wouldn't that be true for a life, or a culture, as well?

It doesn't matter what field we're in or what life journey we're on, the stories we hear and see are what shape the narratives we write for ourselves. They give us permission to stretch, to try new things, to take risks. *I didn't know someone like me could do that. Or be that.* When that dawns on us, it's as if an unseen door opens and we get to peer into worlds we may have felt were closed off to us before. Those who go before us can make all the difference, and so do the ways they are represented—or not represented. When you see someone doing what you aspire to do— someone who looks like you, loves like you, thinks like you, or moves through the world like you—you realize that could be you someday. That's what happened for me when I listened to Sally Ride tell her story. And that's exactly why an important part of my mission today is being a storyteller myself—sharing my own journey and creating space for the voices of others to be heard, especially those that too easily get missed.

At NASA, this often meant ensuring that women and people of color were represented when we were sharing stories about our work. One time, a major network was making a show, *Live from the Space Station*, but the crew on the ISS at the time consisted of six white guys. To me, this was almost a national emergency. Girls (and boys) around the world would be watching this show, and it was unthinkable to me that they would not see a single woman or person of color. It simply wasn't okay that in the twenty-first century, a cool show about space would come with a subliminal but very clear message to anyone who wasn't a white man: *No. Not for you.* I raised this issue with the production company, and we made it a priority to augment the live portion of the show with women in Mission Control, and other video scenes of astronauts including women and people of color at work: spacewalking, doing experiments, performing repairs, and living in space.

I have continued to do this kind of work since retiring from NASA. When you've been privileged to have extraordinary experiences—and I know without a doubt that the things I've done and seen are a rare and invaluable privilege—you have a platform and a responsibility to bring people along with you and to open possibilities for others. Space belongs to all of us, but so few of us actually get to go there. Storytelling is the way I give back. I feel as if I'm honor bound to share those experiences, because they don't belong just to me. Many of my fellow astronauts feel the same, and I'm constantly humbled by the creative and visionary ways they use their platforms to highlight issues of equity, racial justice, sustainability, and so much more.

When I get an opportunity to represent my role and my field, I strive to maximize its impact. I was on the fence about attending the reunion of Massachusetts Institute of Technology alumni astronauts on the fiftieth anniversary of Apollo 11 until I realized that none of the other women were able to attend. I changed my plans in order to be there—and made sure to wear bright colors so I'd stand out in the photos. Future classes at MIT, which trains top engineers and scientists from around the world, would see those photos, so it was essential that women were included and clearly visible. Changing that picture and those like it are central to my mission.

In 2017, when the eclipse was crossing North America from Oregon to South Carolina, I was asked by CNN to narrate a segment from Blackwater, Missouri. An eclipse is one of those moments when we suddenly see the universe at work. When something that seems as unchanging as the sun disappears before our eyes, we experience the same kind of awe and wonder that I felt looking down at the Earth from space. It's also a moment when science comes into the public eye. Families around the country would be watching the coverage together, and future scientists would find their calling that day. With all of this in mind, I was happy that I and another woman, as well as two men, would be narrating the coverage. But I wanted it to do more. I wanted kids to see themselves in the middle of that event, not just a bunch of adults. So I suggested to the production company that my segment would be even more impactful if it included a group of local girls.

To their great credit, the production company made it happen. They got some of the local Girl Scouts to join the broadcast. If I'd known how challenging the actual filming would be—hours and hours on a brutally hot day—I might not have asked, but the crew did understand how hard it would be, and they did it anyway, because they picked up on my vision for how we would make more ripples if we succeeded. The girls were amazing during the eclipse, documenting their observations and keeping track of the critical timing for wearing our safety glasses. We changed the spirit of the coverage, and our segment had several times the viewers the other segments had. We'll never know how many girls—and boys— watched, but I'm sure it made a difference.

More recently, I worked with the same creative team to showcase a Morgan Stanley project about the need to design spacesuits that fit women better. At this stage, it is just a prototype, and I don't know if it will ever develop into something real. But what mattered was that they made a documentary about the project that included a diverse group of teenage girls evaluating the suit and putting it through its paces. They also created an interactive exhibit about the project in New York, where they invited kids from the area to come and explore the world of space-suit design. The girls from the documentary were featured on a billboard in Times Square, six stories high, with their faces looking through the spacesuit's visor.

Expanding the Circle of Inclusion

When it came to women and girls, I was naturally attuned to opportunities for representation through storytelling. But I also had the chance to learn about other stories and experiences that were less visible, and to participate in helping them be seen and heard. My world at the Johnson Space Center changed when Steve Riley, one of the robotics flight controllers who had helped me navigate some tricky robotics situations when I was a CAPCOM, asked me to participate in a video he was making for Dan Savage and Terry Miller's "It Gets Better" project. These videos were created to address the suicide crisis among LGBTQ+ teens who feel alone, unseen, or afraid to come out. Thousands of people contributed videos sharing their stories of how they made it through hard times and came out the other side. I didn't share the LGBTQ+ experience, but I knew how it felt to be different, and I was honored to be part of it. At NASA, we were proud to lead the way by being the first government organization to participate in the project under Dr. Ellen Ochoa's leadership at the Space Center. I was amazed at how many people came up and told me how much the video meant to them. There was one guy who worked on the same floor as me, the floor reserved for astronauts and a few select engineers like him. He told me he hadn't felt comfortable putting his family's photo on his desk before now, but this video had made him feel differently. This shocked me—that in a place I thought I'd known so well, there were people who still felt unable to be fully themselves at work. It was humbling to realize that we'd inhabited the same hallways, the same world, and yet their experience was clearly so different than I could have understood.

Another humbling and powerful experience I've had in recent years has been advising the AstroAccess group, whose goal is to advance disability inclusion in space exploration. I help coach their ambassadors, people with disabilities who are carrying out flight investigations on the zero-g airplane. I worked most closely on the first two flights with two extraordinary women, Dana Bolles, a NASA space-flight engineer and science communicator, and CeCe Mazyck, a U.S. Army veteran paratrooper and Paralympics gold medalist. Seeing Dana, born without arms or legs but maneuvering herself more precisely than any first-time zero-gravity flyer I had ever seen, made me rethink what's possible, both in space and here on Earth. CeCe, who uses a wheelchair, was speechless after she took her first "flight" down the center of the airplane. She looked at me as if she had suddenly been transported to another world. Finally, she said, "Cady, I can go ANYWHERE up here!" Her eyes lit up with the freedom of flight. It was powerful—and uncomfortable—for me to realize that as inclusive as I try to be, I had been leaving an entire group of people behind in terms of the abilities they could bring to a team.

Again, I don't share the experience of people with disabilities, and I can't know how it feels to move through a world that is often unaccommodating and inaccessible. But from my own experience, I do know what a difference it makes when environments and equipment fit—and when they don't. Will people with disabilities be able to be part of the future of space travel? Certainly today they are already flying on commercial space flights and are an integral part of many space teams. With the world of human space flight changing by the hour, and different ways of flying as crew members opening up, the answer is yes. And their lifetime's experience of problem-solving and thinking creatively would make them invaluable crewmates. Of course, there are safety considerations. But we shouldn't forget that not long ago, people thought it was unsafe—impossible, even—for the Mercury 13 women to go to space. That should make us question our assumptions. And it's beginning to happen. As I write these words, the European Space Agency just announced the selection of John McFall, an amputee and former Paralympian, as an ESA parastronaut feasibility study member.

One thing I know for sure is that the more effort we make to include people who don't happen to fit into a standard mold, the more likely we are to achieve mission success. The more we design to be inclusive, the better that design serves all of us. There are many examples, both on Earth and in space. A simple one that applies to both: When we create multiple ways—visual, audible, and tactile notifications—for people to be aware of an emergency situation onboard a spacecraft, or in a theater, we create positive redundancy, and it's better for everyone. I think of the labels on the ISS indicating the nearest oxygen masks and fire extinguishers, and how much more useful they would be in a smoke-filled module if the directional arrows were raised up and tactile. If we design a place to be more easily navigable for people with visual impairment, we make it safer for everyone in emergencies involving smoke or darkness.

The work of inclusion confronts all of us with the limitations of our own perspectives and hidden biases. It requires us to have difficult conversations with one another, and with ourselves. We each see the world through the lenses we've grown up with, shaped by our education, experiences, socioeconomic circumstances, and the people around us. Whether we are part of a group that has been marginalized or consider ourselves an ally, there is so much for all of us to learn about creating more space for diversity in our personal and professional worlds.

We Are the Crew

I'm grateful for the ways in which having been to space has broadened my perspective and changed my way of looking at life, and people, back on Earth.

When you're circling the Earth aboard the ISS every ninety minutes, our planet doesn't seem that far away. It filled my field of view every time I looked out of the window, and I often felt as if I could almost reach out and touch it. It never grew old because it never looked quite the same—the shifting lights and textures that reflected the changing weather and seasons were always captivating. I loved seeing the different continents—each with its distinctive colors—coming closer and closer until they were right above my head, and then I'd spin around and watch them recede into the distance. Whether I was tracing the tangled threads of the Nile delta, or marveling at the vastness of Australia, or learning to distinguish the particular shades of red and gold that told me which desert was which, I never got tired of watching. The oceans were infinite varieties of blue. Within the outlines of each landmass, the planet sparkled and pulsated with life. At first, I was drawn to identify the places I was from and the places I'd been, but after a while I felt like I was from *all* the places I saw moving majestically beneath my gaze. In fact, soon after my mission, I met a cab driver from Egypt and my first thought was, "I was just there!"

Even though I was one of only six humans *not* on the planet, I felt so connected to the billions of people down there. More important, it was startlingly clear to me how connected they all could be to one another. If only they knew that, I often thought, how much easier it would be to solve the challenges that we face here on Earth. From space, you see very few national borders or political boundaries separating humans from one another. You understand—not as an abstract ideal, but as a visceral, obvious reality—that we are one human family sharing a precious, life-supporting home planet.

Another profound shift in perspective that comes from being in space is the realization that *we have always been in space.* When I'm living on a space station, I'm just a little farther from the surface of the Earth, a little farther from home. When you are down in your particular corner of planet Earth, fixing dinner, taking a nap, or running errands in town, you're *also* in space. That's a perspective that's difficult to grasp unless you've seen the Earth from far away. Space isn't just that place above our heads; it's our neighborhood, where all of us live.

Earth itself is like a spaceship, sailing along in our universe, and we are its crew. When I lived on the space station, it was clear that the six of us on board were the only ones in sight who could carry out the mission. If something needed to be done, it was indisputably up to us. It's a little harder to feel that same urgency and personal responsibility when there are so many of us living here on the planet. And yet, if you fly yourself just a few hundred miles out into space, you see that indeed, there is no one else. Only us. And we are few.

That's why I feel, these days, like I've received a new mission assignment with my feet firmly planted on the ground. I feel that urgency every time I step up to a microphone—like the recent talk I gave to a specially selected group of more than a hundred young women in engineering, most of them women of color. I realized that I had only thirty minutes with these exceptional young women who will shape our future. Only thirty minutes to impart the tools from my tool chest that I thought they might need: How to be heard, how to be seen, who to connect with when things seem terrible, and how to laugh at the things you can't change. How to be the best possible crew members for our planet.

As crew members, we're essential—each and every one of us. Our voices, our votes, our unique perspectives, and our individual contributions are all critical to our shared mission. And it truly is shared. We still

have so much work to do when it comes to including everyone in the resources and opportunities that our home planet provides. Perhaps, over
time, our home will expand to include outposts in space or even on other
planets. I like to think that in some small way, the work I did helped
make that just a little more possible, someday. But in the meantime, it's
become my mission to do my part in making space for everyone, right
here on planet Earth.

Acknowledgments

It may take a village to raise a Cady, but I've learned that it takes several villages and an extensive ground crew to get a book off the launchpad! I've been fortunate to have so many crews over the years, during my time at NASA (in space and on Earth) and in the years before and after. All of you are precious to me. This book couldn't possibly include all of our stories, and you are too many to name here, but I hope you know how I feel.

To my cowriter, Ellen Daly: You are truly a wizard, not just with words, but with weaving together stories into a three-dimensional quilt and bringing them to life. What you've given me goes beyond the book, helping me to think more deeply about my life, and I can't thank you enough. (And Carter and Piper too!)

I'd like to thank my marvelous editor at Penguin Life, Laura Tisdel. Laura, it has been marvelous to be on the receiving end of your thoughtful, incisive—and so often hilarious—edits. I loved meeting the rest of your team in New York, like a squad of superheroes, each bringing their own superpower to make this book a reality.

I want to thank my agent, Jim Levine, at Levine Greenberg Rostan Literary Agency, for his help narrowing my book down from three hundred of my favorite stories to one larger story that I wanted to tell. Jim's assistant, Courtney Paganelli, now an agent in her own right, brought important insights and perspective at every stage of the process. And many thanks to author, friend, and neuroscientist Heather Berlin, for her generous introduction to LGR.

I'm grateful to have met Peter Smith, who worked with me to shape the vision for this book in its early stages. Thank you for the right questions and the right dose of humor.

Thanks to Ty Stiklorius, Jeremy Gruber, and the passionate team at the Friends at Work company, who understood that being an astronaut brings with it a platform that can be used for the power of good—and supported me in my quest to do just that. And thanks also to Billy Hallock at CAA Speakers, the best of speaking agents, who has been a partner on that quest, and also gave valuable insights on the manuscript.

With immense gratitude, I'd like to thank my assistant, Erica Beade. Words don't do justice to your contributions. For every step of this project, you have been my thought partner, friend, and a true friend to the book itself. You have a kind of X-ray vision when it comes to details while also keeping hold of the big picture. Because we work virtually, you don't see the dance I do at my desk when I hear the words, "Would you mind if I tinkered with that a little bit . . . ?" You are truly a force multiplier!

Stacey Severn and Libby Willson have helped me navigate the world of social media with skill and enthusiasm. Olivia Gaissert, Amanda Major, and Shira Lander have taken turns supporting me for years, all while working as white-water kayaking instructors. And my amazing daughter-in-law, Vivian Black, who provided book feedback and introduced me to the aforementioned amazing women.

I'm indebted to friends who helped me navigate the writing process, read endless versions of the manuscript with pencils in hand, and encouraged me at every turn. There are too many of you to name, but special thanks to Libby Koponen, Patricia Klindienst, Martha Ackmann,

Mary Robinette Kowal, Andy and Vicki Chaikin, Cori Lathan, Bill Gibson, Diane Flaherty, and Dayna Steele.

I so appreciated my son Jamey's friends who reviewed an early version of the manuscript, particularly Loey Bull, Aarushi Sahejpal, Eddy Ruggieri, and Nick Valbuena.

Thanks are due to my NASA family, and especially my space crews, for reading parts of the manuscript, conferring on stories and facts, and answering questions. Many of you went above and beyond, including: Eileen Collins, Ron Garan, Mark Polansky, Nicole Stott, Jeff Ashby, Mike Fossum, Danny Olivas, Don and Micki Pettit, Scott and Amiko Kelly, and Chris and Helene Hadfield.

My good college friends were instrumental in large and small ways with their suggestions and support: thanks to Kim Elcess and Laura Kiessling in particular. Thanks also to Megan Smith, a close friend since our MIT Crew days—whose wealth of experience and generosity profoundly impact how I see the work that needs doing in the world, and who introduced me to Susan Alzner, who helped catalyze this book with a collaborative deep dive into the history of NASA's spacesuit and its future.

I owe many years of thanks to my Houston-based girlfriends. You shared your opinions and reflections freely, reinforcing that despite how much we have in common, you each bring a different and valuable lens. Stacey and Mary, you interviewed extensively with Ellen and me for the book, for which I'm immensely grateful. Stacey, a science fiction author herself, led the pack by reading every version of the book and giving advice whenever I asked.

It would be impossible to list the many women and men who have mentored and supported me over the years. I particularly appreciate everything I learned from Kathy Sullivan, Kathy Thornton, Eileen Collins, and Pam Melroy. A special thanks to Jackie Parker, one of the first woman test pilots, and flight test engineer Eileen Bjorkman, for introducing me to their world and encouraging me to join it. Barbara Barrett, who I met later in my career, was kind and thoughtful about introducing me into situations where I could learn more about the world outside of NASA.

So many thanks to Catlin Donnelly and Hampton Watkins, who have been at the core of my world when I need . . . anything and everything. I love that you always send me away with a wider perspective and a pocket full of solutions.

There are times when the planets align, and much is learned in a single evening. I'll never forget dinner with a dozen amazing aerospace women at Arizona State University's Space Futures Convening, where we exchanged our best and worst career stories. Thank you for that inspirational, hilarious, toast-inspiring conversation that added to this book in important ways. I'm betting mine won't be the only book to emerge from that evening.

I'd like to thank my musical friends, from my buddies in Bandella to my western Massachusetts crowd. I loved our jams together—on stages, in Rosie's and Terry's living rooms, and in the Gallery with those Minstrels. You helped me to remember who I am outside of someone who hadn't finished writing their book.

To the people who have been my village for so many years: Jann and David Tenenbaum, Diane Flaherty and Bill Gibson, Susan and John Clopton, Nancy and Paul Schwartz, Laura Kiessling and Ron Raines, Meg and Keith Clark—I really can't thank you enough for everything, including your immense support during this book-writing journey.

I owe a big thanks to my neighbors and friends Sandy Clark, Debbie Lane, Nancy Ghitman, and Joanie Bianchi, who offered support throughout the process, often while getting me out of the office to walk together in the hills of western Massachusetts.

Writing a book is truly a family affair. If I were to launch into space again, my extended family would fill the entire bus allocated for guests.

All of you are part of my life, but I wanted to thank Jamey, Cari, Kip, Ben, and Tom for keeping the manuscript-review roasting to a minimum.

I'm grateful to Lindy Elkins-Tanton and Michael Crow for welcoming me into the Interplanetary Initiative at Arizona State University as their Global Explorer in Residence and trusting me to launch the *Mission: Interplanetary* podcast with theater professor and producer Lance Gharavi and my marvelous cohost, Andrew Maynard. Our weekly interviews with exploration experts helped me realize the importance of bringing a range of diverse voices to the table when discussing our planet's future in space.

I brought a current version of the book along on our family vacation to Puerto Rico, thinking that Jamey and Josiah might want to take a look. I remember being so pleased when Josiah beamed at me and said, "Cady, this is a really good book!" His and Jamey's support has always meant a lot to me; it's a tricky thing—and certainly intrusive—to share our family's experiences with people that we don't even know. I appreciated their candor and generosity of spirit.

Infinite thanks, appreciation, and love to Josh Simpson, my partner, husband, and friend. We share so much, including a love of bringing people from different worlds together. Your patient and detailed reading of different chapters always led to insights I hadn't thought of. Your courage to explore the universe in your own unique and visionary way has always given me courage for my own explorations.

Appendix 1

How to Pee (and Poop) in Space

Step 1: Meet the Space Toilet, or the WCS (Waste Collection System), as we call it. The toilet is a machine like a very fancy vacuum cleaner (but *please* do not attempt this at home). In space, everything is weightless, even the pee and the poop, so we use suction to get those things to go where we want them to go. Our "vacuum" provides suction to a long hose that we can easily pee into, and to a tiny toilet-like thing that will suck in, as I tell the kids, everything that is yucky or dirty. The poop, the paper, the wipes. All of those are trapped by a plastic bag the size of a large sandwich baggie that is stretched over the mouth of the toilet. The bag has holes in it—enough to let the vacuum work, but not so big that yucky stuff goes through the holes! Okay, you've got the basics, now it's time to try it out!

Step 2: Let's Pee!

    A. Present yourself to the space toilet. Forward? Backward? Well, except for pooping, the possibilities are almost limitless. You can be right side up, upside down, or sideways, although it is highly recommended that you tuck your toes under the foot straps to avoid floating around during this delicate operation. (None of this out-in-the-woods camping, trying hard to get your butt close enough to the ground that you don't pee on your shoes. Peeing in space is *easy*!)

    B. Turn the WCS fan on and check for the gentle flow of air into the hose: our vacuum system at work!

    C. Now hold that yellow funnel up to where pee comes out of your body and—well—the rest is up to you, but I'll advise you to relax and trust that all of your pee will go into that hose, into the big storage tank, get recycled, and come out later next week as your drinking water.

Step 3: Pooping. Let's face it. Pooping is a personal thing. And luckily the fan on the space toilet is like a jet engine and it is so loud that your privacy is assured!

A. Lift the lid and turn on the fan, checking again for airflow. Then float yourself reasonably close to the vicinity of the toilet bowl, and—again, it's up to you. Use all the paper that you need, and just make sure that everything yucky is in the bag that is stretched across the mouth of the toilet.

B. Now, pull up on the red tab of the bag. The top will scrunch together to keep everything inside, and you push that bag of stuff you'd rather not see again down into the toilet, past a little swinging door, and you'll never see it again!

Note 1: At approximately 3:00 a.m., either you or one of your crewmates will use the bathroom and realize that the "poop container" is full, and you can't leave it that way for your pals. So, you pop off the toilet part, put a cap on the can, install a new can, secure the full one into the trash ship, and try to go back to bed. As you might suspect, this never, ever seems to happen during the day.

Note 2: For future Mars folk, you'll be keeping those cans of poop to grow your food when you get to the red planet.

So, to sum it up: clean, neat, and easy. All of those stories about "chocolate nut candy bars" floating around the cabin are designed to scare people away from our space paradise.

While we're on the subject, here is a list of just a few of the other unusual places I have been privileged to pee while training for space flight:

• In my bathtub, trying to see how diapers work (or don't) prior to my shuttle mission, when we'd be lying on our backs on the launchpad for a few hours.

- Antarctica: Peeling off three layers of clothes while wearing three layers of gloves. I would remind myself that it was good training—spacewalkers couldn't pull their gloves off either.

- In the brand-new sparkling clean bathroom next to the cosmonaut offices in Star City, Russia. Marked with a giant metal *M* attached to the door to indicate Mooshina (Men, in Russian). The women's bathroom was incredibly far away, so I started turning the *M* upside down before I went in, to make a *W*. For all of us. One of the cosmonauts asked if I was sure that this was both a men's and a women's bathroom. "Oh yes," I said. "I'm very sure!"

- And the worst to date? Underwater (during my stay in the Aquarius underwater habitat), fighting off giant angelfish (several feet long, no kidding) by waving one of my fins frantically in front of me, all the while knowing that Aquarius Mission Control was announcing to the whole world, "Coleman is going out to the gazebo. We repeat, Coleman to the gazebo." Thankfully, no cameras were present, but just the thought that everyone knows you are out there, doing *that* . . .

So, as you can see, peeing in space was a piece of cake!

Appendix 2

How to Spot the Space Station—and Why You Should

It's 6:00 a.m. on a cold morning in western Massachusetts. Am I asleep? No. I'm racing over to our local diner to share the exciting news with whomever might be there: in just a few minutes, the International Space Station is going to pass right over Shelburne Falls! It's not the first time that I've burst in, eager to drag neighbors outside with me so that they can look up and see the space station, looking like a bright star, sailing across our deep, dark sky. It's dark for us on the ground, but the station, high above the Earth, is already lit up by the sun. Why bother, you might ask. I wanted them to know that next winter, I'd be living up on that space station, and thinking of my family and friends down there as I flew overhead. But I also wanted them to know that the space station was something that they could see with their own eyes.

It still seems unbelievable to me that people can go to space, let alone *live* there. But when you actually see this bright star going by and realize that there really are seven people inside, it brings the reality to life. They're up there—so why not wave hello?

Seeing the space station for yourself expands the *feeling* of what's possible. It's one thing to know that the space station circles the Earth every ninety minutes. But it is another to see it yourself. In some sense, you travel to space too.

So, how do you see the station? You'll need to know: WHERE to look, and WHEN to look, and HOW LONG you might see it. The NASA website "Spot the Station" (https://spotthestation.nasa.gov/) will give you the detailed steps, as will several other apps and websites. But first, before you look for the data for your location, let's talk about what the station will look like when you do see it.

If you've picked a clear night or morning with very few clouds, the station will look like a really bright star slowly sailing purposefully across the sky. Not zipping quickly by, but moving slowly, gracefully as it orbits the Earth. In fact, if we could watch the station cross the whole sky, from one horizon to the other, it would take about eight minutes!

So now that we know what to look for, we need to know how to spot it. The website will tell you the direction you should be looking, so you'll need to know where north, south, east, or west are from your location. But equally important is how high you are looking in the sky, referred to as the elevation. To give you an idea, if you were standing with your arm stretched out in front of you, level with the horizon, and the station was just above your fist, then it would be at ten degrees elevation. That's pretty low for spotting, and buildings or mountains might block the way. When you are first starting, look for sightings that are at least forty degrees up in the sky. Four fists or so, about halfway up in the sky.

Now look in the correct direction per the website, and look up, per the elevation. If it's forty-five degrees, your head will be tilted up. If it's sixty-five degrees, you'll feel like your head is all the way back and you are looking straight up in the sky. Don't stare at one spot but scan the sky in that area.

It won't always be easy to tell what's moving and what's not at first, and you might be asking yourself, "Is that star moving? Or that one?" But then suddenly, you won't wonder. You'll just know. THAT STAR IS MOVING. One of the brightest stars in the sky is moving gracefully and slowly across the sky. And that star is not a star at all; it is the space station.

When I walk outside to spot the station, as I often do, I will follow it across the sky until I suddenly can't see it, maybe because I want to savor every minute of being on that journey with the crew up there, even if it's only for a short time. And I'll be thinking about the people on board. Are they asleep? Working? Talking on the "phone" with their families? If it's evening time for you on the East Coast of the U.S., then likely they are supposed to be in bed by now. But maybe they are awake, and looking out their windows at the Earth. Maybe at YOU!

So now you're ready. Put your location into NASA's "Spot the Station," and just like that, you'll know when the space station might be flying over your neighborhood!

You see, space is for sharing—and by coming out to watch for the International Space Station, you'll be sharing space with the seven or so people who are lucky enough to be living up there.

So when you see the station, please say hello from me too. And next time, maybe recruit a few new friends to spot the station with you. When they see it go overhead, really see it, you'll see their eyes light up. And just like that, you've changed their view of the world.

Appendix 3

Sharing Space Acronyms

AC1: Alternating Current Phase 1

ASAP: As Soon as Possible

ASCANs: Astronaut Candidates

ASHOs: Astronaut Hopefuls

CAPCOM: Capsule Communicator

DPC: Daily Planning Conference

ESA: European Space Agency

EVA: Extravehicular Activity

HTV: H-II Transfer Vehicle

ISS: International Space Station

IUS: Inertial Upper Stage

KSC: Kennedy Space Center

LCVG: Liquid Cooling and Ventilation Garment

LOS: Loss of Signal

MECO: Main Engine Cut Off

MIT: Massachusetts Institute of Technology

NASA: National Aeronautics and Space Administration

NBL: Neutral Buoyancy Lab

NOLS: National Outdoor Leadership School

ROTC: Reserve Officers' Training Corps

RTLS: Return to Launch Site

SRBs: Solid Rocket Boosters

STS: Space Transportation System

T-38: T-38 Talon USAF training jet

USAF: United States Air Force

VR: Virtual Reality

WCS: Waste Collection System (toilet)